# Techniques and Issues in Abuse-Focused Therapy With Children & Adolescents

# Interpersonal Violence:
# The Practice Series

## Jon R. Conte, Series Editor

*In this series...*

LEGAL ISSUES IN CHILD ABUSE AND NEGLECT PRACTICE, Second Edition
by John E. B. Myers

CHILD ABUSE TRAUMA: Theory and Treatment of the Lasting Effects
by John N. Briere

INTERVENTION FOR MEN WHO BATTER: An Ecological Approach
by Jeffrey L. Edleson and Richard M. Tolman

COGNITIVE PROCESSING THERAPY FOR RAPE VICTIMS: A Treatment Manual
by Patricia A. Resick and Monica K. Schnicke

GROUP TREATMENT OF ADULT INCEST SURVIVORS
by Mary Ann Donaldson and Susan Cordes-Green

TEAM INVESTIGATION OF CHILD SEXUAL ABUSE: The Uneasy Alliance
by Donna Pence and Charles Wilson

HOW TO INTERVIEW SEXUAL ABUSE VICTIMS: Including the Use of Anatomical Dolls
by Marcia Morgan, with contributions from Virginia Edwards

ASSESSING DANGEROUSNESS: Violence by Sexual Offenders, Batterers, and Child Abusers
Edited by Jacquelyn C. Campbell

PATTERN CHANGING FOR ABUSED WOMEN: An Educational Program
by Marilyn Shear Goodman and Beth Creager Fallon

GROUPWORK WITH CHILDREN OF BATTERED WOMEN: A Practitioner's Manual
by Einat Peled and Diane Davis

PSYCHOTHERAPY WITH SEXUALLY ABUSED BOYS: An Integrated Approach
by William N. Friedrich

CONFRONTING ABUSIVE BELIEFS: Group Treatment for Abusive Men
by Mary Nõmme Russell

TREATMENT STRATEGIES FOR ABUSED CHILDREN: From Victim to Survivor
by Cheryl L. Karp and Traci L. Butler

GROUP TREATMENT FOR ADULT SURVIVORS OF ABUSE: A Manual for Practitioners
by Laura Pistone Webb and James Leehan

WORKING WITH CHILD ABUSE AND NEGLECT: A Primer
by Vernon R. Wiehe

TREATING SEXUALLY ABUSED CHILDREN AND THEIR NONOFFENDING PARENTS:
A Cognitive Behavioral Approach
by Esther Deblinger and Anne Hope Heflin

HEARING THE INTERNAL TRAUMA: Working With Children and Adolescents Who
Have Been Sexually Abused
by Sandra Wieland

PREPARING AND PRESENTING EXPERT TESTIMONY IN CHILD ABUSE LITIGATION:
A Guide for Expert Witnesses and Attorneys
by Paul Stern

TREATMENT STRATEGIES FOR ABUSED ADOLESCENTS: From Victim to Survivor
by Cheryl L. Karp, Traci L. Butler, and Sage C. Bergstrom

HOMICIDE: THE HIDDEN VICTIMS—A Guide for Professionals
by Deborah Spungen

TECHNIQUES AND ISSUES IN ABUSE-FOCUSED THERAPY WITH CHILDREN
& ADOLESCENTS: Addressing the Internal Trauma
by Sandra Wieland

ASSESSING ALLEGATIONS OF SEXUAL ABUSE IN PRESCHOOL CHILDREN:
Understanding Small Voices
by Sandra K. Hewitt

# Techniques and Issues in Abuse-Focused Therapy With Children & Adolescents

## Addressing the Internal Trauma

Sandra Wieland

Interpersonal Violence:
The Practice Series

**SAGE Publications**
*International Educational and Professional Publisher*
Thousand Oaks   London   New Delhi

*For information address*:

SAGE Publications, Inc.
2455 Teller Road
Thousand Oaks, California 91320
E-mail: order@sagepub.com

SAGE Publications Ltd.
6 Bonhill Street
London EC2A 4PU
United Kingdom

SAGE Publications India Pvt. Ltd.
M-32 Market
Greater Kailash I
New Delhi 110 048 India

Printed in the United States of America

*Library of Congress Cataloging-in-Publication Data*

Wieland, Sandra.
   Techniques and issues in abuse-focused therapy with children &
adolescents: Addressing the internal trauma / by Sandra Wieland.
      p.  cm.—(Interpersonal violence; v. 22)
   Developed out of a series of workshops presented by the author in Ottawa.
   Includes bibliographical references (p. ) and index.
   ISBN 0-7619-0481-6 (cloth: acid-free paper)
   ISBN 0-7619-0482-4 (pbk.: acid-free paper)
   1. Sexually abused children—Mental health.  2. Sexually abused
teenagers—Mental health.  3. Psychic trauma—Treatment.
4. Hypnotism  Therapeutic use.  I. Title.  II. Series.
RJ507.S49 W544  1998
618.92'8583606—ddc21                     98-25306

This book is printed on acid-free paper.

98  99  00  01  02  03  04  7  6  5  4  3  2  1

| | |
|---|---|
| *Acquiring Editor:* | C. Terry Hendrix |
| *Editorial Assistant:* | Fiona Lyon |
| *Production Editor:* | Sherrise M. Roehr |
| *Editorial Assistant:* | Nevair Kabakian |
| *Typesetter:* | Lynn Miyata |
| *Indexer:* | Juniee Oneida |

◆ ❖ ◆

To my colleagues
at the Centre for Treatment of
Sexual Abuse and Childhood Trauma
and to the dream behind the Centre

◆ ❖ ◆

# Contents

Preface      xi

PART I. The Child's Trauma

1. Understanding the Child's Trauma:
   The Internalization Model      2
      Models for Understanding the Dynamics and
        Effects of Sexual Abuse      4
      The Internalization Model      6
      Summary      19

PART II. Techniques

2. Addressing the Child's Internalizations: Therapy      21
      Responding to the Internalizations      23
      Responding to the Individual Child      39
      Summary      41

3. Working Within: Imaging                                      43
   Imaging                                              45
   Uses of Imaging                                      50
   The Process of Imaging                               68
   Summary                                              77

4. Placing the Abuse in Context: Genograms, Timelines,
   Messages, and Myths                                  79
   Genograms                                            80
   Timelines                                            94
   Messages and Myths                                  103
   Summary                                             112

PART III. Issues

5. Engaging the Parts: Working With Dissociation                114
   From Normal to Dysfunctional Dissociation           115
   Diagnosing Dissociation in Children and Adolescents 120
   Treatment of Dissociation in Children and Adolescents 129
   Summary                                             148

6. Reconnecting to the Body: Sexuality                         150
   Children and Sexuality                              151
   Therapy                                             155
   Therapeutic Process                                 174
   Summary                                             178

7. Avoiding the Thoughts: Resistance                           180
   The Child's Resistance                              181
   The Parent's Resistance                             197
   The Therapist's Resistance                          200
   Summary                                             202

PART IV. The Adolescent's Experience

8. Therapy: The Adolescent Comments                     205
    Therapy as a Negative Experience             206
    Therapy as a Positive Experience             208
    Summary                                      214

    References                                   217

    Index                                        228

    About the Author                             237

# Preface

My previous book in this series, *Hearing the Internal Trauma: Working With Children and Adolescents Who Have Been Sexually Abused* (1997), developed out of a series of workshops I presented in Ottawa for therapists working with children and adolescents who had been sexually abused. When the series was over, my colleagues said that they did not want to stop talking. There were too many questions, too many issues still to be talked about. How are we going to accomplish with these children what we have set out to do?

More than 5 years later we are still meeting, still talking, and still have issues to be thought through. This volume is a result of these conversations and, most importantly, of the conversations my colleagues and I have had with the children and adolescents with whom we work. Working from a developmental perspective, we have tried to identify the information a child, then adolescent, takes in about herself and her world when she is abused. In working to find ways to access and address these perceptions, we have tried a variety of techniques, along with play and conversation. Many of these techniques—drawing, making lists, writing letters—are well covered in the present literature on working with children who have been sexually abused. Other techniques that have proved quite helpful—drawing genograms, making timelines, listing family messages and myths, imaging—have not been discussed in this literature. These techniques are described in this book.

My colleagues and I have found that several issues keep coming up in our conversations—dissociation, sexuality, resistance—and feel that these need their own separate discussions. The chapter on dissociation in this volume is a chapter in process. Although recognition of dissociation has progressed considerably, far more learning needs to be done in how to help a child reassociate all that has been split off. The present literature on therapy with children has given only cursory attention to the issue of sexuality. Recognizing the importance of addressing sexuality with these children, my colleagues and I have struggled through our own inhibitions and have found our conversations around sexuality extremely valuable. As we have worked, we have naturally encountered resistance. We started asking, What does resistance mean? What role does the child play, does the parent play, do we play? How can we move on?

This is a different type of book from *Hearing the Internal Trauma*. That volume presents a conceptual framework, the internalization model, for understanding the effects that sexual abuse has on a child's sense of herself and her world and for recognizing what a child is presenting in therapy. It describes psychodynamic trauma-focused therapy for children, adolescents, and parents, and discusses the therapist's own experience within the therapy session.

This volume builds on the ideas developed in *Hearing the Internal Trauma*, but also stands totally on its own. The issues are those of children who have gone through the experience of sexual abuse, not the issues of a theoretical model. These are issues that need to be considered by all therapists working with these children, regardless of therapeutic orientation. The techniques center on recognizing and addressing the trauma internalized from the abuse, from the child's unique perception of the abuse, and from the family experience. With the exception of the chapter on sexuality, the ideas in this book are as relevant for children who have been physically abused, emotionally abused, or neglected as they are for children who have been sexually abused. With the exception of parts of the chapter on dissociation, the ideas are as relevant for working with adults who were abused as children as they are for working with children. Because my primary concern, both as a therapist and as a teacher, has been children and adolescents who have been sexually abused, the book is written and examples are chosen from that perspective.

Chapter 1 presents a brief review of the internalization model. Those who have read *Hearing the Internal Trauma* may wish to skip this chapter and move immediately to Part II, which comprises discussion of techniques and issues. The techniques discussed include addressing specific internalizations, imaging, genograms, timelines, and listing of messages. Imaging is a technique that allows the therapist access to the child's internal perception of herself and her world. Imaging helps the therapist to move the therapy beyond such comments from the child as "I'm just fine," "There's a deadness inside and that's the way it is," "I don't know what's making me so angry," and "I let it happen." Chapter 4 discusses techniques for helping a child understand the context—family and society—in which the abuse happened and the false messages taught as the abuse happened.

The chapters in Part III consider three issues that are particularly relevant for therapists who work with children who have been sexually abused—dissociation, sexuality, and resistance. There are many more issues that could be included and that, indeed, need to be part of the therapist's thinking. As my colleagues and I meet this fall, we will be talking about the effects of trauma on attachment and how to address these effects in therapy. We have reviewed the literature on the physiological effects of trauma, but need to do more thinking around how this can be addressed in therapy. But, just as there needs to be an end point for each therapeutic session and each therapy case without all the issues being addressed, so there needs to be an end point for this book.

This end point is provided in Chapter 8, which presents the results drawn from interviews with 15 adolescents and young adults who had been sexually abused in childhood or adolescence and who received therapy as adolescents. Both negative and positive experiences are reported. What hindered these individuals in therapy and what helped them we, as therapists, need to know.

The ideas presented in this book have not been submitted to empirical research. They are presented as ideas that my colleagues and I have found helpful as we have struggled to help children. We have watched children sort through abuse experiences and acquire new experiences. We have watched children become more relaxed and more sure of themselves. We have watched children start to take better care of themselves and relate more appropriately with family and friends. I offer these ideas for you to think about and to use when appropriate.

As in *Hearing the Internal Trauma,* the terms *victim, survivor, disorder,* and *sexually abused children* are not used in this book. We work with children who have had things happen to them that never should have happened, but they are children who need to be seen as just that: children with the potential to grow and develop, the potential to discover and create, the potential to love and be loved. It is far more important for a therapist and, indeed, a parent to see and to connect with these aspects of the child than with victim, disorder, or abuse.

Many case examples are presented throughout the book. Therapy is a dynamic interactive process and, thus, needs a dynamic interactive description. The child's and the therapist's reactions and responses provide this description. Each example is drawn from an actual occurrence in therapy. All names are changed and, in some cases, ages and scenarios have been changed slightly to provide complete confidentiality. Both male and female pronouns are used in the descriptive sections. Gender pronouns are consistent within sections and are applied on an alternating basis between sections.

Many people have encouraged and helped me in my thinking. Sandy Ages, Ann Lees, Jill Frayne, Maggie Mamon, and Penny Dearing, among others, have encouraged the thinking through of ideas and pushed for more conversations. Linda Seppanan, Thérèse Laberge, Helen Pigeon, Bev Cimermanis, and Lalita Salins have brought cases, raised questions, created ideas, and read chapters. Ellie Kanigsberg and Susan Oke were particularly helpful with the chapter on dissociation. To Jon Conte, I owe a particular thanks for suggesting this book and for suggesting a chapter on resistance, which I was, indeed, resisting. His comments on the text helped me to clarify ideas and, thus, have contributed considerably to this book. And a special thanks to Chris Whelan, who read and reread sentences, paragraphs, and chapters and kept encouraging me as I worked my way through my own resistance.

# PART I

*The Child's Trauma*

# 1

# *Understanding the Child's Trauma: The Internalization Model*

When a child or adolescent is sexually abused, she is used to meet another person's needs.[1] Her body is looked at or touched in a way that does not match her developmental level. Her world is made unsafe.

Depending on the age of the child and the context of the abuse, this reality may or may not be experienced consciously. No matter what the child's age, the child's internal experience of herself and the world is affected. Bowlby (1971, 1973), in his thought-provoking work on children and their relationship to others, describes the child as creating within herself "working models" of self, of mother, of mother in relation to self, of the world, and of self within the world. These internal models reflect a child's previous experience and, in turn, shape the way a child "perceives events, forecasts the future, and constructs his plans" (Bowlby, 1973, p. 236). As future events impinge on the child, she internalizes further information about self, others, and the world. The child's internal working models shift.

When an individual is sexually abused, abuse-related information about the perpetrator, the world, and the self is internalized. For an adult, who already has a clarified working model of self and of the world and who has the conceptual ability to view situations separate from herself, the impact of an assault may be, after the initial shock and stress, in just that order—new information about the perpetrator, the world, the self. For a child or adolescent, whose model of the world is still taking form and who experiences herself central to events that occur, the abuse has impacts, first and foremost, on the self. It is the child's working model of the self that is most affected, then the child's understanding of the world, then her perception of the perpetrator.

For the child who has had early positive attachment experiences, abuse-related internalizations are cushioned by an earlier internalized positive model of self and the world (Pearce & Pezzot-Pearce, 1997; Wieland, 1997). Rather than becoming a predominant part of the child's working model, the abuse internalizations have less effect ("*I am different,*" not "*I am damaged*") or the area of the child's life affected by the internalization is more circumscribed ("*I, as a sexual being, am damaged,*" not "*I am damaged*"). For the child who has experienced early neglect or maltreatment leading to negative attachment experiences (Karen, 1994), the impact of abuse-related internalizations will be greater (Friedrich, 1995; Prior, 1996).[2]

As a child's internal world shifts, her perceptions of and reactions to new experiences shift (Bowlby, 1973). Research has indicated that children who have been sexually abused experience depression, suicidal ideation, and revictimization significantly more often than do either nonabused well-adjusted children or nonabused highly distressed children (Beitchman, Zucker, Hood, daCosta, & Akman, 1991). Particularly prevalent among children who have been sexually abused is increased sexualized behavior (Eibender & Friedrich, 1989; Friedrich, 1988; Friedrich et al., 1992; Friedrich, Urquiza, & Beilke, 1986). Increased anxiety (Gomez-Schwartz, Horowitz, & Cardarelli, 1990; Mennen & Meadow, 1995; Mian, Marton, & LeBaron, 1996) and negative thoughts about oneself (Mennen & Meadow, 1995; Morrow & Sorell, 1989) are also reported. Distrust of people and of the future permeates the child's thoughts (Terr, 1991). These shifts in mood and behavior reflect the internal change, the change in a child's understanding of self, world, and others.

The therapist needs to have in mind the event(s), the context within which the event(s) occurred, the changes in the child's environment during and following the event(s), the changes in the child's behavior, and the shifts in the child's sense of self and other. Whereas the event, the environment, and the behavior can, with careful information gathering, be identified, recognition of shifts within a child's internal world is often more difficult. Young children are not able to verbalize these shifts, and older children and adolescents are reluctant—indeed, in some cases unable—to talk about them. For this reason, my colleagues and I have worked to develop a schema for conceptualizing what a child internalizes when sexually abused. With this schema as a framework, we have found it easier to recognize abuse-related internalizations in our work with children and adolescents.

The internalization model, which I have described in detail in *Hearing the Internal Trauma: Working With Children and Adolescents Who Have Been Sexually Abused* (Wieland, 1997), examines the experience of a child when sexually abused, the child's internalizations as a result of that experience, and the effects of these internalizations on subsequent reacting and behaving. This model is not a replacement for other models, but rather an additional perspective on what occurs for a child who is sexually abused, a perspective that centers on the child's internal processing of the abuse experience.[3] This perspective can be particularly helpful for the therapist as he works within the therapy room.

The following discussion briefly considers the models developed over the past 15 years to help us understand the dynamics and effect of sexual abuse. A description of the internalization model is then provided.

❏ **Models for Understanding the Dynamics and Effects of Sexual Abuse**

The traumagenic factor model developed by Finkelhor and Browne (1985) identifies four characteristics of the abuse experience: betrayal, stigmatization, traumagenic sexualization, and powerlessness. Each of these factors alters "children's cognitive and emotional orientation to the world and create[s] trauma by distorting children's self-concept, world view and affective capacities" (Finkelhor & Browne, 1985, p. 531). These areas are highlighted as needing to be discussed within therapy.

Hartman and Burgess's (1988, 1993) information processing model describes the pretrauma phase (child's characteristics and previous experiences), the trauma encapsulation phase (the experience, the coping that occurs, and the memory held), the disclosure phase (either disclosure or no disclosure), and the posttrauma phase (child's behavioral response). This model considers how the effects of abuse experiences vary, depending not only on the type of experience but also the child's own background, the child's way of coping, and whether telling is possible. The therapist is helped to understand individual differences in abuse effects and to be more aware of these differences when working with the child.

Friedrich's (1995) integrated contextual model takes into consideration the child's interpersonal experience (attachment); the child's neurophysiological, behavioral, and cognitive reactivity to trauma (dysregulation); and the development of sense of self and other (self-theory). Each of these areas affects the impact that abuse has on the child and is, in turn, affected by the experience of the abuse. This model, by incorporating these different perspectives, has encouraged therapists to look at and address the effect of abuse on different areas of functioning. Of particular importance is Friedrich's incorporation of recent physiological research on trauma and maltreatment into the therapeutic literature.

The models described above extend our understanding of abuse dynamics and of the effects of abuse on a child. They highlight concerns that need to be considered in therapy. But the therapist in the room with the child needs more. The therapist needs a framework through which she can observe the child—the child's play, behavior, or conversation—and recognize the internalizations that have come from the abuse, the internalizations that are now shaping the child's internal model of self and world. The therapist also needs a framework that will help her to understand the basis of abuse-related internalizations. Only when a therapist understands where, within the child's experience, the abuse-related internalizations are formed, can she talk about them in a way that will help the child separate those internalizations from himself.

## ❏ The Internalization Model

All children's experiences of sexual abuse differ as a result of the characteristics of the abuse: the child's relationship to the abuser (Adams-Tucker, 1982; Finkelhor, 1979; Russell, 1986); the extent, frequency, and duration of the abuse (Burgess, Hartman, McCausland, & Powers, 1984; Friedrich et al., 1986; Sirles, Smith, & Kusama, 1989); the presence or lack of violence (Beitchman et al., 1991; Friedrich et al., 1986; Mennen & Meadow, 1995). Yet within these differences, sexual abuse experiences have common characteristics. These characteristics form the beginning point of the internalization model, depicted in Figure 1.1; they are presented on the left-hand side of the figure. The first four characteristics occur with all sexual abuse experiences. The second three characteristics occur, in addition to the first four, when sexual abuse is perpetrated by someone close to the child. The last four characteristics occur when abuse is extreme. Figure 1.1 is divided horizontally to indicate these different areas.

Each of these common characteristics has some impact on the child. The extent of the impact is influenced by the child's own characteristics: developmental level, temperament, quality of attachment, and present understanding of herself and her world (Friedrich, 1990, 1995). From this impact, the child internalizes information about herself and her world. These abuse-related internalizations (Figure 1.1, middle column) become part of the child's internal world. These internalizations may be moderated or may be intensified by the child's temperament, the child's earlier experiences, and the responses of other people in the child's world. The internalizations affect the child's internal model of self and world and, thus, shape the way the child perceives and reacts to future situations (Figure 1.1, right-hand side).

Like any model, the internalization model is a simplification. Each internalization may arise from several different aspects of the experience. As well, each internalization influences many areas of behavior.

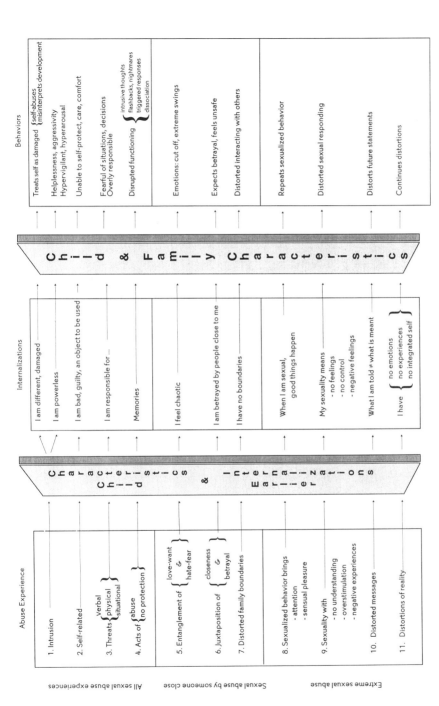

**Figure 1.1.** Internalization Model

7

Simplification provides a framework that can help the therapist, as he watches and listens to a child, to identify what the child is "saying." It can help him hear the child's internal trauma and recognize internalizations that need to be addressed and shifted for the child to experience her future separate from the sexual abuse. By following the play, conversation, and behavior of the child in the therapy session back to an underlying internalization, the therapist is better able to identify the issue most relevant to a child at a particular moment. The therapist can address this internalization, and thereby the abuse, even when a child does not talk or play directly about the abuse. Therapy can be direct without being intrusive.

The internalization model has been developed from research findings in the areas of sexual abuse, child development, early attachment, and trauma as well as from clinical work with children, adolescents, and adults who have been sexually abused. The first four internalizations occur with each instance of abuse and, although developed separately from Friedrich's model (1995), closely parallel his self issues.

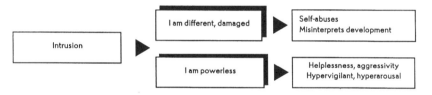

Sexual abuse is intrusive. It intrudes on a child's physical body, sexual development, and sense of self. This intrusion is experienced both emotionally and physically, and, for older children, cognitively as well.

During the infant and toddler years, sexual abuse intrudes into the child's preliminary development of a sense of self, trust in others, and ability to self-regulate (Cole & Putnam, 1992). During the early school years, as the child becomes more aware of internal psychological processes and of himself in relation to others (Harter, 1983), sexual abuse affects this awareness. With adolescence and increased self-reflection and awareness of others' opinions (Elkind, 1967), sexual abuse intrudes into the adolescent's self-definition. This intrusion has been described by children, adolescents, and adults as a sense of being internally different or damaged in some way. The intensity of the feeling varies depending on the characteristics of the abuse and the characteristics of the child, but there is, in some form, a feeling of "yuck," differentness, or damage. And this is internalized, *"I am different . . . damaged."*

The internalized sense of yuck or damage distorts a child's sense of self and of body schema (Santostefano & Calicchia, 1992), including sexual awareness (Hindman, 1989). The child, experiencing himself as negative, treats himself in that way—he becomes self-abusive. Whereas alcohol, drug use, and self-mutilation can readily be labeled, other forms of self-abuse are less obvious—the child may withdraw from friends or family, engage in abusive relationships, behave in ways that will bring punishment, overexert himself, adopt destructive eating patterns, or neglect his body. Once the sense of being different/ damaged is inside, the child is all too likely to interpret normal developmental changes in sexual awareness (increased curiosity, sensations, arousal) as abnormal and as proof that there is something wrong with him.

Intrusion also leads to a sense of powerlessness. Infants, children, and adolescents gradually develop control over their environment. Until this control is developed, parents and caretakers need to be aware of a child's needs and react to the child within the context of those needs. Sexual abuse is determined by the perpetrator's "needs." The child is acted upon. From this experience of intrusion, the child internalizes, *"I am powerless."* This sense of powerlessness appears to be even greater when the child has no way of knowing when the abuse is going to occur. Depending on the other experiences the child has had and on the extent of the abuse, the internalization of powerlessness may be linked by the child to only some situations, to many situations, or to all situations. Response to a disclosure, both within a family and through the court system, also affects—either lessening or strengthening—this sense of powerlessness.

Powerlessness leads to two opposing responses: learned helplessness (Seligman, 1975) and aggressive behavior (Friedrich, 1995). For some children, the sense of powerlessness and the response of helplessness or aggressivity occur with almost all interactions. For other children, these responses occur only when a situation becomes sexual.

Reactions of hypervigilance, hyperarousal, impulsive responding, and aggressivity also reflect, for some children, a physiological effect. If a child is abused at a young age, when there is still considerable plasticity in the biological startle mechanisms, the child's basic arousal mechanism may become overstimulated, thus increasing physiological reactivity (Pynoos, Steinberg, & Goenjian, 1996). This child becomes anxious and out of control far more easily and more quickly than do other children. Severe trauma in middle childhood can lead to a disruption of the inhibitory control of the startle response (Ornitz & Pynoos, 1989). This child has less control and responds impulsively. Severe trauma at any age may also lead to neurologic hypersensitivity and hyperexcitation (Everly, 1993; van der Kolk, 1996b). This child experiences the contrasting effects of arousal and numbing as described in posttraumatic stress symptomatology. Friedrich (1995) labels these effects dysregulation.

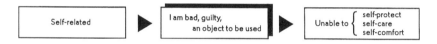

Sexual abuse occurs to an individual child and, in most cases, occurs alone with the child. The young child, because of egocentric thinking (Piaget & Inhelder, 1969), experiences herself at the center of the activity and internalizes that she is bad. As the child moves out of egocentric thinking, she becomes increasingly aware of other people's statements: the abuser's statements ("You enjoy this"; "If it were not for me, you would just be a dropout on the street"), the nonperpetrating parent's statements ("You are too young to go with us, you'll have to stay with the baby-sitter"; "Don't sit like that, it isn't ladylike"), and statements made in abuse prevention programs ("Say no"; "Tell someone"). The child, not being able to recognize the unfairness of these statements and the incredible difficulty of saying no or telling, internalizes that she is bad. This sense continues even when the child knows she is not to blame.

The child continues to develop, both sexually and socially. Sexual curiosity is part of growing up. In situations of abuse where fear is not overwhelming, the child is curious about bodies, about sexual feelings, about sexual reactions. And because all children enjoy attention, the child may enjoy part of the abuse scenario. If the child is placed in a favored position within the family or within some group related to the abuser, the child, being a normal child, enjoys and wants to hold on to that status. Awareness of this curiosity, the wish to be special, and the enjoyment of sexual sensations contribute to a child's internalization of being bad or guilty.

For the adolescent there are additional dynamics occurring. Reacting with age-appropriate efforts to control her world, an adolescent may shape when and how the abuse occurs. She is then likely to experience herself as playing a role in, or even causing, the abuse.

From these experiences of abuse, the child internalizes, *"I am guilty, bad, an object to be used."* Although attention is given during disclosure procedures to assuring the child she is not at fault, a sense of guilt has already been internalized. Friedrich (1995) describes internalized guilt as the basis of shame, an inner sense of being looked down on or diminished (Fossum & Mason, 1986). The internalized guilt or shame becomes embedded in the child's working model of self. Thus, although the child may be able to verbalize that she is not at fault, a sense of guilt and shame often continues within.

Self-blame may also occur when the abuser is someone important to the child and the child does not want to blame that individual. If the child is blamed by the parent, this internalization is strengthened.

A child with an internal sense of badness or shame does not take care of herself, protect herself, or comfort herself. The child is unable to tell herself that she is a good person and to integrate the positive experiences that do happen.

The threats from sexual abuse may be verbal ("Your mother will go crazy if you tell"; "Nobody will believe you"), physical (the use of a weapon, the size of the abuser), or situational (the abuser being admired and valued by the family). In addition, when the abuser is a parent or a parent figure, telling involves a threat of abandonment.

These threats place the child in a position of control at the same time he is experiencing powerlessness, a double bind. The child becomes responsible for holding together the family or the family's position in society, a responsibility inappropriate for a child. The child internalizes, *"I am responsible for . . . ,"* and what he starts to feel responsible for has few limits. This sense of responsibility occurs whether the child does or does not disclose. When a disclosure does occur, with all of its ensuing disruptions, the child feels responsible not only for what happened during the abuse, but also for the present emotional and, often, financial strain on the family.

Responsibility for keeping the world "stable" for the family, while at the same time needing to protect himself, places the child in an impossible position. Both alternatives, telling and not telling, lead to negative situations. The child develops a fear of new situations and a fear of decision making. The internalization of being responsible leads to a feeling of responsibility for other people and other events.

When a child is abused, she has two experiences: an experience of being abused and an experience of not being protected. These experiences, depending on the child's age and on the level of stress experienced during the abuse, will be recorded in implicit (sensorimotor/emotional) memory, a function of the basal area of the brain, or in explicit (declarative) memory, a function of the hippocampus (LeDoux, 1994, Tobias, Kihlstrom, & Schacter, 1992; van der Kolk, 1994).

Events that occur during the first 3 or 4 years of life, before mylination of the hippocampus is complete, are encoded through the basal area of the brain and, thus, are held within sensorimotor/emotional modalities (van der Kolk, 1996b). These early memories are reflected in a child's behavior and body sensations. Memory after 4 years of age is, for the most part, recorded through the hippocampus and held within the verbal memory modality. When, however, a child is highly stressed, the levels of corticosteroids released within the brain can increase to a level that inhibits hippocampal activity (Nilsson & Archer,

1992; van der Kolk, 1996b). Highly stressful events may, as with early memories, be recorded through the basal area and, thus, are held within a sensorimotor/emotional, not verbal, context (LeDoux, 1994; van der Kolk, 1996b). A child may experience fright or shift her way of behaving when she sees a person or people with particular characteristics, yet have no verbal knowledge of anything that happened with that person or type of person.[4]

This knowledge—*memories of abuse, memories of lack of protection*—is internalized and affects the child's working model of self and others. For some children, the memories remain active and intrude persistently into the children's thinking. For other children, the memories are suppressed—that is, not thought about or felt on a regular basis but still available to active recall. For still others, the memories are repressed (not available to verbal recall but still part of the core self) or dissociated (not part of or available to the core self). In whichever form memories are held, they are part of the child's internal world.

These memories, as part of the child's internal world, affect the child's future experiences. Active memories that are not worked through are likely to cause intrusive thoughts and a sense that the abuse, even though it is over, is pervading the present. Flashbacks, nightmares, anxiety attacks, and trigger responses may occur whether memories are active, suppressed, or repressed.[5] When internal memory has been dissociated, the child is left with a sense of "not being all there" or of "something being missing" when particular types of situations occur.

For children who have been sexually abused by someone within the family or by someone close to them, the abuse experience has additional characteristics and additional internalizations.

When an abuser is someone unimportant to the child, feelings of distress, fear, or hate toward the abuser are not problematic. When, however, the abuser is someone the child loves or someone who is important to the child in some way, the child ends up feeling both love and want and hate and fear toward the same person.

The child's normal ambivalent feelings become heightened to the point that the child may feel out of control. He hates himself for loving the person and hates himself for hating the person. Children and adults describe this as a crazy-making feeling. It is this feeling of chaos and of being alone within the chaos that is internalized, "*I feel chaotic*," and becomes part of the child's sense of self. For the child whose early attachment experiences fit within the category of disorganized attachment (Karen, 1994; Main & Solomon, 1990), the sense of chaos is likely to be even greater. For the child who experiences early abandonment or neglect, the pull toward the perpetrator, a person who is attending to him, is particularly strong (Prior, 1996). Both love and hate become intensified.

Feelings come to represent chaos. The child in future emotional situations either experiences extreme emotional swings or, to be protective, cuts off feelings. This reaction is particularly strong when a child starts to feel emotionally close to someone.

When a child is abused by someone close to her, she experiences closeness and betrayal at the same time. When the abuser is an early attachment figure or has provided the support and security that early attachment figures did not provide, the sense of rejection or betrayal is particularly strong (Alexander, 1992; Friedrich, 1995).

As the child internalizes this link between closeness and betrayal, "*I am betrayed by people close to me*" becomes part of her working model of "others." Depending on the characteristics of the original abuse, this link between closeness and betrayal may relate to all other people or may relate only to people with whom the child becomes sexually intimate. The child's expectation of betrayal all too often becomes a reality as the child chooses friends and partners who betray, as the child "sees" betrayal even where it does not exist, and as the child treats other people as if they have betrayed her to such an extent that those people take on that behavior. Disruption in an individual's sense of personal and world safety and trust has been described by Pearlman (1997) as a primary effect of childhood sexual abuse.

Sexual abuse is disrespectful of personal boundaries, both physical and emotional. The child, with a right to privacy and to having his needs met, is used by others to meet *their* needs. In families with intergenerational abuse, boundaries between individuals, between family subsystems, and between the family and society are distorted (Alexander, 1985; Trepper & Barrett, 1989). Children are used to care for adults, both sexually and emotionally. When abuse occurs within a single generation, there are also distorted boundaries. The boundary between the perpetrator and the child is too porous, and that between the child and the protecting parent(s) is too opaque. The child internalizes, "*I have no boundaries.*"

A child who has not had an opportunity to internalize appropriate personal boundaries is likely to allow others to intrude inappropriately on him as well as to become overly intrusive with others. The child is often "parentified," and with this loses normal childhood experiences.

To this point in the discussion, characteristics common to all sexual abuse experiences and to abuse perpetrated by someone close to the child have been considered. There are additional aspects of the experience of abuse when the abuse is extreme. Researchers have defined extreme sexual abuse in terms of the type of intrusion, the extent of force used, and the duration of the abuse. Within the present discussion, I use the term *extreme* to refer to abuse that severely impacts a child's sense of sexuality and reality.

Sexual abuse provides attention and, in some cases, pleasurable sensations for a child. Both attention and pleasure are important and enjoyable for children, and especially for children who have had little attention and pleasure in their lives. Sexual abuse may give a child special status in the family, may help the child to avoid punishment, or may bring other rewards. This attention, pleasure, and importance reinforce the behaviors of the child during the abuse—that is, sexualized behaviors. These behaviors may include particular ways of sitting or moving the body or may include interest in particular types of pictures or activities. The child internalizes, *"When I am sexual, good things happen."* When a child recognizes this connection between sexual behavior and positive outcome, his sense of being bad or guilty is likely to intensify.

Behaviors that bring positive reinforcement are repeated. Indeed, the occurrence of sexualized behaviors has consistently been found to distinguish children who have been sexually abused from children with psychiatric problems who have not been sexually abused (Beitchman et al., 1991; Friedrich et al., 1986, 1992; Gomez-Schwartz et al., 1990).

When sexual abuse occurs, the child experiences sexual responding, either her own or that of the perpetrator, at an intensity beyond her developmental level. For some children, sexuality becomes connected with a sense of fright or being out of control. For children who protect themselves by cutting off body feeling, sexuality becomes linked to a lack of sensation or a sensation of freezing and rigidity in the body. When pain and manipulation occur with the abuse, sexuality may become associated with pain and manipulation.

For the adolescent who is in the developmental stage of solidifying her sexual identity and of exploring relationships combining emotional and sexual attraction, the abuse and the dynamics surrounding the abuse become not only part of her sexual identity but also part of her understanding of sexual relationships. This may occur for the individual abused during adolescence or the individual abused during childhood who brings into adolescence the dynamics linked to earlier abuse.

Even though sexualized behaviors, because they bring attention and pleasure, may be experienced as positive, the child's sexuality, the emotional and physical experiencing of self as a female or male, can take on negative meaning. This negative internalization, *"My sexuality means no feelings, no control, negative feelings,"* disrupts the child's chance to develop understanding, appreciation, and respect for her body and for her body's responding. Without this development, the child, as she matures, continues to connect sexuality with no sensation or negative sensations, with no feelings or negative feelings. Sexual relationships are likely to exist separate from emotional caring.

A child who is severely sexually abused may be told that he is being cared for and that he is safe, yet he experiences the opposite. He hears people saying that people are not to hurt, and yet he experiences these people hurting him. What he is told does not match his reality. These children experience that people in their world do not mean what they say. *"What I am told is not what is meant"* is internalized and becomes part of the child's inner reality. For some children, this applies to the world in general; for others, it applies to a few specific people.

This internalized understanding is extended to new situations. Future statements are not believed—indeed, the child may distort statements in such a way that situations that are safe appear dangerous.

For a child, the happening of the abuse may be too frightening, too painful, or too overwhelming to be absorbed into her conscious awareness. Denying that anything happened or that what happened meant anything ("He was drunk so it doesn't count") allows the child to protect herself (Femina, Yeager, & Lewis, 1990). A child may also protect herself by blocking memories from retrieval (Briere & Conte, 1993; Herman & Schatzow, 1987; Williams, 1994).

Another escape mechanism is dissociation. The child, either emotionally or cognitively, disengages from what happens during the abuse. The connections among feelings, thoughts, behaviors, and memories are disrupted (Briere, 1992). A child may remember the abuse but feel no distress or feel as if she were not there. For some children, the dissociative defense becomes linked with a part of the child's self, thereby creating a dissociated part (Kluft, 1984). This is discussed further in Chapter 5.

As a result of distortion of reality, the child ends up with abuse memories but no emotions, with negative emotions but no memory, or with a self but no sense of wholeness. This distorted reality is internalized by the child, *"I have no emotions, no experience, no integrated self."* And because it is protective—the world feels safer—the child continues to distort experiences. As denial, repression, and dissociation are used for coping mechanisms, a child does not have the opportunity to learn more positive coping. Cole and Putnam (1992) note that when a child has had to rely on immature coping strategies, the coping skills of playing out, reflecting on, or reasoning about a situation do not develop. Immature impulsive responding in difficult situations continues. Distortion is used for coping, even in nontraumatic situations.

The internalization model does not contradict Finkelhor and Browne's traumagenic model, Hartman and Burgess's information processing model, or Friedrich's integrated contextual model, nor does it take the place of any of these models. Rather, it provides an additional perspective from which to understand the child's experience, a perspective that highlights the child's concept of self and other that comes from a sexual abuse experience.

In addition, the internalization model provides a framework the therapist can use while working within a therapy session with a child who has been abused. The internalization model, by providing a link between event and internalizations, encourages the therapist to move, in his thinking, from the abuse event to the child's internal sense of self and world. The internalization model, by providing a link between behaviors and internalizations, helps the therapist move, in his interventions, from the behavior displayed in the child's play, conversation, and behavior to the internalization behind the behavior. Rather than centering on the causative event or the symptomatic behaviors, the therapist can, from the event and the behaviors, recognize the abuse-related internalizations that need to be addressed.

Once the abuse-related internalizations are shifted, the child's internal model of self and world is no longer dominated by the abuse. The child's future experiencing of the world is no longer shaped by the abuse.

## ❏ Summary

When a child or adolescent is sexually abused, he has a new experience of himself and his world, an experience that alters his internal model of self and world. The internalization model describes the abuse-related internalizations that occur when a child is sexually abused and behaviors that occur as a result of these internalizations.

This model has been used clinically by therapists working with children and adolescents. Therapists report that it helps them (a) to understand a child's way of thinking following abuse, (b) to recognize what a child or adolescent may be expressing in a therapy session, and (c) to develop a new experience that can shift abuse-related internalizations.

## ❏ Notes

1. To simplify the discussion, I use the term *child* to refer generally to both children and adolescents. When the discussion pertains only to adolescents, I use the term *adolescent*. When the discussion pertains only to children, I designate the specific age group—for example, the preschool child.

2. Negative parenting behavior has been found to be predictive of posttraumatic stress response following exposure to severe stress (reviewed in Shalev, 1996).

3. *Internal processing* refers to the ongoing organizing of information (both implicit and explicit memory) in a pattern from which the individual then responds to the world. This pattern has been variously described as a cognitive map (van der Kolk, 1994), mental schemata (Piaget & Inhelder, 1969), and an internal working model (Bowlby, 1971, 1973). Internal processing differs with the developmental level of the child; for example, young children employ egocentric thinking, whereas adolescents recognize the roles of others. With early trauma, a child's internal processing can become stuck at the early developmental level.

4. Terr's (1988) research with young children who have been traumatized describes the effects of nonverbal memories.

5. Trigger responses occur when something in the individual's present world is similar to something in the past and, because of this similarity, the individual's experiencing and capabilities from that time are triggered. The individual is left trying to deal with adolescent or adult situations with the resources of a child.

# PART II

*Techniques*

# 2

# *Addressing the Child's Internalizations: Therapy*

Therapy for individuals who have been sexually abused has developed, over the past several decades, toward an abuse-focused model. This model recognizes that the distress being experienced is a result of abuse trauma, not a disorder within the individual (Chaffin, Bonner, Worley, & Lawson, 1996). This distress and the trauma behind it are addressed sensitively but directly in therapy. The abuse is described and explored on both cognitive and emotional levels, and the individual is helped to separate the experience from himself.

The internalization model highlights the importance of addressing in therapy a child's internal experience. External, symptomatic behaviors are starting points for understanding what is going on inside a child. The therapist needs to address these behaviors directly to provide relief and a consistent, supportive external world for the child. But addressing the behaviors is not enough. These behaviors need to be understood as the results of the child's experiences and the abuse-related internalizations that have shaped the child's sense of self and world, that is, the child's internal working model. This internal model needs to be addressed in therapy if a child is to be able to grow up without the abuse affecting future experiences and interactions.

Using a psychodynamic abuse-focused approach (Wieland, 1997), a therapist can observe and notice the content a child brings to therapy. This content may include descriptions of the abuse events or the sequelae of abuse (for example, intrusive thoughts, flashbacks), descriptions of feelings, or descriptions of the child's ongoing world at school, at home, and with friends. These descriptions are expressed through the child's play and the adolescent's conversation, through the child/adolescent's general behavior in the session, through the child/adolescent's response to the therapist (transference), and through the therapist's own reaction to the child/adolescent (countertransference). The therapist also takes into account the behaviors described by parents, foster parents, or group home workers.

The therapist responds to this content through discussion of the play or events reported, through discussion of the reactions noticed as well as reactions that seem to be notably absent, and through her relationship with the child. In my previous discussion of therapy with children and adolescents who have been sexually abused (Wieland, 1997), these presentations and therapist responses are described in detail. The internalization model is used, within that discussion, as a framework for helping the therapist recognize and respond to an individual child's internal experience. The internalization model can also, by highlighting the distorted information a child holds about the abuse and about himself and his world, alert the therapist to issues that will need to be addressed during therapy.

The present emphasis on abuse-related internalizations is not meant to minimize the importance of addressing in therapy other aspects of a child's experience. Early attachment experiences shape a child's internal view of self and others. Temperament and environment influence coping mechanisms and general behavior. Anxiety can come from many experiences. Feelings pervade—consciously or unconsciously— all areas of a child's life. And all of these aspects of the child's world— as they pertain to the sexual abuse and as they pertain to other areas of the child's experience—need to be addressed in therapy. As Putnam (1997) notes, owing to the limited ability of children and adolescents to self-observe, interventions often need to be implicit (not directly labeling the abuse but dealing indirectly with abuse issues or effects) as opposed to the explicit interventions (directly addressing the abuse) used with adults.

Discussion and ideas for psychotherapy with children who have been abused are offered by a number of authors, including Deblinger and Heflin (1996), Gil (1991, 1996), Karp and Butler (1996), Friedrich (1990, 1995), James (1989), and Pearce and Pezzot-Pearce (1997). These ideas, even if they do not fit with a therapist's particular approach, stimulate thought and encourage a therapist to expand her repertoire of skills for working with children. The present emphasis is an invitation to readers to add another perspective to their work with children, a perspective that emphasizes the information and self-messages taken in by a child when sexual abuse occurs. These internalizations need to change for the child to be able to put the abuse behind him.

In this chapter, I use the internalization model as a framework for identifying issues related to the experience of sexual abuse and for developing ways of helping children shift abuse-related internalizations. The importance of responding to the individual child and his individual experiences is also discussed.

## ❏ Responding to the Internalizations

> I am different, damaged

Owing to the innate intrusiveness of sexual abuse, the child internalizes this abuse as a part of her. No separation is placed between herself and the abuse. Some parents are excellent at talking about or describing the abuse as an external event—something outside the child. In other situations, because of parental distress or parental denial, the parents' reactions unfortunately may reinforce the child's sense of being irreparably different or damaged. Within therapy, the abuse can be described as a happening, not the child. It was a happening that never should have happened and a happening that left confusion and feelings inside, but the abuse itself is not inside the child. The abuse can be defined as belonging to the abuser. That is where it originated, thus that is where it belongs.

Sometimes a child feels that the abuser abused because he or she was abused, and this illustrates the existence of abuse inside the individual who has been abused. This child needs information on the number of people who have been abused who do *not* abuse.[1] Some children feel that their sexual curiosity or their sexual feelings mean the abuse is inside them. The difference between sexual abuse and sexuality needs to be highlighted for these children (see Chapter 6). Their sexual reactions come from a normal physiological process. That this process could have been intensified or, indeed, cut off by their experience can be discussed. But this physiological process does not represent the abuse inside them.

For some children, particularly if they are experiencing flashbacks that include body memories, the sense of the abuse being inside is very strong. For these children, learning that bodies can have physical sensation memories—even if they never rode a bicycle again, they would be able to remember the feeling of their legs pedaling uphill or the feeling of the wind in their faces—but that a memory is not the event can be helpful.

A child talking about herself when she was a baby or a young child—the time before the abuse began—can help connect the child to herself before and, therefore, separate from the abuse. The child can draw or bring in a picture of herself. Similarities between herself then and herself now can be highlighted. These would include attitudes, reactions, and feelings, not just external characteristics. The differences between the self before the abuse and the self after the abuse—the feelings and behaviors arising out of the abusive events—can then be listed. The working through of these differences can be labeled as the job of therapy.

Increased fears, anxiety attacks, hypervigilance, feeling out of control, and other posttraumatic stress reactions can be described as normal, *given what the child has gone through.* They are to be expected, *given what the child has gone through.* These reactions are not crazy and do not indicate that the child is abnormal or damaged. The child's knowledge of the world includes dangers that were not there before, her emotions include reactions beyond a child's normal experience, and her physiological arousal system may have been hypersensitized. These reactions can be defined as resulting from the event(s). Once the child is removed from situations causing hyperarousal, the experiences are worked through—the abuse-related internalizations are shifted—and the child has opportunities to learn to relax and experience physiological desensitization, these reactions will decrease and, in time, disappear.[2] The fact that reactions are often greater following disclosure than following the event itself needs to be explained. The therapist may say, for instance:

> While the abuse was going on, it wasn't safe to recognize the effect—our bodies do a wonderful job of holding on to things until the world is a bit safer. What did your body hold on to until now?

It is particularly important that the therapist, in working with parents and other individuals in contact with the child, reinforce the idea that the child is not damaged—hurt, yes; confused, yes; angry, yes—but not damaged. The use of diagnostic labels, including *disorder,* may be helpful for professionals but is seldom helpful for a child. Anxiety is a normal response to frightening experiences and carries over until the event is worked through. Anxiety is not something wrong with the child. Dissociation is an important and helpful coping defense that can become too automatic and, therefore, needs to be worked through, not something wrong with the child. Parents and workers need to be encouraged to avoid pejorative labels such as *victim* and *damaged goods.*

Another area often affected by the intrusion of sexual abuse is a child's development of sexual awareness (Hindman, 1989; Maltz, 1991) and understanding of her own sexual development. As a child becomes curious about sex and starts to be aware of her own sensations and arousal, she may link these with the abuse and not with normal development. The child may come to see her physical development as bad or ugly and her sexual reactions—and thus herself—as perverted rather than as part of normal development. Providing information about normal sexual development can be an extremely important part of therapy; this is discussed at greater length in Chapter 6.

| I am powerless |

Because of the internalization of powerlessness, the child's interrelating with other people, including the therapist, will be affected. To counteract this, it is important for a child to feel a sense of control in therapy. The play or conversation within a therapy session should revolve around the child's, not the therapist's, agenda. When a contract for therapy is being made with an older child or adolescent, the therapist can engage the child in a discussion of objectives. Although the therapist may suggest a certain number of sessions, the child should be the one to decide the number. The decision to talk or not talk directly about the abuse should be the child's. At the same time, the therapist should reserve the right to draw links between what is happening now and the abuse.

When the child's play, behavior, or conversation shows considerable helplessness or aggressivity, the therapist can wonder about feelings of powerlessness. The therapist can link this powerlessness to the experiencing of the abuse or, if the child is extremely defensive and is not able to discuss the abuse, the therapist can discuss the sense of powerlessness in general. Throughout therapy, the therapist can emphasize what the child knows now and highlight the difference between *now* and *then* (the time at which the abuse occurred), even if the *then* was just a week ago.

The therapist can encourage parents, while providing safety, not to overprotect a child following a disclosure of abuse. In addition, parents can be encouraged to provide opportunities for their child to say no. For parents who are autocratic, the therapist can describe this as teaching the child the skill of saying no.

Because the aggressivity observed in a child who has been abused may also reflect neurobiological effects (Friedrich, 1995), in particular a disruption of the arousal system (Everly, 1993; Ornitz & Pynoos, 1989; Pynoos, Steinberg, & Goenjian, 1996; van der Kolk, 1996b), helping a child think through his reactions and his behavior is an important part of therapy. Friedrich (1995), in his work with children experiencing dysregulation, emphasizes the importance of clear structural guidelines, techniques for self-soothing and decreasing anxiety, opportunities for children to label and talk about the distress being experienced, and direct discussion of sexual feelings and behaviors. Working with parents to create a calmer setting at home can help lower the ongoing level of stimulation the child is experiencing and, in time, may reduce arousal level within the nervous system (Everly, 1989).

> I am bad, guilty,
>                an object to be used

The child's sense of guilt and badness comes from her understanding of the abuse when the abuse was happening. As the therapist works with the child, therefore, he needs to be aware of the child's age when the abuse started and the stages of development the child went through while being abused. During each stage, different ways of thinking and different content became connected to the child's sense of guilt and shame. These ways of thinking and this content need to be part of the therapy.

It is important to explain to the older child or adolescent that seeing oneself as causing events is a result of the limited breadth of a young child's thinking (egocentric) and is not from the reality of the situation. A therapist can explain the development of thinking from (a) being aware of one's own thoughts and behavior and therefore thinking that everything is a result of oneself, to (b) being aware of another's thinking and behavior and therefore realizing that others play a role in what happens to oneself, to (c) being aware of social (including familial) influences on thinking and behavior and therefore realizing the many dynamics that influence behavior and events. Helping the child, as she is now, notice the roles of other people and, if appropriate, of social influences and then asking her how she would explain all of this to a child the age she was when the abuse first started can be helpful.

It is important for the therapist to explain that looking for attention is normal child behavior. Children cannot thrive without emotional attention; therefore, they are drawn to individuals who give them that attention and a sense of importance. Wanting and asking for attention is *not* wanting and asking for sexual abuse. When these occur together, however, they become connected in the child's mind. A therapist needs to clarify the difference.

Infatuation with an older person is part of normal pre- and early adolescent emotional responding and behavior. For some pre- and early adolescents, this infatuation is directed toward a singer or movie star, for others it is directed toward a teacher, relative, or family friend. These feelings are a normal developmental stage. Although they may lead to a wish to have a relationship with the individual and indeed to flirting, they do not cause sexual abuse. It is the adult's responsibility not to take advantage of a child's infatuation. The therapist needs to normalize and legitimate the child's feelings and place the responsibility for any abuse of these feelings with the older person.

It is important for the therapist to explain that trying to gain control over situations is normal adolescent behavior. Deciding when abuse will occur or how it will occur is not causing the abuse, it is reflecting a normal adolescent's efforts to control her world. The therapist can help the adolescent understand rather than condemn herself by talking with her about how she, as an adolescent, tried to control what was going on—some children do this by avoiding, others by planning.

Sexual curiosity and, as the child gets older, a wish to experience sexual feelings are part of normal sexual development. When curiosity and feelings are explored with a peer in a nonthreatening manner, these experiences are at a level that can be absorbed within the child's understanding and are part of normal growing up. When the demands of someone older or in a threatening position are imposed, the sexual experiencing is shifted from the child's level to an older level, and the experience becomes abuse. It is not the child's curiosity or wish to experience something sexual that created the abuse, but the exploitation of this by someone older or threatening. Discussion along these lines with the therapist can help the child realize that her own increasing sexual awareness was normal and did not cause the abuse.

The therapist can inquire whether the child thinks she played a role in what happened and, if so, what that role was. There may be behaviors, like going into someone's apartment, that the child will wish she had not done. The therapist can listen to the child's sadness or anger at herself around those decisions. Dismissing or minimizing those behaviors may mean that the child's worry around them will continue to fester inside. The therapist can then differentiate between those behaviors, however unwise they may have been, and the abuse. The abuse resulted from a decision made by the older or more powerful person.

Cognitive explanations by themselves are seldom sufficient to relieve an internal sense of badness, guilt, and shame. Because the internalization is held within the processing of the younger child, having the child draw a picture of herself at the age the abuse occurred or image herself at that age and then talk with this younger self can be helpful. Encouraging the child to remember and to notice things about her younger self can help build a more positive sense of self. This is particularly important for children who have experienced considerable neglect. As the therapist comments on characteristics about the child and notes similarities between the earlier and present characteristics, the child can gain a sense of being noticed. Asking the child or having the child play out how she would have cared for, comforted, or protected the younger self can help the child learn present caretaking.

The therapist can help the child to list self-protective (putting on weight), self-caring (learning to read), and self-comforting (listening to music) activities she did at the time of the abuse. The child can review these activities and decide which are helpful now. Lists for present-day self-protecting, self-caring, and self-comforting can be developed.

| I am responsible for... |

Whether the abuse was intrafamilial or extrafamilial, it placed the child in a difficult position. For the child to tell, he was talking about things that should not have happened. For the child not to tell, he was keeping secret things that should not have happened. Whichever happens, the child is left feeling responsible. For the child in therapy, a disclosure has occurred and the child, all too often, takes on responsibility for all that happened after the telling.

Both the child and the child's family may need help in separating what happens after disclosure from the child's telling. A mother's getting upset is a result of her distress at having something happen to her child, at learning that someone she trusted cannot be trusted, and at realizing that what she dreaded is a reality. Unfortunately, some parents do get angry at the child and blame the child. These parents need a place, separate from the child, to vent and to sort out what has happened (Wieland, 1997).

The child's telling can be described as a behavior that has given the child safety, has given the nonperpetrating parent a chance to protect, and has given the perpetrator a chance to learn new ways to behave. Yes, the telling did set in motion many different things, but it did not cause them. The investigation is a result of our society's statement that sexual abuse should not happen and children need to be protected. A trial is a result of an offender's choice not to tell what happened. A finding of guilty or not guilty is a result of the judge's or jury's understanding of what happened. The sentence is a result of the judge's decision.

Helping parents to avoid putting inappropriate responsibilities on the child and helping them to assume responsibility for not having been aware of the unsafe world that existed (Trepper & Barrett, 1989) may be the most helpful intervention a therapist can make in relation to a child's internalization of responsibility.

Creating a setting in which the child is not responsible for the adult—the therapist—and is not responsible for making therapy successful can provide the child with a new experience. Therapists are often tempted when a child does not want to talk about something or wants to drop out of therapy to talk about the negative effects of not talking or not having therapy. This places responsibility back on the child. To take pressure off the child, the therapist can talk about how it might be possible to make the therapy sessions more helpful or about a time in the future when therapy could be more helpful.

| Memories |

Memories that have not been worked through can disrupt the child's functioning through intrusive thoughts, nightmares, trigger responses, anxiety attacks, and visual, auditory, or body flashbacks. Although working with memories can be one of the most beneficial parts of therapy, children may not be ready to do this and seldom are ready when they first enter therapy. The child needs to be able to do some self-caring and self-comforting before starting memory work (McCann & Pearlman, 1990). She needs to feel comfortable with the therapist and feel that the therapist can keep the setting safe. She also needs an outside support system—family or friends who are available to her. While this setting is being built, the therapist will want to help the child with the thoughts, flashbacks, nightmares, trigger responses, and anxiety attacks.

When intrusive thoughts occur for an older child or adolescent, she can write them down and keep them carefully to take to therapy. If the child follows through and brings the thoughts to therapy, this process of putting aside thoughts can be quite successful. If the child does not follow through, intrusions usually continue to occur. Within therapy, the child can describe the thought, what worries her most about it, and what she would like to do to or about the worry, and then practice doing that.

Some young children are able to say whether they think about the abuse and what their thoughts look like. Others simply deny any thoughts, because for a young child denying is a way of trying to make something not real. Parents and therapist are then left to infer intrusive thoughts from the child's high level of distractibility or from the child's play. When abuse themes do appear in the play, the therapist can comment on them and encourage the child to talk about them. For some children, however, the working through of abuse remains within the metaphor of the play, with the therapist verbalizing what happened.

Both flashbacks and anxiety attacks can be extremely scary, and a child needs techniques for grounding herself. An older child or adolescent can identify something about herself that represents the age she is now (a new ring, a hairstyle) that she can touch to help her reorient to the present and to her present ability (Dolan, 1991). She can learn to hold tightly to the chair and press her feet down on the floor in order to feel herself where she is (Briere, 1992). She can take hold of a comfort object, such as a favorite stone kept in her pocket or a stuffed toy. Relaxation exercises (Friedrich, 1995) or distracting activities (Briere, 1992) can be helpful. Then, within the therapy setting, the adolescent can talk through or use imaging to work on the flashback or the anxiety attack. Both the beginning (what triggered the anxiety or flashback) and the ending (the part of the flashback that is seldom experienced because it is too scary and the adolescent tries to stop it) need to be worked on. As the adolescent describes what was going on before, the therapist listens for similarities to the abuse scenario, recalling that this scenario included experiences of nonprotection as well as experiences of abuse. When these similarities are recognized, the therapist can encourage the adolescent to differentiate between what happened in the now that triggered the flashback or the anxiety and what happened at the time of the abuse. Within the conversation or imaging (see page 54), the therapist encourages the adolescent to recall present resources and to use those resources as she continues the flashback through to the end. Experiencing that flashbacks do end and that the world is different now is an important part of the processing.

Trigger responses occur when something in the present is similar to the abuse scenario and triggers emotions or behavior inappropriate for the present situation, but similar to the response that occurred at the time of the abuse. A 16-year-old can find herself able to respond only at a 5-year-old level. When an older child or adolescent experiences a trigger response, she and the therapist can work together to determine the trigger and then practice reorienting, through discussion or imaging (see page 66), to the present.

Working through the memories themselves can be, for some adolescents, an important part of therapy (Gil, 1996). For others, it may be more important at that point to get on with their lives (Herman, 1992). When reworking is appropriate, it can (a) provide new information about what the adolescent experienced and how she handled what happened (Gil, 1996); (b) bring together the content, sensations, and emotions; (c) provide the adolescent a chance to vent the confusion, terror, rage, and grief that could not be expressed at the time; and (d) provide an opportunity to add the adolescent's new resources of understanding and comforting. The therapist's availability throughout this process is essential (Herman, 1992). Briere (1992) refers to the working through of accessible memories as having a generic effect, that is, a relationship to all painful memories. The adolescent is no longer overwhelmed when recalling what happened and experiences a decrease in flashbacks, nightmares, and anxiety attacks.

For young children, memories are usually presented through play. Replay of memories, if not shifted in some way, can, however, retraumatize the child (Terr, 1990). Pynoos and Nader (1993) emphasize that play related to traumatic happenings needs to include (a) control over what is happening, (b) expression of prohibited affect, (c) cognitive reworking, and (d) a satisfactory ending. As these conditions occur within therapy (Wieland, 1997), disruptions in the child's functioning have been observed to decrease. Until long-term outcome research on therapy with children is carried out, the long-term effect on memories will not be known.

As highlighted in much of the literature on working with individuals who have been sexually abused and emphasized by the debate on false memories, therapists should not go looking for memories. Repression or dissociation of memories occurs as a protective mechanism. As the individual—child, adolescent, or adult—feels safer and stronger, if working through memories is important, these memories will emerge either directly as memories or indirectly as flashbacks or anxiety. It is then that memory work should be done.

| I feel chaotic |

When the abuser is someone important to the child, the child both wants and fears that person, both loves and hates the person. The therapist can help the child make sense of the chaotic feeling by labeling this dilemma. Recognizing that the child knew two different aspects of the person or wished for a different aspect of the person—the individual who cared for her, played with her, made her feel important and the individual who abused her—helps the child make sense and be able to feel all right with the different feelings.

Because *hate* is a strong word and some children have been told not to hate people, the therapist should avoid this word unless the child uses it first. It is sometimes easier for a child to talk about good feelings and bad feelings. The child's fear of losing the abuser's love can also be talked about. If the child describes having no feelings, the therapist can talk about the experience other children have of mixed-up feelings.

The therapist can also increase the child's tolerance for ambivalent feelings by recognizing the child's ambivalent feelings toward therapy and toward the therapist himself. What does she dislike most about therapy or about the therapist, and how is she able to tolerate that in order to be there? The therapist must talk about this carefully, for he must never imply that the child should have tolerated the abuse. What is important here is the permission to have multiple feelings toward one person and permission to talk about those feelings.

| I am betrayed by |
| people close to me |

The experience of being betrayed by someone important—both the abuse and the nonprotection—is central to the child's experience and needs to be talked about in therapy. Because most children are protective of the nonperpetrating parent, they may not be able to talk about feeling betrayed. They may, however, be able to talk about what they wish the parent had noticed. The child may also be protective of the abuser, particularly if this person has been important to him and if the child wants to have a future relationship with this individual. Encouraging the child to talk about the protective feelings and then inquiring about the betrayed feelings can be helpful.

Ongoing experiences of betrayal often occur for the child who has been abused. This may take place as a result of the child's behavior (transference) within his environment. Children behave in familiar ways, and if a child's behavior patterns were established within an abusive setting, the child's present behavior will include abuse-response behaviors (Littner, 1960). If parents, foster parents, or group home workers do not recognize what is happening, they are likely, by reacting to the child's abuse-response behavior, to be pulled into abusive dynamics and may behave in ways similar to the child's earlier experiences. With this will come a new experience of betrayal. A therapist, being aware of the abuse dynamics, can help parents and workers avoid these patterns and, thus, avoid a repetition of betrayal.

Even when a therapist is careful, a child often feels betrayed in therapy—the therapist goes away on vacation, a flashback comes back even after a session is spent working through the flashback, the therapist forgets to bring a particular toy she promised, the therapist's mind wanders during a session, the therapist asks an intrusive question. What makes therapy different is that the therapist can name what happened. She can take responsibility for not attending better, not remembering better, not working thoroughly enough, or not being there.

In addition, the therapist can carefully set and describe the boundaries of therapy—when she can be available, what toys can be played with, what can or cannot be taken out of session, what will or will not be talked about with other people—in order that children are not misled. A therapist also needs to be realistic as to the extent to which she can help a child. A therapist who tries to do too much may become burned out or may start to resent and dread seeing a particular child. The child will then feel the closing down that occurs within the therapist and feel betrayed again.

Distrust or even fear of the therapist is seldom expressed directly but is often there and expressed indirectly. The child may pull back from the activities in therapy; the adolescent may stop coming to appointments. The therapist can express interest in how the child is feeling, can note how hard it is to trust someone when abuse has happened, can talk about the discouragement and disappointment a person can feel when therapy is not making things feel better. The therapist can note the people in the child's life—not just the abuser—from whom the child has experienced betrayal. The therapist can help the child look at how his life and he himself is different now. But most important will be the therapist's providing a place that feels safe and stays safe.

I have no boundaries                      The child who has been abused by someone known to her has not had her boundaries, either physical or emotional, respected. Her role as a child, as someone to be cared for, has not been respected. Within the therapy session, the therapist can carefully set and adhere to boundaries. Outside of the therapy session, the therapist can work with parents to help them establish appropriate roles and boundaries in the family.

Clarifying boundaries in therapy is an ongoing task. There are the concrete boundaries of starting and stopping times, of what objects get used and how. There are the role boundaries of the child being tended to and the therapist being the one who does the tending. And there is the physical and psychological boundary that no one gets hurt in therapy. Boundaries are not set to indulge or to frustrate a child but to empower the child—she knows what to expect and can trust that expectation to occur—and to enable a good working relationship (Herman, 1992). With some children, boundaries become a major issue, and the therapist needs to think through clearly the behaviors or use of objects that not only are therapeutic but also within the therapist's range of tolerance. If a boundary needs to be changed in the middle of therapy (the floor can no longer be banged on because of complaints from others, the table can no longer be knocked over because the therapist is concerned it will get broken), the therapist can highlight the reasons and the need to respect others. With other children, children from homes where boundaries have been more clearly respected, boundaries are simply a framework within which the work is done.

If sexualized behaviors appear within the therapy, appropriate boundaries—our bodies are private; rubbing oneself for pleasure is fine, but it is a private activity—need to be clearly stated. If a child asks for a hug from time to time and there is no sexualized content in the session and the therapist feels comfortable, this can fit within the guidelines of therapy. If, however, the child is constantly asking for hugs or there is any sexual feel to the hug, the therapist needs to think about and address the issue behind the request. If the therapist needs to touch the child to restrain her, he needs to verbalize what he is doing and why he is doing it, and, following the incident, he should discuss with the child what the touching was like for her.

Parents of both young children and adolescents often need help in identifying appropriate boundaries and role definitions in the family and then need encouragement while enforcing them. Privacy of rooms or of particular spaces within a shared room, of clothing, or of particular objects may need to be discussed and implemented. Who goes to sleep where and when? Who takes care of whom?

Lack of appropriate boundaries may be a multigenerational issue within the family. Drawing genograms and identifying distorted family messages, discussed in Chapter 4, can be particularly helpful with adolescents.

> When I am sexual,
>                good things happen

A child may be sexual in therapy to enjoy a physical sensation, to gain the therapist's attention, to feel important, to check out the therapist's reaction, or to let the therapist know past experiences and present confusions. If the therapist is able, by her observations, to separate out the reason for the behavior, she can address the underlying issue. Whether she is or is not able to do this, she still needs to name the child's behavior and draw appropriate guidelines. The behavior can be (a) named specifically (such as taking off a shirt, rubbing against the therapist's leg), (b) described as something the abuser *taught* the child people wanted, (c) defined as something the therapist and other people do not like because bodies are private, and then the therapist can (d) suggest and encourage a new behavior that allows the child and therapist to interact in a healthy way. The use of the verb *taught* rather than *learned* is important in that it places the action and the responsibility with the abuser, not the child. The reality of the child's world—that some people do want that behavior—needs to be recognized. Particularly for adolescents who are aware of and often caught in pressures to be sexual, the meaning of these pressures can be discussed.

An adolescent is more likely to bring sexualized behavior into a session through the clothing worn, comments made, or stories told. The therapist can comment directly on what she notices. Not commenting may be interpreted by the adolescent as approval and would, therefore, reinforce that when the adolescent is sexual good things happen.

The parent or group home worker does the most important work in relation to sexualized behavior. Because of the anxiety that is generated in each of us when sexualized behavior occurs in inappropriate places, parents and other caregivers often find it difficult to talk directly about what the child has done. A child is told to "stop *that*" but may have no idea what *that* means or why it should be stopped. The child may indeed stop the behavior because he stops everything he is doing right then, but then continue the behavior later because he is not aware that *that* is what he is not to do. Clear and specific guidelines need to be established and alternative ways to gain attention need to be taught. The therapist can work with the parents or with the parents and child together to identify inappropriate behaviors, suggest alternative behaviors, and encourage supportive responding by the adult.

A child's right to attention and to pleasure needs to be reinforced. The error was not in the child's wanting attention or pleasure but in the teaching given by the perpetrator. The therapist can ask about other ways the child gets attention or notices other children getting attention. These behaviors can then be encouraged. The child's right to sexual feelings and to being curious about sexuality is supported.

My sexuality means { no feelings / no control / negative feelings }     The child's sense of sexuality and of herself as a sexual person is distorted by sexual abuse. The importance of talking about sexuality within therapy has been mentioned several times, and is discussed in greater detail in Chapter 6. The willingness of the therapist to ask questions and to listen carefully to the child's responses can help reestablish sexuality as something important and valuable. These discussions can help separate sexuality from sexual abuse.

What I am told ≠ what is meant     When a child has internalized that people do not mean what they say, the child applies this internalization to foster parents, group home workers, and therapists. When talking with this child, the therapist needs to be aware that the child may be hearing something very different from what the therapist has meant. The therapist can check with the child about what she thinks is meant. Even more important is for the therapist to discuss the difficulty of believing in what people say and how the child will start to know when it is safe to believe what someone says.

The therapist can talk with parents, during their own session or in a family session, about a child's distrust or misinterpretation of what a parent has said. Improving communication within the family is an important part of family work.

```
┌──────────────────────┐
│          ┌ no emotions
│  I have  ┤ no experience
│          └ no integrated self
└──────────────────────┘
```
As the child protects himself from the reality of the abuse, he separates off emotions, experiences, and, in some cases, aspects of himself. The therapist can acknowledge the child's wish to avoid the feelings or memories that come from being abused or from not being protected. This avoidance was protective and helped the child survive. Dissociation, in particular, can be described as a creative response to frightening situations. A child can be encouraged to draw, write, or talk about the feelings that did occur and what feelings might have occurred if it had been safe for them to be there. As the therapist notices what is happening in the child's play (the baby doll being placed on the roof of the house, the wild animals coming into the house), she can comment on the types of feelings a child might have in those situations. As the therapist notices the events described by the older child, she can comment on what those situations would have been like for a little child who needs closeness and attachment. She can ask the child how he thinks a little child would have felt.

Of equal importance is the therapist's inquiring about the child's experiences and feelings now. When a child reports no feelings or feelings that contradict the reality of the situation, the therapist can note the old pattern of protecting and can express interest in hearing about other feelings.

When a child has used dissociation as a way of coping, dissociation will also occur within the therapy session. The child may be at one moment a kitten, at another a guard dog, at another a *Tyrannosaurus rex*, and at another a wolverine. The feelings or attitudes expressed by the child may shift dramatically. The functioning age level of the child may shift from moment to moment. The therapist needs to notice each of these shifts and needs to encourage the child to talk about them. Even when the child avoids the discussion or denies what happened, the therapist's accepting and describing together all of the aspects of the play or the behavior creates the possibility of these different aspects existing together. Working with children who dissociate and with their parents is described in Chapter 5.

For the child who has used denial, repression, or dissociation, addressing these distortions is not enough. The child needs to learn new ways of coping. The child needs to have opportunities to talk about feelings, to problem solve situations, to address directly what has happened, and to incorporate self-care into daily activities. Therapy can encourage these behaviors, first within the therapy setting and then within the child's outside world.

## ❏  Responding to the Individual Child

Just as a child's cognitive understanding of sexual abuse cannot, on its own, relieve the internal hurt, so a therapist's cognitive understanding of sexual abuse cannot, on its own, enable the therapist to help the child. A therapist needs to be sensitive to when a child needs distance from the abuse as well as when the child needs to be encouraged to address the abuse. A therapist needs to be sensitive to the child's feelings—those she is expressing and those she cannot express. Therapy needs to be not only abuse-focused but also child-focused and relationship-focused.

In child-focused therapy, the therapist attends intently to that particular child—what that child is doing or saying, what that child's play, behavior, or conversation means. The therapist holds in mind that particular child's present situation and past experiences. As highlighted by Friedrich (1995) and Pearce and Pezzot-Pearce (1997), this includes both abuse experiences and attachment experiences. The therapist watches and listens for the internal experience—is the play or conversation about powerlessness or betrayal, about internal chaos or sense of responsibility, about a sense of damage or guilt, about memories or about distortions of what happened, about sexual behavior or sexual feelings, about having no sense of boundaries or not being able to believe what others say or do, about abandonment or lack of respect, about intrusiveness or rejection? Then the therapist can talk with the child, not just about the content of what the child is doing or saying, but about what may be the child's internal experience behind this event. The therapist can talk with the child about where that experience came from—the abuse or early relationships. The therapist can provide a new and healthier experience for the child.

The therapist needs to be constantly aware of the ages at which that particular child was abused and thus the stage or stages of self-development that were disrupted (Cole & Putnam, 1992). By being aware of the developmental tasks—recognition and integration of self, development of coping mechanisms, awareness of self in relation to others, recognition of social values, sexual awareness—that have been disturbed, the therapist can seek to provide opportunities for working through specific tasks.

In relationship-focused therapy, the therapist attends to what is happening between the child and himself—the child's relationship to the therapist and his own relationship to the child. The child's relationship will reflect earlier relationships, in particular the early attachment relationships (transference). When early attachments have been secure, there will be a basic sense of trust and the child and therapist can deal more directly with the abuse and abuse issues. When early attachments have been problematic, and especially with disorganized attachment (Friedrich, 1995; Karen, 1994; Main & Solomon, 1990), the child is likely to be both demanding and wary; the child will want to feel close but then feel threatened by the closeness and misbehave or refuse to come to therapy. In that setting, abuse cannot, and should not, be a constant topic. Availability (within the therapy boundaries) and acceptance do need to be constantly there.

The therapist's relationship to the child (countertransference) will reflect (a) the therapist's own early experiences together with the processing the therapist has done around those experiences (Wieland, 1997) and (b) the response pulled out of the therapist by the child's reaction to the therapist. The therapist can learn a great deal about the child's experience—neglect, hurt, demands, sexualization—by recognizing his own reactions (Davies & Frawley, 1994). By (a) attending to these reactions (mind wandering, asking intrusive questions, overprotecting, ignoring sexualized behaviors), (b) recognizing how the reactions continue the dynamics of the child's earlier negative relationships, and (c) shifting reactions (staying with the child's play or conversation, keeping comments to the issues the child is raising, encouraging the child to protect herself, and addressing sexualized behaviors), the therapist provides a new experience for the child. By being aware of the child's early experience with the mother figure—any early emotional or behavioral neglects or intrusions—the therapist can consciously work toward establishing a setting and a relationship that provides what the child did not have (B. Saxe, personal communication, 1997).

As the therapist works with an individual child, he moves from cognitive interventions (providing information on abuse and child development, normalizing the child's experience) to behavioral interventions (making lists and practicing caretaking, drawing genograms and recognizing messages, encouraging problem solving and reality checking, talking about the abuse and the feelings emanating from the abuse, meeting with the child and parent) to emotional interventions (being attentive to the child, asking what it feels like inside, identifying and helping the child connect to early emotions, recognizing and responding to the different parts of the self, imaging and encouraging caretaking of the younger self).

❏  **Summary**

Abuse-focused therapy has been recognized as essential for children whose experiences of abuse are negatively affecting their care of themselves and their interaction with the world. The abuse and the internalizations from the abuse need to be addressed. This chapter has considered many of the issues that arise for a child as a result of sexual abuse. Ideas for addressing these issues, for shifting abuse-related internalizations, and for providing the child with new and healthy experiences have been suggested. These new experiences are sometimes cognitive, sometimes behavioral, sometimes emotional, and sometimes all three. Indeed, all three types of experiences are needed, because abuse is experienced on all three levels. The following two chapters describe in greater detail a technique that addresses primarily the child's emotional experience (imaging) and techniques that address primarily the child's behavioral experiences (genograms and timelines).

Therapy also needs to be child-focused. The child's individual experience of abuse and of early caretaking needs to be addressed. The therapist needs to keep in mind the age during which the abuse occurred and, thus, the particular developmental tasks that were disrupted and need now to be experienced.

And therapy needs to be relationship-focused. The therapist needs to be aware of that particular child's early attachment experiences and the issues related to attachment that are likely to occur within the therapy. The therapist needs to attend to how the child is relating to him and how he is relating to the child. A healthy adult-child relationship is essential for therapy.

❏  **Notes**

1. In a 1987 review of the literature, Kaufman and Zigler estimate that 70% of parents who had been abused during their childhoods did not abuse their children. In a more recent study of young males (ages 18-27) who had been sexually abused during childhood, 87% of those who had been abused on one occasion had not sexually abused a child, and 63% of those who had been abused on multiple occasions had not abused a child (Bagley, Wood, & Young, 1994). These are conservative figures based on no overlap between abuser groups.

2. For ideas on how a child can learn to relax, see Friedrich (1995) and Pearce and Pezzot-Pearce (1997).

# 3

# Working Within: Imaging

Although it is possible to construct a general model of the internalizations resulting from abuse, it is not possible to know specific perceptions or specific reactions. Each child's experience is unique; each child's experiencing, coping with, and processing of all that happened is unique; and each child's internalization of that experience is unique.

The child's behavior and conversation during therapy help the therapist and child understand both the experience and the internalizations. Much of the internal experiencing, however, remains hidden. The child is, after all, an expert at hiding what is painful. For some children in some situations, imaging can provide a process for further accessing their internal worlds.

Traumatic imaging occurs when a flashback intrudes into an individual's present awareness. The individual experiences an emotion or perception from a time other than the present. This usually comes with an out-of-control feeling. Therapeutic imaging occurs when an individual within a safe setting turns his mind inward and accesses—

through a sensory or thought-flow experience—emotions and perceptions blocked out of conscious awareness.[1] Now in a safe setting, the individual can start to sort through his internal experience. The individual starts to feel in more control. Imaging is a natural internal process that can be frightening or reparative.

Just as traumatic imaging occurs as a result of an individual's experience and yet is not an exact replica of that experience, so also therapeutic imaging reflects, but is not a replica of, the child's experience. Although images come from events that have happened, these images come from the individual's experience—not an outside view—of those events. Imaging of earlier experiences reflects the younger child's perspective and emotions. Indeed, this is the value of imaging—being able to grasp the early experience, not just the present rational (or irrational) thought about what happened back then. Imaging is used to follow an individual's internal experience, not to search for experiences. Imaging is a therapeutic, not an investigatory, process.

Imaging, as an internal process, must be used carefully. It should be used in a way that is not intrusive to the individual. It needs to be used in a way that enables a child to increase his understanding of his own internal experience and to care for and comfort himself. As a process that heightens a child's awareness of the emotions and perceptions from the time of the abuse—emotions and perceptions that may have been blanked from conscious awareness—imaging can help a child process feelings and shift abuse-related internalizations. It is not a process for working with the factual events or narrative memory of abuse. Because imaging has been identified by critics as suggestive, it is recommended that it not be used if a child is or may be going to court.

This chapter describes the use of imaging with children who have been sexually abused. Both imaging's similarities to and differences from hypnosis are noted. Situations in which imaging should *not* be used are also discussed. The second part of the chapter addresses the use of imaging within abuse-focused therapy for children. The process of imaging—starting, facilitating, and ending—is described in the third part of the chapter.

This chapter is not meant to teach a therapist how to do imaging. Training within a workshop setting that includes opportunities for a therapist both to experience and to facilitate imaging is a necessary prerequisite for the use of imaging in therapy. This chapter provides, for therapists who have not used imaging, a description of how this technique can facilitate their therapeutic work. Based on this description, they may decide to take part in training in imaging. For therapists who have used imaging, this chapter reviews important points and describes ways in which imaging can be helpful in work with children who have been sexually abused.

## ❏ Imaging

Imaging has been described as an experience that enables an individual, by narrowing the focus of attention, to bypass rational thought (McMahon & Sheikh, 1986; Sheikh & Panagiotou, 1975). The individual becomes more aware of her internal experiencing of present and past happenings, more aware of reactions to these happenings. As the individual talks about the image, rational thought is reintroduced and the individual starts to process the experience.

Alternatively, imaging may be providing a process whereby the individual, by detaching herself from present pressures and defenses, is able to access emotions and experiences that have been defended against. Once accessed, these emotions and experiences can be processed.

Imaging is distinct from hypnosis in that no trance is applied externally to shift awareness. Imaging is produced by the individual's own inward focusing of attention. Some individuals describe themselves as being very aware of where they are and what is happening in the therapy room during imaging. Others describe an experience that indicates that they have self-induced a trance state. They describe feeling outside the therapy room and in a different time and space. One adolescent described a feeling of going a long way away but keeping a view back to herself in the therapy room.

Although the therapist may encourage the individual to let her mind float, to allow a certain emotion to be present, or to go back to an earlier time, the therapist does not suggest an image or an active behavior, as is often done in hypnosis. Although the therapist may ask the individual to describe what is happening or to take care of herself, the therapist does not state how the individual should do this.

Imaging is different from guided imagery in that the image originates from the individual and the individual's internal world, not from the therapist or the therapist's hypothesis of what an individual needs. Because it is not possible for a therapist to know all the situations that may have been connected with danger for a particular individual, there is the possibility that guided imagery could produce for an individual a dangerous-feeling image. Even if a therapist could guarantee safety, the image created by the individual is far more relevant and, thus, leads to more important processing. There may be times within imaging—for example, when a new skill is being taught—when some guided imagery is appropriate and helpful.

Hypnosis and hypnotherapy have been used in the treatment of adults who have been sexually abused to access memories of the past, to work with multiple aspects of the self, and to increase present functioning (Barnett, 1991; Briere, 1992; Courtois, 1988; Putnam, 1989). With the debate around false memories, therapists are becoming increasingly aware of the importance of not influencing an individual's memory retrieval process (Courtois, 1996). Although therapeutic work under hypnosis can be done carefully, the danger of suggestibility exists. For this reason, hypnosis is increasingly not recommended for work with individuals who have been sexually abused. An additional concern related to hypnosis is that an individual can, but may not necessarily, be influenced to take an action that she may not be ready to take. This could place additional stress on the individual and put her in a vulnerable position.

Imaging has received only limited attention within the literature on treatment of sexual abuse (Grove & Panzer, 1991; Hyde, 1990). This may be a result of its being overshadowed by hypnosis—initially because hypnosis appeared to be quite effective and then because hypnosis appeared to be risky. The role of imaging—a process whereby an individual can become more aware of the feelings and perceptions from the time of the abuse as well as feelings and perceptions occurring in the present—within therapy with individuals who have been sexually abused has been overlooked.

With the increased awareness of and concern for the possibility of creating false memories or pseudomemories (Courtois, 1996), therapists using imaging need to be clear, in their discussions with adults and with children, that imaging presents an individual's internal experience (for example, feeling frozen) and not necessarily objective reality (for example, actual freezing). Therapists need to be careful that factual event assumptions are not made from images.

Inevitable questions arise: Can imaging cause someone to believe that something imaged did happen exactly that way? Can imaging shape subsequent memories? Experimental research is not available to answer these questions. Clinical experience indicates that with careful discussion between the therapist and the individual (described in a later section), the adult or child does not interpret an image as objective reality. Clinical experience also indicates that an individual's feelings (feelings being held in implicit memory) concerning an event can shift without the narrative knowledge of the event (narrative knowledge being held in explicit memory) shifting.[2] An individual can move from feeling terror to feeling anger or grief, from being self-condemning to understanding a behavior, without the memory of the factual event changing. The feeling state around future recovered memories may be affected, but there is no evidence that the content of these memories would be affected.

## HYPNOSIS AND IMAGING WITH CHILDREN

Until recently, hypnosis with children has been used primarily in connection with medical problems or procedures. Gardner and Olness's 1981 review of hypnosis with children included only short discussions of the use of hypnosis for phobias, social anxiety, sleep fears, behavioral disorders, and somatoform disorders. A few examples of hypnosis have been reported with children who had been sexually abused (Levine, 1980; Rhue & Lynn, 1991a, 1991b) and more particularly with children who had experienced high levels of dissociation (Dell & Eisenhower, 1990; Kluft, 1984, 1985). Rhue and Lynn (1991a) describe the use of hypnosis through storytelling. Within the stories, a safe place is established and situations or issues similar to what the child experienced are introduced. Suggestion and metaphor are used to create a sense of mastery and well-being during this discussion. Friedrich (1995) has used hypnosis and hypnotherapy to help a child calm herself, process flashbacks, and manage compulsions, panic, or conversion disorders.

The advantages of using imaging, rather than hypnosis, with children are similar to those discussed for adults. Because imaging is based on the child's processing, compared with the therapist's direction or suggestion, it is less intrusive and addresses more specifically the child's unique experience. Hypnotic suggestions based on a therapist's theories or assumptions regarding a child's reactions to abuse (see, for example, Levine, 1980) may or may not reflect a child's experience. With imaging, the child is in control of the process. Situations, reactions, and issues come from her and not from the therapist.

### WHEN IMAGING SHOULD *NOT* BE USED

If a child has difficulty differentiating fantasy from reality, if the process of imaging bears any similarity to the child's early negative experiences, or if the child may be involved in a court case, imaging should not be included in therapy. If a child is experiencing extremely high anxiety or is denying emotions or events that would, if recognized, disrupt the world in which he is currently living, imaging should not be used to explore these areas. If a child does not wish to use imaging, he should not be pressured to do so.

If, in the assessment of a child, there are any indications of schizophrenia or of the child's having difficulty differentiating between fantasy and reality, imaging would not be appropriate. A child needs to have attained the ability to move from concrete thought to abstract thought for imaging to be effective. For a child engaged in concrete thinking, play or sand tray therapy would be more appropriate. Play therapy, like imaging, provides a process through which a child can express and become more aware of emotions and perceptions.

If psychic reasoning or ritual abuse has been part of a child's earlier experiences, imaging is not recommended, because there is a danger that therapy could start to feel like the earlier abusive experiences. Feeling completely present in the here and now and in control of their thoughts is important for these children. Because imaging moves away from the here and now, it could be frightening for these children.

A fourth situation in which imaging should not be used is when a case is going to court. Court cases that must rely on child witnesses are extremely difficult to prosecute. Although research has shown increasingly that children can serve as accurate witnesses (Fivush, 1993;

Ornstein, 1995), children's vulnerability to suggestion is also well documented (Ceci & Bruck, 1993, 1995). In cases where a child will be going to court, it is important that therapy not include activities that provide, or appear to provide, suggestion. Imaging, even very carefully done, can appear to provide suggestion. Imaging should not, therefore, be included within a child's therapy until after a court case is completed.

For many children who have been sexually abused, court action is not carried out because of lack of clear evidence or inability of the child to testify clearly. Although for these children court cases are not pending, there is always a possibility of a court case in the future, when more evidence becomes available or the child is better able to testify. Because imaging can be a positive therapeutic experience and can help a child shift abuse-related internalizations, eliminating all imaging from therapy under these circumstances seems extreme. Although therapists need to be conscious of legal considerations, the legal system should not shape therapy. Careful attention to the research on memory[3] and child development,[4] to the literature on clinical theory and practice, to the type of phrasing that can create suggestion,[5] and to the experiences of the children therapists work with should provide a guide to positive therapeutic work. If a case has not gone to court, imaging related to specific memories can be avoided.

When a child is extremely anxious, techniques related to grounding and building ego strengths are more appropriate therapeutic interventions than imaging. The child needs a stronger sense of herself and of herself in the here and now before therapy should start to explore inner experiences. A child who is extremely anxious may start to experience a flashback—traumatic imaging—during therapy. When, with grounding, the child's anxiety lessens—the child has connected with herself in the here and now and with the safe therapeutic setting—processing the flashback through therapeutic imaging would be appropriate. If the child's anxiety does not lessen, the therapist would continue helping the child ground herself and not pursue the imagery of the flashback at that point. Discussion of the flashback and ways to relieve anxiety would be important.

A therapist needs to be sensitive to a child's defenses. A child may push emotions or past experiences out of present awareness in order to be able to function in his present environment. Imaging that might open up these emotions or experiences before the child is able to handle them would not be appropriate. For example, a child living with his mother who had allowed an abuser to stay in the home even after she knew of the abuse may report, and even wonder about, feeling no anger at his mother. Imaging related to anger or to feelings or experiences connected to his mother may bring up reactions or memories that would frighten the child or destabilize his present situation. The child, feeling that his world is threatened, is likely to leave therapy. Questions that help a child to think about the lack of anger and what would happen if he were angry—in other words, cognitive rather than internal processing—would be more appropriate for this child.

If a child does not wish to use imaging, his concerns can be discussed and perhaps resolved, but he should not be pressured to use imaging. Some children find the idea of imaging—of not consciously controlling their thoughts—frightening. At times, children who have already used imaging and have retrieved frightening images will not want to image again. In such a case, discussing the past imaging experience and how it affected (a) the child, (b) the therapeutic relationship, (c) the child in her home situation, and (d) the child's present feelings is important. This discussion may help the child feel comfortable with further imaging. If not, imaging should not be pursued.

Whenever imaging is used, it should be carefully documented in the therapist's notes—both the comments made by the therapist and the images reported by the child. It is important for the therapist, either before or after imaging, to discuss with the child the difference between objective reality (factual events) and emotional reality (the child's emotional experiencing; see pages 70-71). Imaging should be used only within a supportive therapeutic setting and should not be used as a way to prod indiscriminately into the past.

The present discussion is applicable to work with children age 8 and older. For young children processing at a concrete level, play objects and drawings can provide a process similar to imaging.

❏  **Uses of Imaging**

The experience of sexual abuse is held at the emotional, cognitive, and physiological level of the child at the time the abuse occurred. The abuse-related internalizations, although shaping the child's present internal world, reflect the developmental level of the child at the time of the abuse, not present cognitive or emotional functioning. As a child talks in therapy, he talks, for the most part, about his present view of past experiences. With talking, this present view may shift and understanding of the past experience may increase. At the same time, however, the early internal experience from the abuse may continue.

> **Ralph** (an 11-year-old sexually and physically abused by his mother between ages 3 and 8) talks about the abuse: "I know the abuse belongs to my mother but it's inside. It's horrendous and it's there."

Imaging helps a child be aware of the internal hurt from the time of the abuse. The experience and the internalizations from that experience can be addressed more directly.

Imaging can help a child to connect with the younger part of him who experienced the abuse and to use his present capabilities to help that younger part. Imaging can be used to process flashbacks and to work through abuse-related internalizations. Specific points of distress and emotions can be explored through imaging. For children who dissociate, imaging can be used to encourage the different aspects of the self to work together. For children who do not have the skills to deal with their present world, imaging, in combination with guided imagery, can help develop needed skills.

## CONNECTING WITH THE PART
## THAT WAS ABUSED

When the child comes to therapy, she is not the same age she was when first abused. She may be a few weeks older or many years older. She tends, however, to judge her "younger self" in terms of what she now knows and what she wishes the "younger self" had known and had been able to do. As a result, she may dismiss either the meaning or the impact of the abuse. She is likely to self-blame and to take on responsibility for all that has happened.

To recognize the experience and emotions felt at the time of the abuse, the child needs to move away from her present thinking patterns, back to the original experience.

**Mary** (a 17-year-old sexually abused by her uncle between ages 4 and 8) talks about the abuse experience. As she talks, her face shows no distress but tears start to run down her cheeks.

**Mary:** I don't know why I'm crying, it was so long ago, and he is dead now and, anyway, it is all over.

**Therapist:** [Realizes that the tears may be coming from the early abuse experience.] Just close your eyes for a minute and let yourself see yourself with tears running down your cheeks. I don't know what you are going to see, I don't know how old you are going to be. But if you start to see or be aware of anything, just let me know by nodding your head.

**Mary:** (after a moment) Yes, I see myself, I'm 5 years old and I'm all alone.

**Therapist:** What do you notice about the 5-year-old who is there, the 5-year-old who is all alone?

**Mary:** She is just there. She is standing there doing nothing but crying.

**Therapist:** What else do you notice?

**Mary:** My family is there.[6] And there is my uncle. My uncle is talking to me but no one else is. There aren't any tears now.

**Therapist:** Where have the tears gone? What happened to the tears that were running down the 5-year-old's cheeks?

**Mary:** They're inside. They are still running down but you can't see them. Nobody sees them. Why doesn't she tell someone, why doesn't she scream? She could have stopped it!

**Therapist:** And I'm thinking of little Mary's sister and how she always screamed. What happened for her? Is she there in that picture?

**Mary:** Yeah, she is there. Nobody likes her screaming, nobody believes what she says. Nobody likes her.

**Therapist:** What was the little Mary, way back then, taught about screaming and telling?

**Mary:** Don't do it, if you want to be loved. But she is crying so inside, why doesn't someone hear her? (continued on page 53)

With imaging, both the child and the therapist become more aware of the hurt experienced at the time of the abuse. The imaged events cannot be assumed to be objective reality. They do, however, represent the child's internal experience and, as such, are the child's emotional reality. Although it is certainly important to recognize and discuss the objective reality of abuse, the trauma cannot be released until the emotional reality is addressed.

## USING THE "NOW SELF" TO HELP THE "YOUNGER SELF"

As the feelings from the abuse emerge—emptiness, fright, loneliness, curiosity, excitement, terror—a child can become quite frightened. A child should never be left in a state of fright. To do so could further traumatize the child. Similarly, the abuse situation should not be changed to something that did not happen. To do so, even within imaging, could reinforce the child's denial of abuse.

A therapist can use a child's present abilities or ego state (Watkins & Watkins, 1992) as a resource for the child's frightened feelings—the abused child ego state. The child's present capabilities can be used within imaging to protect, to comfort, and to care for the younger, abused ego state. As this occurs, the child has a new experience, an experience of protection and nurturing. This experience can lead to new and healthier internalizations.

**Mary:** (see page 52) Why doesn't someone hear me? I am so lonely.

**Therapist:** Can you take the "now you," the 17-year-old Mary, into that picture with the 5-year-old Mary with tears inside, that picture with all the other people around who do not notice what is happening to little Mary? And when she is there, just let me know. (Mary nods.) Where is the 17-year-old Mary?

**Mary:** She is standing next to little Mary.

**Therapist:** What does little Mary need?

**Mary:** She needs to have someone notice her tears, notice what is happening.

**Therapist:** Can the "now you," the 17-year-old Mary, do that? (Mary nods.) . . . What is happening now?

**Mary:** I'm hugging the little Mary and telling her I know how she feels.

**Therapist:** Is there anything else the now you could do for the little Mary?

**Mary:** Yes, she wants *everyone* to realize the type of person Uncle was. Everyone thought he was such a kind person to have us all there and he wasn't
at all—he was a scheming, manipulative, dirty, old man. My parents, even
knowing about the abuse, still think he was basically a nice guy. Why don't
they hate him? I want to tell them how awful he was.

**Therapist:** Why don't you and see what happens.

**Mary:** She's doing it. My mother is listening, she goes over by the little Mary.
But my father can't hear. Now I'm shouting. He's just going away. What a
chicken! I never knew my father was the chicken, I thought I was.

Although the therapist, within this imaging, is making a suggestion—
take in the "now you"—there is no suggestion related to the scene or
to the early experience. The therapist uses questions, not directives, to
encourage the child to care for herself. At times, because the younger
self feels frozen or the now self feels hopeless, little interaction may
occur between the two. Raising the possibility of caring for oneself
does, however, in itself create a new perspective for the child.

### WORKING WITH FLASHBACKS

When memories are held inside and not processed in any way,
children often experience flashbacks. With a flashback, the child experiences something from the past as happening now even though in
reality it is not. To stop the flashback, the child forces her mind away
and, therefore, seldom experiences an end to a flashback. It is often the
lack of ending that makes flashbacks so frightening. The child feels
caught in an abuse that is going to go on forever.

Imaging can be used to help a child, within a safe setting, process a
flashback all the way through. The imaging allows the child to bring
her present capabilities into the reexperiencing of the past. With this
new experience, she realizes she can survive the flashback. In addition,
imaging can help the child and therapist identify the distress symbol-
ized by the flashback and the situations triggering flashbacks. When
flashbacks are adequately worked through, they usually do not continue to occur.

Jenny (a 16-year-old sexually abused between ages 12 and 15 by her father, who was extremely violent) talks about how terrifying her flashbacks have been.

**Therapist:** Some young people find it helpful to work through flashbacks here in the office. We can, knowing that you are here in a safe place, look at the flashback, use the skills and resources you have developed to handle the flashback, and then talk about the flashback and what it means.

**Jenny:** I don't know. I really don't want to have one, they're awful.

**Therapist:** They do feel awful and if you don't want to work on the flashback today, we don't need to. Often, however, once a flashback is figured out, it stops occurring.

**Jenny:** All right.

**Therapist:** Before we start to work on the flashback, let yourself go to a place that is peaceful and calm for you. . . . And now, knowing that you can go back there, that that place is there for you, let your mind float back to the flashback you had yesterday. And when you are back there, nod your head to let me know. (Jenny tenses and nods.) Tell me what it is you see or what it is you sense.

**Jenny:** I'm back in the living room at home and my father is threatening me with a knife.

**Therapist:** What do you notice yourself doing or saying?

**Jenny:** I'm telling him to stop, that I'll tell on him.

**Therapist:** And what is he doing?

**Jenny:** He is laughing. He is saying no one will believe me. Nobody will help me.

**Therapist:** What is happening now?

**Jenny:** He is chasing me.

**Therapist:** And what do you have now, that you didn't have then, that you can bring into the picture?

**Jenny:** Marie from the group home, she is coming to the door and she is ringing the bell, but my father yells at her. She tries the door but it is locked. She goes away. Now he is chasing me around the couch, he is going to catch me.

**Therapist:** And knowing how scary that would be for you, give yourself a bit of time. What do you see happening now?

**Jenny:** Detective Morris, he is there at the door. But my father won't let him in. My father scares him with the knife and he goes away. My father just laughs.

**Therapist:** Knowing that you are here, that that happened then, but that you are here now—knowing that, watch and see what happens next.

**Jenny:** I'm running to the door, I'm unlocking the door. My father is yelling at me that I can't leave, but I do. I'm out and running down the street.

**Therapist:** And let yourself feel that running, and feel the opening of the door and feel the running. And that running is you and you are the one who created it, who did it. You are the one who helped you. (pause) And when you have felt that running and enjoyed the feeling of the running, let me know what is happening.

**Jenny:** I'm walking, it's great, I'm just walking.

**Therapist:** Tell me about that place where you are walking. (Jenny describes.) And, when you are ready, let your mind go back to that place that was peaceful and calm, that place that was for you. (pause) And when you are ready come back to the room. . . . What did you notice about what was going on in the flashback?

**Jenny:** Well, no one could help me, just like he said.

**Therapist:** But someone did help you.

**Jenny:** I guess I did.

Although it would be inappropriate to suggest a child change the imaging of an abuse event—either denial of the event or self-blame that the event was not handled differently could occur—changing a flashback, an event in the now, is appropriate. The difference between now and then is highlighted. The working through of the flashback, as described above, is similar to desensitization. The process of this desensitization is, however, created by the child, not the therapist.

Within the process of imaging, it is important for the therapist to believe in the child's ability to problem solve. The grounding provided by the therapist's voice and by the reminder that the child is in a safe place now allows the child time to access her problem-solving skills.

## WORKING THROUGH THE ABUSE-RELATED
## INTERNALIZATION OF SELF

When a child is sexually abused, he experiences an intrusion of both his physical self and his emotional self. He internalizes a sense of being different or damaged. Direct assurances and clear demonstration that the therapist does not see the child as damaged or as different from others are important, but this is not always enough to shift a child's internalized sense of damage. Imaging can help a child to concretize the feeling of damage, to identify the depth of that feeling and then, through a symbolic process, to repair the damage. The possibility of existing without damage is created.

> Susan (a 13-year-old sexually abused by her father for 3 years) talks about therapy being a waste of time, that it will not make any difference. She states that she has been abused and that simply is the way she is.

Therapist: It sounds as if you feel there is something wrong with you. You were abused and the abuse is something wrong, something that never should have happened. But you're *not* the abuse. You're okay. Your father's hands, your father's penis are not in you anymore. Yes, there are a lot of feelings and confusion inside. And it is our job to work on that. Tell me about that feeling inside.

Susan: Yucky!

Therapist: What does that "yucky" feel like; what does it look like? (no response) Why don't you close your eyes just a moment and look at the "yuck." What do you see?

Susan: (pause) It's a pile of shit—a big, big pile of shit.

Therapist: What's the shit like?

Susan: (shuddering) Gooey, gooey brown.

Therapist: And that gooey brown shit, the gooey brown shit of the abuse, the gooey brown shit that is not Susan but is there with Susan because of the abuse. What would you like to do with that pile of gooey brown shit?

Susan: Shovel it away.

Therapist: All right, go ahead and do it. Shovel it away until there isn't any more. Let me know when it is all shoveled away. . . . (Susan nods.) What do you see now?

**Susan:** A wound and it's bleeding, it's deep and it's sore.

**Therapist:** And that's understandable. A child would feel hurt—hurt because she wanted to do things with her father, hurt because she wanted her father to love her, hurt because she trusted him and then he touched her on her body. What could we do for that deep, sore wound?

**Susan:** Bandage it.

**Therapist:** Look around, is there anything you can use?

**Susan:** Some cotton balls.

**Therapist:** What would you like to do with the cotton balls?

**Susan:** Clean it.

**Therapist:** And as you clean the wound, knowing that it often hurts to clean a wound, let little Susan know that you know she was hurt, but that hurts can be cleaned and hurts can heal. That she is okay. What's happening now?

**Susan:** It's clean now, but the cut's still there.

**Therapist:** And that makes sense. It takes a while for cuts to heal but they do. Does this one need some stitches or will it heal smoothly without stitches?

**Susan:** It's okay without stitches.

**Therapist:** What would you like to do for it now?

**Susan:** Put a bandage on.

**Therapist:** All right. Put a bandage on. And when you have done that, nod your head to let me know. . . . (Susan nods.) And, as with all bandages, this one is going to need to be checked and changed and we can do that each week when you come. Is there anything else that we should do now for the cut, for this cut that is going to heal and be all right?

**Susan:** Not now, but it's still sore.

Imaging, by itself, does not shift abuse-related internalizations. It can, however, create an internal sense of new possibilities.

### IDENTIFYING POINTS OF DISTRESS

Children who have been abused often experience general distress without being able to link it to anything specific. Without this link, both the child and the therapist may be at a loss to understand or to process the feeling. A therapist can encourage a child to feel the distress (Barnett, 1981) or to form an image of the distress (Grove & Panzer, 1991) and then use this sensation or image to move back to the source of the distress.[7]

> **Jane** (a 15-year-old sexually abused by her uncle from ages 10 to 11) returns to therapy after several months. She comments that she does not know why she still feels so awful. She states that she has talked to her mother, has read books, has "told off" her uncle, and has "done" therapy, so why does she still feel awful?
>
> **Therapist:** Why don't we trace that awful feeling and see where it is connected.
>
> **Jane:** All right, but it is just there.
>
> **Therapist:** First tell me more about the awful feeling. . . . Where do you feel it? . . . And this awful feeling in your stomach, what does it feel like? . . . And this awful throbbing feeling in your stomach, let it get a bit stronger, knowing that you are here in this safe place, and when it is a bit stronger, just nod your head to let me know. . . . (Jane nods.) Now let yourself float back on that awful throbbing feeling in your stomach to another time, maybe the first time, you felt that feeling, and when something comes into your mind, just let me know by nodding your head. . . . (Jane nods.) And if it feels all right to tell me about it, nod your head. (Jane nods.) Tell me about it.
>
> **Jane:** I'm in the bedroom and my uncle is there on the bed next to me.
>
> **Therapist:** What do you notice happening?
>
> **Jane:** He is sliding his hand down the front of my pants. I never saw this before, oh, I hate it. Stop it. The picture's stopped, but I don't want to be there.
>
> **Therapist:** Can you take the "now you" in, into that picture of the younger Jane and her uncle and when the "now you" is there, nod your head to let me know. (Jane nods.) Watch and tell me what happens.
>
> **Jane:** I'm taking the little Jane by the hand, she shouldn't be there. I'm going to take her out of there. She shouldn't be there!! Why did *she* let me go there!! Why did my mother let me go there!! She knew what he was like! She never let my sister go there! Why did she let me go there!?! I am so angry!!

For each child, the distress will be linked to different parts of the experience of the abuse and different internalizations. As these are identified, the conversations in therapy can become more specific and more helpful.

### EXPLORING EMOTIONS

Exploration of emotions is an essential part of therapy with children who have been sexually abused. Exploring emotions can, however, be extremely difficult when the child has spent years, as well as considerable energy, blocking either the emotions or the source of emotions. Imaging, by enabling the child to move away from ongoing pressures and defenses, helps the child to access emotions.

> **Sally** (a 10-year-old sexually abused by her stepfather from ages 7 to 9) talks about how tense she becomes when her stepfather comes over to the house to visit her younger brother. The therapist raises the possibility that she is scared he might touch her again. This Sally vehemently denies.

**Therapist:** Why don't we take a look at that feeling of tension that comes when your stepfather is over at the house.[8]

**Sally:** All right.

**Therapist:** Just close your eyes and let yourself float back to some time when you were at home and your stepfather arrives at the house.

**Sally:** I don't want to close my eyes, it's too scary.

**Therapist:** That's fine. Just leave your eyes open, you can see yourself inside your head when your eyes are open or when they are closed. When you start to see yourself, just let me know by nodding your head. (Sally slowly nods.) Where are you?

**Sally:** I'm in my room standing in front of my mirror.

**Therapist:** What do you have on?

**Sally:** (startle response) Pajamas!

**Therapist:** [Realizes from Sally's mentioning the bedroom and pajamas that it may be the abuse setting that has been imaged. Also realizes that the image is Sally's emotional reality and not necessarily objective reality.] Look in the mirror and look around the room. What do you notice?

**Sally:** I'm alone. Wait, I can see my stepfather coming in and he is looking at me with that smile and he is coming toward me. I'm so scared I can't move. (see page 63)

* * * * *

Jocelyn (a 15-year-old sexually abused between ages 7 and 11 by the next-door neighbor) talks about feeling angry. This anger, she says, is so disconnected from her that she cannot do anything about it.

**Therapist:** [Knows that Jocelyn is fearful of losing control and that to ask her to close her eyes might be too stressful for her.] Just looking at the wall where you are already looking, let yourself go back to the first time you felt this anger, the first time you felt the anger that feels so disconnected. If anything comes into your mind, if you start to see or feel anything in your mind, let me know.

**Jocelyn:** (pause) I see myself, I'm 9 years old.

**Therapist:** What do you have on?

**Jocelyn:** A white T-shirt, yellow shorts.

**Therapist:** Look around you for a moment. Where are you?

**Jocelyn:** There are bushes.

**Therapist:** Tell me about the bushes.

**Jocelyn:** They're the bushes between Steve's house and our house and I have just come back through them.

**Therapist:** What else is happening?

**Jocelyn:** I can hear the car. My mother, father, and sister have just arrived back. My sister is running up to me, telling me that my parents are angry at me because I came back from Steve's before they called.

**Therapist:** You must have been angry. You had just taken yourself out of an abusing situation—quite a task for a 9-year-old—and then you were being criticized for just that, for leaving Steve's house. (pause) What's happening now?

**Jocelyn:** Nothing. I'm just sitting down on the steps. I don't feel anything.

**Therapist:** I'm thinking how scary it is as a child to be angry with parents, how scary to be angry at the people who are so important. But know that it is all right to be angry at them, you can be angry at them without hurting them, without them getting hurt. It makes sense that you were angry at them and that anger can be there without anyone getting hurt.

## FOR CHILDREN EXPERIENCING DISSOCIATION: ENCOURAGING COMMUNICATION BETWEEN PARTS

A child who is severely abused often protects herself by dissociating herself from the abuse experience. When this happens occasionally, part of the child's experience or emotion is separated off. When dissociation is used repeatedly—as with children who are severely or repeatedly abused with no one available to help them make sense of their world—it can cause a child to experience herself as having multiple aspects of self or multiple identities. (For a complete discussion of dissociation, see Chapter 5.)

For a child experiencing multiple aspects of self, imaging can be used to help the child become more aware of the various parts, to bring the parts together in one space, to encourage the parts to work together in responding to ongoing events, and, if appropriate, to integrate the parts. For a child experiencing moderate dissociation—perhaps negative emotions or experiences have been dissociated—imaging can be used to encourage recognition and integration of those feelings or experiences.

> Emily (a 12-year-old severely neglected and physically abused from a young age to age 8; sexual abuse is suspected but has not been reported) talks about how she cannot remember her early years. She says she was living with her birth parents then, but has little sense of what things were like.

Therapist: That sense that you do have, what is it like?

Emily: Lonely.

Therapist: Tell me about the lonely you.

Emily: I don't know.

Therapist: If you close your eyes, can you see the lonely you? . . . (Emily nods.) Tell me what you see.

Emily: She is so little and seems so far away.

**Therapist:** Can you bring her here with you or to some space that feels safe? . . . (Emily nods.) What is happening?

**Emily:** Well, she is on my lap. This is weird. But she is still lonely.

**Therapist:** Can she tell you what she sees?

**Emily:** There is a window and people are fighting on the other side of the window. She doesn't want to look through the window, she doesn't want to know what is happening. She doesn't know.

**Therapist:** Seems like it was too scary for you to know about your parents fighting so you took yourself away from it. That was good protection then, but can leave a very lonely feeling. It's important for us to get to know that lonely feeling you have. Tell me more about it.

Imaging can help to strengthen the child's connection with and the therapist's knowledge of dissociated aspects or parts of herself.

### LEARNING NEW SKILLS

As the child works through the abuse and the dynamics related to abuse, there are usually new skills that she needs to learn. These skills may relate to becoming more assertive with others or caretaking of herself. They may relate directly to the abuse or may be part of helping the child be less vulnerable in all situations. Both role-play and imaging or a combination of the two can be helpful. With imaging related to learning new skills, a therapist will need to be more directive than with other imaging. Checking on the child's own experience of what is happening continues to be important.

Sally (see page 61) sees, within the image that comes from the tension she is feeling, her stepfather coming into her bedroom.

**Sally:** I'm so scared, I can't move.

**Therapist:** Yes, you're feeling scared. And it makes sense that you would be feeling scared because of all that has happened. But *now, not back then when the abuse was happening,* but now, you may know new things that you can—even with that scared feeling inside—do.

**Sally:** Tell him to go away.

**Therapist:** All right, watch and see what happens.

**Sally:** I can't do it, I can't say anything.

**Therapist:** That's all right. Telling him to go away is hard and something you will learn sometime. But right now, what ideas do you have for what you could do now?

**Sally:** I could run away.

**Therapist:** Yes, you could. That was something you didn't have a chance to know how to do back then but something you could use now. Anything else you could use now? Watch carefully, what is happening?

**Sally:** I could tell him that if he touches me, I am going to tell my mother.

**Therapist:** Yes, you could. Let's practice that.

**Sally:** If you touch me, I'll tell my mother.

**Therapist:** Say it louder, let's be sure he hears. (Sally repeats louder.) What's happening now?

**Sally:** He's turning away.

When working on new skills or behaviors, the therapist needs to be careful that the child does not assume she should have been able to do those behavior at the time of the abuse. The time between the abuse and a particular point in therapy has brought new experiences for the child. Recognizing these experiences, realizing the new skills that can come from these experiences, and practicing these skills can help the child to feel stronger and safer than she did at the time of the abuse.

Specific behaviors may also need to be taught. When children internalize sexual behaviors as positive, they repeat these sexualized behaviors. In many cases, they will need to learn to control these behaviors and to develop new behaviors. Imaging, together with guided imagery, can provide a setting for practicing new behaviors.

> **David** (a developmentally delayed 12-year-old sexually abused by his mother from a young age to age 8) has been spending an inordinate amount of time in the washroom at school. In discussion with the therapist, David explains that he is spending the time in the washroom masturbating because he feels aroused each time he sees a girl.

**Therapist:** Sounds like it is really hard to stop thinking about the girl and about the arousal you are feeling. What happens when you try to think of something else?

**David:** It doesn't work; I just keep on thinking about the girl. If I go to the washroom and masturbate, it's okay.

**Therapist:** Would you like to figure out something else that would take her out of your mind? (David nods.) Something other boys have found helpful is to imagine that the girl is on TV and then to change the channel to something else. Shall we try that? (David nods.) All right, close your eyes and pretend in your mind that you are walking down the hall at school. Can you see yourself there? (David nods.) Now look down the hall, you may find that a girl is coming toward you. If you see someone, just let me know by nodding. (David nods and smiles.) Describe her to me. . . . As you look at her, you may start to notice a tingling in your body, in your penis. (David smiles.) All right, take that picture you just described, the picture of the girl, the picture that gives you a tingling feeling, and put it up on a TV screen. (pause) Can you see it on the TV? (David nods.) Describe the TV and describe the picture on the screen to me. . . . Now I want you to take a remote control in your hand. And I want you to change the channel of the TV. What do you like to watch on TV? (David talks about cartoons.) All right, now, press the channel change button on the remote control. Press it until you come to the cartoons. What do you see?

**David:** (surprised tone) London Bridges Falling Down!

**Therapist:** And stay with London Bridges Falling Down until you find that all of the tingling feeling has gone away and the picture in your head of the girl has gone. And when the picture and the feeling have gone, nod your head to let me know. (David nods.) Let's practice that. Switch back to the channel with the girl. There she is—blond hair, red shorts—and you are starting to feel a bit aroused. Let me know when you see her. (David nods.) Do you feel any tingling in your penis? (David smiles and nods.) Now press the channel change button, back to London Bridges Falling Down. What is happening now?

**David:** I'm back there. (The switching of channels, each time checking David's response, is practiced several times.)

Imaging in relation to skill learning is unlikely to be successful unless the child wants to change his behavior.

A skill important for children who have been sexually abused is the ability to recognize abuse triggers and to reorient to the present. When a child's behavior in a situation is less capable than the behavior she usually exhibits, the child may have experienced a trigger response.

Something in the situation reminded her, on a conscious or unconscious level, of the abuse situation and she is "triggered" back to the child she was at the time of the abuse. She no longer is able to access her present level of functioning but responds with the level of capability she had at the time of the abuse. This often occurs for adolescents around sexual situations and therapists can sometimes identify this response by asking adolescents about unwanted sexual experiences. Imaging can help an adolescent learn how to reorient to her present capabilities.

Before doing imaging around trigger responses, the child and therapist talk about and identify similarities between the present situation and the abuse situation. Depending on the amount of work that has already been done in therapy differentiating *now* from *then*, they would refer to or talk about the differences between the present situation and the abuse situation and, in particular, the differences between the child now and then. They then identify the regression in functioning that was experienced. Imaging can provide a chance for the older child or adolescent to, in the image, go back to the situation in which the trigger occurred, experience the regression, and then practice reorienting to present functioning. For a younger child, role-play may be a more effective practice than imaging.

> **Kaitlyn** (a 16-year-old sexually abused at age 6 by a friend's father, who would come up behind her and start rubbing against her) has been doing very well and is no longer in therapy. She is active in school politics and speaks out on a number of issues. She has established good boundaries with family and friends. Kaitlyn calls and asks if she can have a therapy session because something has happened. When she comes in, she reports that over the weekend she ended up in a sexual situation she didn't want. She explains that at the beginning of the evening, she was sitting on the front edge of a chair talking to friends. A boy she doesn't particularly like came and sat behind her, pressing against her. She found that she froze and was not able to tell him to move away or able to move away herself. Finally he moved away and things got better. But later in the evening, he moved up close behind her again and started whispering in her ear. He asked her to go upstairs with him. She had no wish to do so but found that she couldn't say anything or even resist when he took her hand and led her up to a bedroom.

**Therapist:** Not saying anything doesn't sound like you, does it? You have become very clear in your statements of what you want and what you don't want. What do you think happened?

**Kaitlyn:** I don't know, it was awful, this feeling of not being able to say anything.

**Therapist:** What happened, each time, right before you couldn't say anything?

**Kaitlyn:** Well, the first time, he sat down behind me. The second time, he came up behind me. It's that "behind me" stuff again. Just the way Ann's father always came up from behind. It gives me the creeps just to think about it. And Bob came up from behind and leaned on me.

**Therapist:** And then what happened?

**Kaitlyn:** I couldn't do anything.

**Therapist:** The "coming up from behind" and "leaning against you" sound like triggers. Sounds as if you went back to the 6-year-old you. The "16-year-old you" would have been able to handle the situation, but a 6-year-old can't handle situations like that. We could do some practicing to help you learn how to bring yourself back to the "16-year-old you."

**Kaitlyn:** I have to do something.

**Therapist:** All right, let your mind go back to that evening and to your sitting at the table talking to your friends. And when you see yourself there, just nod your head to let me know. . . . (Kaitlyn nods.) And now Bob comes over and sits behind you and leans against you. (Kaitlyn seems to pull into herself.) I want you to look at your hands, the hands of a 16-year-old. Notice the fingers of a 16-year-old, not the fingers of a 6-year-old. Notice the fingernails of a 16-year-old, the length of the fingernails, not the fingernails of a 6-year-old. And when you can see and can feel the hands of a 16-year-old, nod your head to let me know. . . . (Kaitlyn nods).

Feel your arms, the arms of a 16-year-old, not the arms of a 6-year-old. (Kaitlyn puts her hands on her arms.) Feel the size of your arms, the arms of the 16-year-old. And when you can feel the arms of the 16-year-old, nod your head to let me know. . . . (Kaitlyn nods.)

Now sense your mind, the mind of a 16-year-old, not a 6-year-old. Feel the capability of the 16-year-old, the ability to decide what she wants and to say what she wants. And when you sense that mind, the mind of the 16-year-old, with all of the capability of a 16-year-old, nod your head to let me know. (Kaitlyn nods.) Now with that mind of the 16-year-old and the body of a 16-year-old, watch yourself and let me know what you are doing.

**Kaitlyn:** I'm telling him to move, but he doesn't. I'm jabbing him with my elbow. Boy, did that surprise him. He moved.

**Therapist:** All right, let's go to that time later in the evening when Bob came up close behind you. . . .

## ❑ The Process of Imaging

Imaging that develops from the conversation between the child and therapist, that follows the child's imaging experience, encourages in-depth processing without intrusion. Although the therapist facilitates, asks questions, and sometimes gives direction to the imaging, it is always the child, not the therapist, who determines the actual content of the imaging. The therapist remains alert, throughout the imaging, for problems that may arise. When imaging ends, the therapist remains sensitive to the child's experience and provides grounding and further processing.

### INITIATING THE IMAGING

The possibility of imaging should not be introduced until a child is comfortable within the therapy setting and feels safe and supported by the therapist. As discussed earlier in this chapter, imaging should not be used with children who are unable to differentiate between fantasy and reality or who show any indication of schizophrenia. If a child had been included in or preached to about psychical activities or involved in ritual abuse, imaging would not be appropriate.

Imaging to explore emotions should not be introduced by the therapist if the child is highly anxious. For a child who is highly defended, imaging should not be used to explore those areas. Imaging related to other issues or for comforting and reassurance can be used as long as the therapist is alert to and avoids areas that could feel too risky for the child. Imaging should not be used if the case will be going to court.

To use imaging, the therapist needs to believe in the child's ability to image. Although most children experience visual images, some children have auditory, body sensation, or emotional experiences. For a few children, nothing is actually imaged, heard, or felt, but they do become aware of thoughts going through their minds. This can be referred to as thought-flow imaging. The therapist needs to believe in a child's ability to access the images—in whatever modality—important for him.

An introduction to imaging can include the therapist's description of the process:

> If you want, we can use imaging to take a look at that feeling. I would ask you to describe the feeling and then, with your eyes closed or open, I would ask you to let that feeling come in. And then, when the feeling is there, I would ask you to let that feeling become a bit stronger and then, when it is stronger, to float back on that feeling to another time when you felt the same feeling. You may find that some image, some feeling, or some thought comes into your mind. If some image, feeling, or thought comes in, nod your head to let me know, and if nothing comes in, that is all right too, and shake your head to let me know.[9]

The instructions for imaging are left somewhat vague to allow a child to move into whichever modality comes most easily for that child.

An introduction may, in some situations, simply provide a beginning:

> Why don't you close your eyes and let yourself see the you who is scared.

Occasionally a child does not develop an image. It is then helpful for the therapist to ask the child what he does see:

> Tell me what is there inside you. Is it gray, is it black, are there lights or stars, is there any sensation or feeling—just describe to me what you are aware of.

The therapist may ask the child to stay with whatever he is aware of and to notice any shift that occurs. The therapist might ask the child to look through or beyond the nothingness that is there and to notice what happens. Or the therapist may ask the child just to stay with the nothingness that is there and let himself relax with that nothingness for a time before opening his eyes.

When a child does not form an image, it may be that he does not feel safe enough in the therapy setting and is, therefore, not ready to let his mind float. The therapist may wish to talk further about the process of imaging, to inquire how the therapy setting could be made to feel safer, or simply to proceed from the child's cognitive response. The resistance reflected in the lack of an image may reflect not a resistance to imaging but rather a resistance to the particular issue being explored. If this appears to be the case, the child should not be pressured to image, but rather reassured that it is all right not to have an image—that not imaging at that point may be an important way for the child to take care of himself. A cognitive approach to exploring the issue would be more appropriate and may provide an opportunity for the therapist to understand better the reason for the child's resistance and to provide the support needed to help the child through his resistance. Not imaging should not be assumed by either the child or the therapist to mean that the child cannot image.

At times, the child will see himself in a space but see no other objects or movement in that space. This may reflect the child's sense of loneliness or the wish not to remember. The feelings of being alone can be explored. Whatever occurs should be affirmed as important for the child at that time, with the option of a different image coming at some other time.

Either before or after the first experience of imaging, it is important for the therapist to discuss with the child the difference between objective reality (factual events) and the emotional reality (the child's emotional experiencing) that is experienced in imaging.

**Therapist:** What was that like for you, Mary (see page 52), seeing yourself at age 5? Seeing yourself back then when the abuse was going on?

**Mary:** It felt so real. Like I was there.

**Therapist:** But it's really important for you to realize that what you are experiencing when imaging is your perception, your experiencing of what happened back then, not the happening itself. Imaging does not give a replay of what actually happened. Imaging gives a replay of your experience of the happening. And your experience would have been affected by other feelings and happenings occurring for you—just as your experience of what is happening right now in this room is different from my experience of it and also different from the actual happening, that is, the words that are being said. Your experience includes your feelings, your perceptions, and your understanding.

   For example, 5-year-olds are less able to understand that events are caused by other people. They often see themselves at the center of events—the cause of something—because the thinking of a 5-year-old is not developed as far as the thinking of a 17-year-old or even a 7-year-old. It may feel to you inside that you could have stopped the abuse because that is the way a 5-year-old would have understood it, even though you did not have the teaching—screaming is okay when something is really happening—that could have helped you stop it.

It may have felt, for the 5-year-old you, that everyone knew about the abuse because 5-year-olds believe adults know things that have happened. Your family being in the image of you with your uncle may or may not be factual. It is, however, part of your experience and part of the hurt from the abuse.

Also, it is important for you to realize that imaging does not create something out of nothing. Something happened that gave you these feelings and these perceptions. What we can't do is assume that your image portrays the factual event. Your image was your experience of what happened. And that experiencing is important for us to know.

**Mary:** Do you mean my uncle may not have abused me?

**Therapist:** No, you have a memory of something happening to you, of abuse that happened to you. Your imaging of it gives you something a bit different from the memory, it gives you a part of your experiencing of the factual events.

Imaging should proceed from some statement or behavior by the child during the therapy session (Mary starting to cry; Jenny reporting a flashback; Jane saying she feels awful). The image itself may be specified by the therapist (Mary: see yourself with tears running down your cheeks) or it may be left open (Jane: float back to another time you felt that feeling). In both cases, specific details of the image would not be mentioned.

If imaging is being used to modify behavior, it may not develop from the material the child brings to the session but rather from someone else's concern (David spending time in the washroom at school). Before doing behavior control imaging, the therapist needs to discuss the behavior with the child to determine the meaning of the behavior and whether the child wants to change. If the child does not want to change, imaging would not be appropriate.

A therapist may be able to help a child move himself from awareness of the room to internal awareness by using a soothing, rather melodic tone. Some repetition of words ("Let yourself have that feeling, that throbbing feeling, that throbbing feeling in your stomach") can be helpful. Some children experience self-hypnosis, whereas others stay very close to the ongoing moment.

When imaging is directed toward processing traumatic material, it is helpful to have a child first go, within his mind, to some place that is peaceful and calm. Because some children are unable to access a place that feels safe, the phrasing "peaceful and calm" is suggested:

> Before we start with the flashback you had yesterday, just let your mind float to a place that is peaceful and calm, a place for you. Maybe a place you have been before, and maybe a place you have never been. But a place for you. (pause) And if any place goes through your mind, just let me know by nodding your head (pause) and if no place goes through your head, that is fine, and let me know by shaking your head.

Having this place provides a sense of balance and security and provides a space to which the child can return following trauma recall.

Expanding the image of a calm and peaceful place helps create a more concrete experience and encourages the child to use multiple senses within imaging. Any descriptive words included in the instructions need to come from the child initially and not the therapist.

> Tell me about the place. . . . And as you look at the trees and the lake, is there anything else you notice? . . . And there on the beach by the lake, are there any colors you notice? . . . And there on the sandy beach by the deep blue lake, are there any sounds that you hear? On the sandy beach with the deep blue lake and the trees around and the sound of a loon, are there any feelings, any sensations in your body?

Once an image of a calm and peaceful place is developed, the therapist can increase the child's sense of safety and that frightening experiences can be contained by letting the child know he will be able to go back to the calm and peaceful image:

> And knowing that this place is yours, and that it is there for you to come back to, let your mind float again . . .

## DEVELOPING THE IMAGE

To help the child focus on and develop an image, the therapist can ask for concrete details:

> What does the "little you" have on? . . . How old is she? . . . As you look around the room, what do you notice?

Asking for, but not suggesting, information about a scene helps the child become more aware of and more connected to the internal image. It may also help the child and therapist understand the image scenario and its connection to the child's past.

The therapist will want to avoid phrases such as "What do you think happened?" or "What happened next?" This wording encourages the child to think rather than allowing his mind to explore internal reactions. Asking the child simply to "watch what happens next" provides more freedom and helps the imaging process not become cognitive.

As the imaging progresses, the therapist's comments need to follow what the child is seeing. Specific questions can, at times, be helpful, but for the most part questions should be open, for instance, "What is happening now?" With imaging in which a therapist is more directive— for example, teaching new skills—checking as to what is happening in the child's image is particularly important. If this checking is not done, subsequent directions may be inappropriate or, indeed, counterproductive.

If the content of the image becomes frightening in any way, the therapist can help the child maintain her connection with the here and now in the therapy space:

> And knowing that you are here in this room, in a safe place as you watch these experiences/feelings from the past, and knowing that the abuse is now over and that we are working together to help that part of you that feels caught back then, let yourself watch and be there for the younger you.

A child should *never* be left in a "negative space." That the child is in reality in a safe place—the therapy room—and that the abuse is not happening now can be repeated. The reason for looking at the image— to understand better the child's experience and to be there for that part of the child who holds the abuse—can be restated. If this grounding does not help lower the child's anxiety, the now self or ego state can be taken into the image or the younger frightened self can be brought into the therapy room. The child should not be left without support to deal with a frightening image and neither should the imaging be terminated without some grounding and reassurance given. If a child becomes frightened when imaging, the therapist needs to remain calm and feel sure within himself that with consistent grounding, reassurance, and staying with the image, the child will find within herself the resources for dealing with the image. If the therapist tries to take over direction of the image or to terminate the image, the child will be left with a sense of not being able to cope.

The "younger self" within the image—that is, the child from the time of the abuse—can be asked to notice things but should never be asked to do something. Having the "younger child" do something implies that the child should have done something at the time of the abuse. The now or present ego state can be used to help the "younger self" in the image. The first time an unusual suggestion is given, such as "take in the 'now Mary,' " the therapist can help the child understand what is meant by providing several possibilities:

> Take the "now you," the 16-year-old you, into the picture. I don't know where in the picture the 16-year-old you will be—maybe he will be over by the "little you," maybe he will be by the door, or maybe he will be outside the picture, looking in—or maybe he will not be there at all. Just let me know.

Although possibilities are listed, the image is not directed and the outcome is left to the child.

Some children do not like to image. This is usually connected to an uncertainty as to where their thoughts will go and the feelings that may come up. This can be discussed, but no one should be pressured into imaging. Imaging around pleasant feelings or a calm and peaceful place can be reassuring and can help a child who experiences anxiety. Other children do not like to image because they are worried about not getting an image and feeling they have failed. This would represent a transference response and should be explored.

Problems can occur with imaging if the therapist has started imaging before the child feels safe in the therapy setting, if a frightening feeling or scene comes back that feels overwhelming for the child, if the therapist tries to do too much work too fast, or if upsetting parts of the imaging intrude on the child outside therapy.

If imaging is initiated before the child feels safe with the therapist or in the therapy room, the child may experience within the imaging a lost and unsafe feeling and become extremely frightened. The therapist will need at that point to do considerable grounding to the therapy room. Because lack of a feeling of safety in therapy is part of the problem, it can be helpful for the therapist to talk about the positive strengths the child now in the therapy room has, the strengths that enabled the child to move out of the abuse situation and to make the progress that she has. Imaging should not be used again until the child feels safe within therapy.

If an image becomes frightening or the child has a flashback during a therapy session, it is important, as discussed above, that the therapist not try to terminate the image but rather help the child work through the image. The therapist can provide grounding and reassurance and can encourage the child to continue watching and noticing what is happening (see Jenny, page 55). Having the child image herself at her present age within the image can also be helpful (see Mary, page 53). The therapist believing that the child has within herself the capability for working through the trauma is an important part of the work. Although it may, at times, feel as if the fright is just going to go on and on, clinical experience has shown that children are able, with the calm support of a therapist, to work through these situations.

If the therapist has been working too fast, has pushed the child to confront too much too soon, the child is likely either to become overwhelmed with feelings and scenes from the past or to feel that her present world is threatened. If the therapist has stayed closely with the content of the session and has avoided, during imaging, areas where the child shows high defenses or high anxiety, this should not happen. The therapist needs to be sensitive to images that in themselves may not seem so frightening but because they represent an area the child is not ready to look at can feel threatening to the child. If such an image does occur, it is important that the therapist have enough time following the imaging to talk with the child about the content of the imaging. How imaging relates to the real world—the child's experience as opposed to objective reality, both back at the time of the incident and now—needs to be discussed. Therapist and child can discuss ways in which the child can put some of the feelings or scenes "on hold" until others are thought through or until they are better understood. If there is not sufficient processing, the child is likely to become more anxious and possibly leave therapy or initiate some action outside of therapy that further disrupts her world.

If frightening feelings or scenes from imaging are intruding outside of therapy, the therapist will want to give more attention both to grounding and to talking about the imaging experience after imaging.

Imaging should, whenever possible, end well before the end of a therapy session. Talking with the child during the imaging about leaving the issues or the fears in the therapy room to be worked on during a future session can also be helpful.

When working with traumatic material, only one issue or feeling should be pursued at one session. A therapist must not get pulled into the feeling that issues or feelings cannot wait. The therapist's belief in containment strengthens the child's ability to contain. At times it is helpful for a child to create an image of a place or to choose a place within the therapy room where memories or feelings can be left between sessions (for example, a locked trunk, the Kleenex box).

### TERMINATING THE IMAGING

At times, imaging terminates by the child simply opening her eyes or turning her eyes back to the therapist. At other times, the therapist terminates the imaging by asking the child "to come back to the room." A positive statement or a reassurance that the younger child within the image can be cared for is made before the terminating statement:

> And letting the little Mary know that you realize how lonely she was and how hurt she was, and letting her know that you will be back to spend time with her and to listen to her, start to come back to this space here and now.

It is often helpful to have the child go back to or take her younger self back to the calm and peaceful place imaged at the beginning of the session.

If the child appears to have gone into a deep trance state, orienting her to the feel of the chair, the sounds of the room, and her eyelids getting lighter and lighter until they are ready to open can be helpful. The therapist needs to be sure the child is able to make good eye contact and carry on some general conversation before the end of the session.

Discussion of the child's experience within the imaging is important—what the experience was like for the child and what the child feels the image means. Imaging often helps the child realize how young she was at the time of the abuse and how the occurrence of the abuse existed outside of her. Any feelings that came up during the imaging need to be thought about and discussed—what does the child want to do with these feelings or for these feelings now? Discussion encourages the child to process on a more conscious level what she experienced on the internal level.

Imaging is one of many therapeutic processes helpful for children. Overreliance on imaging can give a child the feeling she is better "by magic" and should, therefore, be avoided.

❏  **Summary**

Both hypnosis and imaging provide access to a child's internal world. Imaging, in that it is directed by the child, not the therapist, is less intrusive and closer to the child's own experience. Although a helpful therapeutic process, imaging should *not* be used if a child cannot distinguish fantasy from reality or shows any symptoms of schizophrenia, if the process of imaging has any similarity to the child's early experience, or if a court case is likely to occur. Imaging should not be used in relation to areas where the child is highly defended or extremely anxious.

Imaging, by enabling the child to become more aware of inner feelings and perceptions, helps him to work through and shift abuse-related internalizations. The child is better able to recognize what his experience was like as a younger child. He can comfort and support his younger self as he experiences new ways of behaving and new ways of feeling. He can sort through flashbacks. He can better grasp feelings of distress and explore emotions.

❏  **Notes**

1.  A few individuals report that they do not, during the process of imaging, have perceptual experiences, but rather find that thoughts separate from what is happening come into their minds. By following their thought flows, as others follow their images, they become aware of emotions and perceptions of which they had not been aware. I refer to this as *thought-flow imaging*.

2. See van der Kolk (1994, 1996a) for discussion of implicit and explicit memory.

3. The difference between implicit and explicit memory (van der Kolk, 1994), the effect of trauma on memory (van der Kolk, 1996b), and the effect of cognitive development on the formation of memory (Pynoos, Steinberg, & Goenjian, 1996) need to be clearly understood.

4. If a child has not worked through the abuse experience, imaging related to early abuse reflects the cognitive functioning (for example, concept of time and causality) of a child at the age the abuse occurred. The therapist needs to be aware of the developmental distortions that may be occurring.

5. Myers (1992) differentiates between focusing questions (content that directs attention) and leading questions (content that includes information).

6. As discussed earlier, imaging presents the young child's perception of the experience. It may or may not be exactly what happened.

7. This is referred to in hypnotherapy as an affect bridge (Barnett, 1981).

8. The therapist would have evaluated whether Sally's present abilities and present environment were such that she would be able to handle recognizing this fear. If the therapist had felt recognition of this fear would be overly threatening to Sally, she would not have proceeded with the imaging (see the discussion on pages 49-50).

9. A similarity between the phrasing used in this example and that used with hypnosis will be noted. In both cases, the therapist is encouraging the individual to narrow his focus of attention. Imaging differs from hypnosis in that a trance is not induced externally. A trance may or may not occur internally.

# 4

## Placing the Abuse in Context: Genograms, Timelines, Messages, and Myths

When a child is abused sexually, he internalizes the experience of himself as an object, as bad, as guilty. Self-blame comes from the fact that the abuse happened to him, not to someone else. It comes from the young child seeing himself at the center of what happens, the school-age child feeling curious about sex, and the adolescent trying to regulate his world. It comes from other people's responses and comments and from the child's wish to have been able to control what happened. Abuse prevention programs, TV shows on sequelae of sexual abuse, and, indeed, therapy itself can heighten a child's sense of something being wrong with him—the child, not the perpetrator, is receiving therapy. Discussions of abuse tend all too often to center on the child, not the perpetrator, family, or society.

It is important, therefore, that throughout therapy the happening of abuse be placed with the perpetrator, that the failure to recognize the abuse happening be placed with the nonperpetrating parent(s), and that negative responses be placed with the people who made those responses. For the child to be able to start shifting the internalization of being bad, the child needs to become aware of the role of the larger system in which the abuse and the reactions to the abuse occurred. This larger system includes the family as it has developed through the generations as well as the society around the family, for example, the church. Genograms, timelines, and listings of the myths and messages passed down through a family or social group can help a child recognize the roles of other people and start shifting away from himself responsibility for what happened.

This chapter discusses the use of genograms, timelines, and family messages and myths within the therapy of children who have been sexually abused. Each activity is described, and the ways it can be used in therapy are suggested.


❏  **Genograms**


During the 1950s, the therapeutic community started to recognize the importance of looking at the entire family and family dynamics when working with any one individual (Hoffman, 1981). At the same time, the scientific community was moving from explanations of linear causality to recognition of circular or reciprocal causality, systems theory. Murray Bowen (1978) combined family theory and systems theory to highlight how patterns repeat within families. He described the manner in which each individual in a family is pulled into the dysfunctional interactions occurring between others in the family. Bowen encouraged therapists to use a multigenerational diagram referred to as a *genogram* to help sort out these dynamics.

The genogram creates a context for viewing both the abuse and the family response to the abuse. The abuse becomes something that happened within a multigenerational family system, not just with the child. It becomes something that happened because of events and decisions outside the child, not because of the child. In addition, the genogram can help both the child and the therapist recognize situations outside the child that have affected the way the child experiences herself and her world.

The diagram of the family is particularly helpful for children in that it sets down in a concrete form both relationships and experiences. Children of 9 or older, the age group with whom genograms and timelines have been used, generally know quite a bit about their extended families. When children know little about relatives and are living at home, this exercise gives them an opportunity to ask questions. If they are living in foster care, they may or may not be able to find out family information. If little information is known, the child's fantasy and whether that fantasy matches the reality of the child's world—being in foster care—can be discussed.

The genogram format described here is based on the system developed by McGoldrick and Gerson (1985). Using squares to indicate males and circles to indicate females, family, stepfamily, and foster family members for at least three generations are diagrammed.

- Solid lines indicate marriages and births.
- Dashed lines indicate common-law relationships and adoptions.
- Dotted lines indicate relationships and foster children.
- A single slash across a marriage or relationship line indicates a separation.
- A double slash across a marriage or relationship line indicates a divorce.
- An X inside a box or circle indicates the individual has died.
- Large circles indicate individuals currently living together.
- A double line indicates a particularly close relationship.

Rather than using dates to identify when births, deaths, separations, marriages, and other major events occurred, as described by McGoldrick and Gerson, the child's age at the time of the event is marked on the genogram (see Figure 4.1).

Although it is important to discuss all forms of abuse, some genograms become too confusing to read if all abuse is diagrammed. It is often easier to mark physical and emotional abuse and neglect in writing with an arrow indicating the direction or directions in which it occurred. All situations of sexual abuse (long-term incest, single-occasion rape by boyfriend, exploitative sexual contact by an older

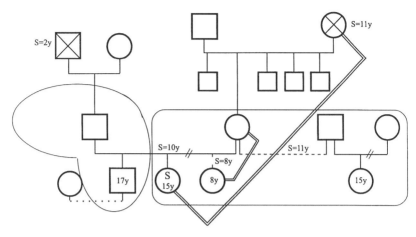

**Figure 4.1.**

sibling) for all three generations should be marked (∧∧∧). Abusers outside the family are indicated by gender symbols, with any relationship to the child or family noted and the abuse line drawn to the child. The child's age or age span during which the sexual abuse took place is marked on the abuse line. Any present contact between the abuser and the family is noted.

Heavy use of alcohol or drugs, periods of emotional distress (such as depression, suicide attempts), and periods of parental involvement outside the family (such as extended travel, affairs, hospitalizations) are indicated for each individual on the genogram. The child's description of family members is marked in abbreviated form on the genogram (see Figure 4.2).

## CREATING THE GENOGRAM

Starting to talk about the abuse and about the guilt, betrayal, and mixed feelings related to the abuse is difficult. Talking about family is often easier. The concrete activity of drawing a genogram helps engage a child who, to protect himself or his family, may pull back from other people and particularly from someone who wants him to talk. The actual drawing is usually done by the therapist, with the child providing information. A younger child can participate by drawing stick

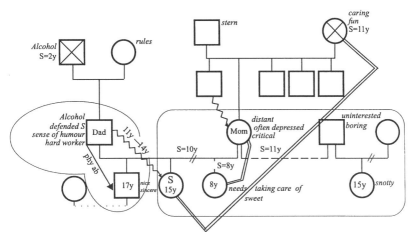

**Figure 4.2.**

figures to represent members of the family. A child who is having difficulty distinguishing between the perpetrator and other adults can be encouraged to draw the faces of each family member for the genogram. Creating a genogram emphasizes that the child is the expert on himself and his world and the therapist is simply a facilitator in sorting through any confusion.

The genogram is explained to the child as a family tree diagram. Large-size paper (11-by-16-inch newsprint) allows ample space for noting descriptions of family members and family messages. The drawing starts with the child's birth family and then expands to include grandparents, aunts and uncles, and stepfamilies. If the child has only limited information about his parent's family, he can be encouraged to find out more, and this can be added in subsequent sessions. Children of the parents' or stepparents' other marriages should be included. If there is extended family abuse, cousins should be included. Patterns similar to the ones in which the child became entrapped often emerge. These patterns highlight the abuse as belonging to the perpetrator's pattern and not the child.

For an early adoption, the child's birth family is placed at the side of the page in small scale, and the child's main or adoptive family is drawn in the center of the page, with the child as a part of the family's child constellation. An arrow (with the child's age at the time of

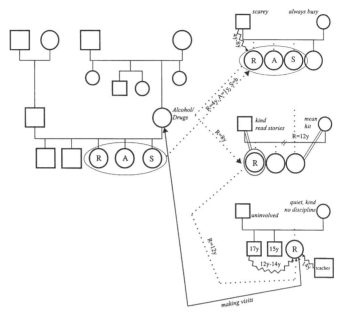

**Figure 4.3.**

adoption) is used to indicate movement between families. For a later adoption or fostering, the birth family would be placed on the left half of the page and would include whatever information and perceptions the child has of that family, with the new family placed on the right side of the page. Foster or group home placements would be diagrammed in order on the right half of the page. The movement of children and intertwining of families over time can present quite a challenge to a therapist as she seeks to create a clear picture of the child's life. Making order out of the chaos of lines helps the therapist appreciate the chaos within which the child has lived and helps the child and therapist find a pattern within that chaos (see Figure 4.3).

As the immediate family for three generations (siblings, parents, grandparents) is drawn, the child is asked about each individual ("Tell me about your mother, what sort of person is she?"). This information is jotted down on the genogram. If the child gives only idealized information, the therapist can inquire further as to what the parent is like when she is angry, drinking, or, less threateningly, tired. The child is asked to describe himself, and this information is included. If the child says he does not know what he is like, he can be asked how someone who knew his inner feelings as well as his outer behavior would describe him. As the child describes behaviors by people important to him, the therapist asks what that was like for the "younger him." This question highlights that the child's behavior, during the abuse and at other times, was in response to the behavior of others. It also highlights that the child's behavior cannot be judged in terms of what the child knows now but needs to be understood in terms of the age and the situation of the child then.

How the people important to the child—parents, siblings—were acting during the period of abuse needs to be clarified. This provides an opportunity for the therapist to ask how the child understood their behavior without the child feeling that someone important to him is being criticized and, therefore, feeling he needs to defend them. The therapist can also highlight the implicit messages the child would have received from other people at the time of the abuse.

> **Patti** (a 16-year-old sexually abused between ages 4 and 10 by her stepfather) completes a genogram of her family.
>
> **Therapist:** When would it be that the abuse happened?
>
> **Patti:** When Mom and Jeff had a fight, Mom would tell Jeff to give her some time alone. She would tell him to go to the cottage and to take the children with him. The abuse would happen at the cottage.
>
> **Therapist:** What was that like for you, Mother telling Jeff to take you to the cottage, the place where the abuse happened?
>
> **Patti:** Mom didn't know what was happening so I certainly don't blame her. Mom needed a break.
>
> **Therapist:** Yes, Patti at 16 is able to recognize what Mom was doing, but I wonder what it seemed like to the 6-year-old Patti.
>
> **Patti:** I thought I had to make things okay for her and Jeff. I liked the attention I got at the cottage so I guess I asked for it.
>
> **Therapist:** All 6-year-olds need attention. Sixteen-year-olds may be able to decide what way they are going to get attention, but not 6-year-olds. With 6-year-olds, adults decide, and that was a decision Jeff, not you, made. [Writes "decided to abuse" next to stepfather's symbol on the genogram

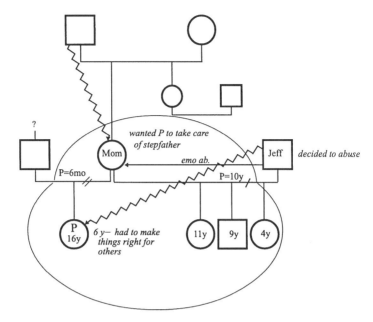

**Figure 4.4.**

and "6 y—had to make things right for others" next to Patti's circle.] What do you think the 6-year-old Patti, who had to make things right for others, would have thought mother wanted?

**Patti:** (sadly) I thought my mother wanted me to take care of stepfather.

**Therapist:** [Writes "wanted P to take care of stepfather" next to mother.] (See Figure 4.4.)

The therapist needs to ask directly about sexual, physical, and emotional abuse happening in the extended family. All abuses are noted on the genogram. At times, the therapist will know, from reading the case history, about situations of abuse the child has not reported. Unless the therapist has been asked to keep this information confidential or there is a reason that knowledge of the abuse would be detrimental for the child, the therapist should share this information with the child, stating clearly the source of the information. Often the child already knows or is aware of, without actually admitting, the information, but feels embarrassed either for himself or for his family. The therapist, by bringing out the information, can relieve the stigma felt by the child and counter the family dictate that abuse should be secret.

> **Mark** (a 13-year-old boy sexually abused by his grandparents, aunts, uncles, and mother and sexually abusive to his sister) reports to the therapist, while working on his genogram, the sexual abuse by his grandparents and his aunts and uncles.

> **Therapist:** [Recalls, as she draws the abuse lines, that the court report had stated that Mark had also been abused by his mother, who had been abused by her parents.] When I first started working with you, I was given a copy of the court report, which included all of the abuses in the family. I am noticing here that you have not mentioned your mother sexually abused both you and your sister and that mother was abused by her parents. It seems that it is easier to talk about the abuse from relatives than the abuse from mother. This makes sense. How did the abuse from mother seem different from the abuse by other people? (continued on page 91)

At the same time as inquiring about abuse from other members of the family, the therapist inquires as to whether the child had experienced or is now experiencing any other abuse or sexually intrusive experience. Experiences with peers that the child wishes had not happened should be included. Placing these on the genogram helps both the child and the therapist understand the child's experience and identify patterns.

## USING THE GENOGRAM

The genogram is helpful to both the therapist and the child. For the therapist, it provides (a) information about family connections (alliances, abuses, losses, shifts), (b) information about family behavior patterns (behaviors the child has learned to expect), (c) information on the role abuse plays in the extended family, and (d) structure to the child's story. Similarly, for the child the genogram provides information about the family. Although the child may have recognized individual facts before, she is unlikely to have linked these facts together into patterns.

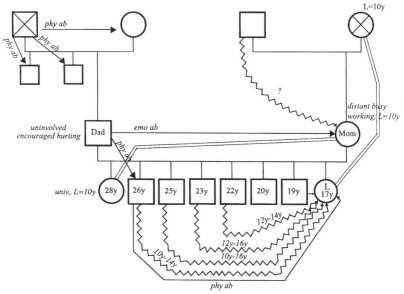

**Figure 4.5.**

*Identifying family alliances, abuses, losses, shifts.* The genogram, by providing a picture of family changes, helps the therapist and child recognize why the child behaved in a particular way at a particular time. This behavior can then be recognized as a result of family dynamics and the child's developmental stage, not a cause of abuse.

**Lisa** (a 17-year-old sexually abused between ages 10 and 16 by four older brothers) describes her family as the therapist draws the genogram. She reports that she was the youngest of eight children, with the eldest being a girl and the six middle children being boys. She describes her father as uninvolved and as encouraging the children to gang up on each other and hurt each other. Her mother, she says, was very close to her older sister. After her sister went away to university, her mother started working full-time and spent little time at home. That same year, when Lisa was 10, her maternal grandmother, to whom she had been very close, died (see Figure 4.5).

When talking about the abuse from her brothers, Lisa states that although some of the abuse had scared her, especially the abuse from her older brother, the abuse from her middle and favorite brother had not hurt and had made her feel special. She feels she had encouraged the abuse because at times she would brag about what she had done with one brother to make another brother jealous.

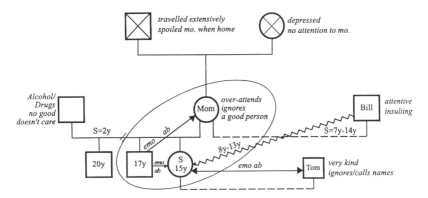

**Figure 4.6.**

**Therapist:** Children need attention and they need ways to be important in their families. Looking at this genogram, I'm not sure where you could have found attention after your sister left home. I notice that Sally left home when you were 10, your grandmother died that year, and your mother went to work full-time. Children need attention, and you had no safe place to get attention.

And then there was the message from your father that hurting was all right. So you were left, trying to manage as best you could. Ten-year-olds seek companionship and attention. Ten-year-olds tend to play one person off against another. You behaved this way, like other 10-year-olds behave that way. Because sexual abuse was occurring in the family, these normal 10-year-old behaviors happened within the abuse. The abuse did not occur because of the 10-year-old behavior.

*Identifying patterns in the family.* A genogram highlights the interactions that have occurred between people in a family. These interactions form much of the child's learning about how people relate.

**Susan** (a 15-year-old sexually abused between the ages of 8 and 13 by her mother's long-term boyfriend) talks about her relationship with her boyfriend. She explains that sometimes Tom is really kind to her and does things for her but at other times he totally ignores her. He pressures her to do certain sexual acts and then calls her names because she does them. Susan states that she gets back at Tom by calling him names and hitting him, but she will not break up with him. She loves him, needs him, and will never find another person to take care of her (see Figure 4.6).

**Therapist:** [Looks at the notes on the genogram and realizes that the dynamics Susan is reporting with her boyfriend are not unlike the dynamics she had experienced from her mother, and her mother from her parents, and not unlike the dynamics occurring in mother's interaction with the abuser.] Tom reminds me a bit of your mother. (points to the notes next to mother) Mother sometimes spends hour after hour with you and then, at other times, forgets about what she has said she will do with you. And that is similar to your mother's experience from her parents. What do you want your experiences in the future to be?

**Susan:** I don't want to be ignored but I can put up with it in order to have the good times.

**Therapist:** Good times can be had without bad times. You can't change how your mother treats you, only she can, but we can talk about it with her. And you can decide what you want from a boyfriend.

**Susan:** I know Tom isn't nice, but I don't want to lose him. Without him, I wouldn't be able to go to parties or do other things.

**Therapist:** That reminds me of your mother. Your mother has stayed in contact with Bill even after you told about the abuse, because she says it is only through her business dealings with him that she can afford the extra treats in your lives.

**Susan:** And I said I didn't want the treats, I just wanted everyone to kick him out. There are all sorts of other things Mom could do, to earn extra money.

**Therapist:** It sounds like you are looking at new ways to handle people who are abusive, ways different from your mother. And it can be hard. What would it be like not to do things with Tom?

When pointing out patterns, a therapist can wonder aloud about what types of patterns the child wants to have now. The ideas presented in narrative therapy can be helpful (White & Epston, 1990).

*Identifying the role of sexual abuse in the family.* In situations where the abuse is perpetrated by someone close to the family, abuse often plays a role within the family dynamics. This role differs from family to family. For a therapist to be able to help a child sort out the destructive interacting, this role needs to be identified, understood, and discussed in therapy.

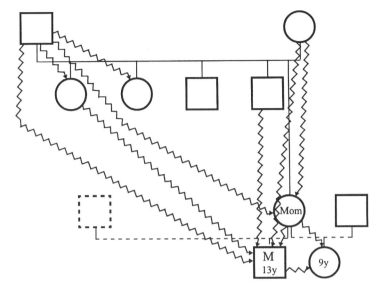

**Figure 4.7.**

**Mark:** (see page 87): Why is everyone making such a big deal about all this? My sister should have just kept quiet, after all I didn't tell anyone, no one else in the family had told anyone.

**Therapist:** (points to the abuse lines on the genogram; see Figure 4.7) Sexual touching, which is abuse when it is between an older person and a younger person, has happened between most adults and children in your family. It seems that it is something people in your family learned as part of behavior within a family, as a way of being close. But, no, everyone has a right to their body privacy. There are many ways people in a family can be close and can do things together that do not have to do with sexual touching. People in a family can be close *and* have their own physical privacy. Are there other things you remember doing with your mother that were special for you?

**Mark:** Sometimes we would play board games. I liked that.

**Therapist:** Let's add a line here between your mother and you and write "games" on it. It becomes a connection between her and you that still allows each of you your body privacy. What about special things you did with your grandfather?

                              *   *   *   *   *

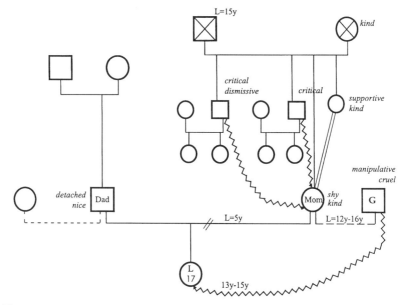

**Figure 4.8.**

**Laurie** (a 17-year-old sexually abused between ages 13 and 15 by her mother's common-law partner) talks about how everyone in the family had ostracized her and her mother following her disclosure of the abuse. They had been called liars and been told they exaggerate by her mother's brothers. These uncles said that if the grandparents were still alive, they would hate Laurie and her mother for talking about this. Laurie says that she feels she and her mother, not the abuser, are being punished for the abuse having happened (see Figure 4.8).

**Therapist:** [Notes from the genogram that the two people who were most critical, Laurie's uncles, had abused Laurie's mother when they were children.] I'm noticing from the genogram that your two uncles who are so critical sexually abused your mother when she was a child. Until you told, abuse was a secret activity. If they recognized and criticized what George did, then they would have to admit that they, themselves, had done something wrong.

*Providing structure to the child's story.* A child who has experienced long-term neglect and multiple abuse tends to have little structure to

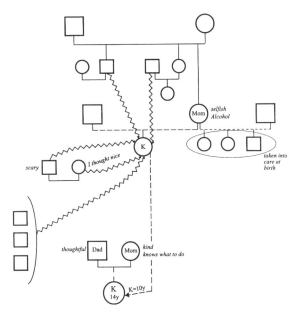

**Figure 4.9.**

her memories. Some events get lost, and others blend together. She may have no sense of attachment and belonging or she may have fantasized attachments. A genogram provides a way to gather information non-intrusively about both the family and the abuse. This information is in a format that makes it possible for the child and the therapist to start understanding what happened. By showing changes in the child's family, the genogram can help the child separate past and present.

> **Karen** (a 14-year-old sexually abused by many relatives and other adults coming into the house, from a young age to age 10, when she was adopted) talks about how frightening everything had been. She tells about her mother getting drunk and passing out. Then, whoever had been drinking with her mother would abuse Karen. Karen then went to live with relatives, and her uncles started abusing her. She ran away when she was 8 and a couple took her in and then abused her. At age 9, she met an older couple who befriended her. When Karen was 10, the couple adopted her and they moved to a new community. Karen says that no abuse happened after that (see Figure 4.9).

**Karen:** The other night was so scary! When Mom was at work and Dad was out, a man called. When I said my parents were out, he said he was going to come get me and hung up. I panicked.

**Therapist:** That might have felt like those times, back with your birth mother when she passed out and then the men in the house abused you. Then you were young. Now you are older. What did you do the other night?

**Karen:** I called Mom at work and she told me to lock the door, call the neighbor, and not answer the phone. I did that and nothing bad happened but now I'm scared every time I'm alone.

**Therapist:** Yes, you panicked inside but it is interesting that you didn't panic outside, you called your mother. Why did you decide to call her?

**Karen:** I didn't know what to do, bad things are always happening to me. That's the way I am.

**Therapist:** Look at the genogram we drew. All of the abuse happened before you were 10. None has happened since you moved away from the community. Bad things happened in that community. But you, with what you know now and where you live now, have kept yourself safe. Why do you suppose nothing bad happened the other night?

Although genograms are generally drawn at the beginning of therapy, they can be used throughout therapy. New information can be added. Reference can be made back to the genogram to highlight early experiences and to differentiate between then and now.


## ❏ Timelines[1]

Although genograms provide cross-sectional views of relationships within a family, they do not provide a longitudinal view. The impact of events occurring within a family may be missed when looking at a genogram. Friedman and colleagues have developed a timeline genogram that includes a vertical axis for important dates (Friedman, Krakauer, & Rohrbaugh, 1989; Friedman, Rohrbaugh, & Krakauer, 1988). The genogram is stretched out vertically, with changes in family attachments or structure indicated at the years in which they occurred.

Although this kind of genogram is more complete, it is difficult to construct and difficult to read. Stanton (1992) has developed a structural timeline in which time is tabulated on a horizontal axis, with family structural changes indicated by mini-genograms at appropriate points along the timeline. Although easier to read than Friedman et al.'s vertical timeline, it is complex and would undoubtedly confuse a child.

A simple timeline, drawn separately from a genogram, is, however, quite easy to read. In addition, it is a concept familiar to older children and adolescents from their studies in history and, thus, is an activity reassuring to the child.

A timeline, by starting with a child's birth—that is, before the abuse—helps the child relate to himself before the abuse. Rather than seeing himself as "the abused child," the child can be encouraged to see himself as a child who had many experiences, one or several of which were abuse. Although abuse may cover a considerable amount of the timeline, it is not the totality of the timeline.

For the child who has experienced neglect or other early abuse, these experiences and their impacts on the child can be discussed. If the child is to have a new experience, one of not being neglected, these early events need to be included.

The timeline includes the entrances and exits of important people in the child's life. A parent's being hospitalized, returning to work, losing a job, becoming depressed, starting to drink heavily, or giving up drinking, as well as the child's moving between schools or families, becoming ill, and joining or leaving particular activities are included. The first memory of the abuse is included, as are changes in type or intensity of abuse. Memories of early sexual experiences are included.

As events in the family are marked on the timeline, family stories around the events can be noted. Both explicit and implicit messages from these events are discussed and noted.

## CREATING THE TIMELINE

A timeline can be started at any point in therapy. Some therapists use the timeline at the beginning of therapy to gather information, whereas others find that it is helpful later, when the discussion of early events starts to become confusing or when therapy is feeling stuck. The idea of a timeline can be introduced when the child or therapist refers to events from the past. An adolescent may say that she does not remember much of her childhood and the therapist may suggest that they put down what she does remember so they have a framework for filling in other parts. A child may refer to an event the therapist had not been aware of and the therapist, noting the number of changes the child has experienced, may suggest that they put down the comings and goings of people and events in the child's life.

The construction of the timeline starts with the child's earliest memory. The therapist then moves back in time to ask about the child's birth and any family stories connected to her birth. The therapist needs to be aware of birth stories, because they form part of the child's internalized sense of self and thus influence the way the child interprets the abuse or other events.

> **Lynn** (a 15-year-old sexually abused during her early years by numerous family relatives and friends when she was left at their homes) reports a family joke related to her birth. When the doctor told her mother that she had given birth to a baby girl, her mother said, "Put her back!" Lynn states that it was okay for her older sister to be a girl because her parents planned to have two children. A second girl was considered unfair and was resented by her parents.
>
> Over the years, Lynn had interpreted the abuse as her fault. If she had been a boy she wouldn't have been left with other people and no abuse would have happened.

The therapist and child can talk about what it was like to be born and to be an infant. Some children think about babies as creatures who only cry and mess their pants. A therapist can introduce the idea that crying and messing are beginnings of communication and body development. The child, as a baby, can be talked about as special and as having positive possibilities but as not being able to control what happens. For the child who was not seen as special by her parents or who may, indeed, have been resented, the therapist can place these attitudes with the parents and their situation at that time. The child as the infant was special.

For the child who was abused at a young age, it is particularly important to talk about the special infant or toddler she was before the abuse. The fact that she is still the child she was before the abuse is important to highlight. Things happened that never should have happened, but she is still that special child.

It is helpful to work through the timeline year by year. Centering on the child's memories may miss important comings and goings within the family. Although the year of birth is marked at the beginning of the timeline, each succeeding year is better marked by the child's age. Indicating the age helps the therapist and child remember how young the child was even if the present child feels she was never young.

The timeline should be continued beyond the time of the abuse and disclosure to encourage a sense of existence beyond abuse. To create a timeline of only the abuse would heighten the sense of being caught within the abuse and, thus, could be detrimental to the child. Some children may want to continue the timeline into the future. This can strengthen a child's sense of moving forward and away from the abuse. For some years, the child may have nothing to mark down. Although some forgetting is normal for all children, extensive blanks after age 5 usually indicate that the child has had to block out something. The therapist can compliment the child on using forgetting as a creative way of dealing with a scary world. She can suggest that part of the work in therapy will be making the past less scary. If the child creates a timeline with only abuse memories, the therapist should inquire about other memories—school or friends, for example. A concept of self separate from the abuse is essential for a healthy internal model.

If it is the abuse memories that have been left out, the therapist can note that the child may be scared that the abuse, if remembered, will take over and crowd out everything else. The therapist can comment on the nonabuse memories already on the timeline and how those memories will continue to be there even when abuse memories are added.

The timeline can be added to at any point in therapy when it seems helpful to place an event within the context of what happened before or after the event. Adding to the timeline should not, however, become a preoccupation of therapy.

When the timeline is completed, or as it is being written, the therapist asks the child what message she, at the age she was when the event occurred, would have understood from a happening. Some therapists find it helpful to write these messages in a different color on the timeline sheet.

## USING THE TIMELINE

A timeline can help a therapist recognize and understand a child's early experiences, both abusive and nonabusive, and the impacts of these experiences on the child. Implicit as well as explicit messages are identified. For the child, the timeline helps to place the abuse—the happening of the abuse—within the context of the environment and with the abuser. In addition, drawing up a timeline helps the child connect to himself before the abuse, himself during the time of the abuse, and himself now.

*Recognizing and understanding early experiences and messages.* A child's early experiences shape his internal world—his model of himself and his model of himself in relation to others. For a child who has been raised in a generally supportive environment and has supportive-type memories, abuse has less impact and a different meaning than it does for a child whose memories include parents being absent, neglectful, or abusive. For abuse-related internalizations to shift, other early negative experiences and the messages from those experiences need to be identified and addressed.

> **Doreen** (a 15-year-old sexually abused between ages 12 and 14 by an older boy living in the family home and raped on several occasions by peers) completes a timeline with the therapist. Her earliest memory, she recalls, is her parents fighting. She was 3 then and the family was living at her grandparents' because of lack of money. Her brother was just a baby and she remembers that everybody ignored her. Going back to her birth, there was nothing special she could recall. There were no stories about her as a baby. She had been told that when she was 2, her baby-sitter beat her and, as a result, her mother stopped work to take care of her.
>
> *birth—uneventful*
> *1 year old—*
> *2 years old—beaten by baby-sitter, mo stopped work*
> *3 years old–father & mother fighting, fam moved to grmo's because of lack of money, brother born, D ignored*

When the therapist asks Doreen what that meant to her, that her mother stopped working to care for her, Doreen replies that maybe that was why they had no money and all the fighting started. When the therapist notes that it might have meant that her parents were worried about her, Doreen looks puzzled and thoughtful. This possibility is discussed.

The timeline is continued:

*4 years old—*

*5 years old—boy in park pulled down pants; told to suck his penis—no one knew; sex play w best girlfriend, didn't like but wanted to keep friend—no one knew; mo caught her masturbating and told her it was bad; older next-door neighbor said "I can't wait until you are older," kissed her, didn't like—no one knew*

*6 years old—brother born; sexual play with 5yo—mo caught and told her she was bad*

*7 years old—took care of brother*

*8 years old—11-year-old cousin mutual sexual touching—no one knew; 12yo baby-sitter sexual touching—D told, parents talked to boy and his parents, mother told D he was just experimenting and had boy baby-sit again*

*9 years old—*

*10 years old—2 boys (8yo, 12yo) told her to take clothes off, fun, no touching—no one knew*

*11 years old—first boyfriend, kissing*

*12 years old—father in psychiatric ward, father invited roommate at hospital (Bob, 17yo from an incestuous family) into home; sister born, D takes over more responsibilities; D started drinking, friend of Bob sexually abused D, D wrote Bob love letter, Bob sexually abused D; ? if parents knew; D raped by 15yo friend—no one knew*

*13 years old—Bob's sexual abuse continued*

*14 years old—B's sexual abuse continued, B attempted rape, D told parents—fa thought okay, mo called her a slut; B moved out; D assaulted by 5 boys at school, felt good but out of control*

*15 years old—heavy drinking, lots of sexual activity, no friends*

**Therapist:** How confusing all of this would have been. I'm noticing that when you were 5 and 6, your mother labeled normal sexual exploration as bad and yet when you were 8 and a baby-sitter sexually abused you, that was labeled as his experimentation. What message do you suppose you got from that?

**Doreen:** Sounds like it's okay for boys to be sexual but not okay for girls. Then she calls me a slut.

**Therapist:** Doesn't fit what happened, does it? You've experienced all sorts of sexual touching that didn't feel all right, but you had no one to talk to and to help you sort it out. No wonder it would have been really confusing when Bob moved into the home and you had a normal 12-year-old crush on a 17-year-old boy.

**Doreen** talks about liking Bob and thinking he was wonderful. All of her friends thought she was so lucky to have him paying attention to her.

**Therapist:** Of course you liked Bob and the attention he gave you. All sorts of things happened when you were 12. Father went into the hospital, your mother had a baby, an older adolescent moved into the home. You were no longer the oldest child in the home, no longer the only girl. You were being asked to do more and more work and given less and less attention. And 12-year-olds need attention. What was that year like for you?

**Doreen** talks about how lonely she was but how Bob made her feel better.

**Therapist:** What, do you think, was the message from that?

**Doreen:** I don't know, sex makes me feel better.

**Therapist:** You didn't have a chance to learn about the many things that can make kids feel better. There were many excursions and fun things Bob could have done with you. It was his responsibility as the older person to stay away from abusive activities. And then, when you told your parents and they didn't hold him responsible for the sexual activity, like with the baby-sitter when you were 8, what was that like?

After talking some more about the abuse, the therapist asks Doreen about other experiences she had had growing up—times at school, times with friends—and adds those to the timeline. (continued on page 101)

Identification of early negative experiences and the messages from those experiences helps a child recognize why she responded in particular ways and why she may still respond in those ways.

*Placing the abuse with the abuser and within the environment.* Many children link events of sexual abuse to themselves—what they did, what they did not do. With this narrowing of focus, the internalization that they are guilty is heightened. Looking at the abuse within the context of other things happening for the child can help the child place the abuse with the abuser.

**Nancy** (a 15-year-old sexually abused between ages 11 and 13 by her sixth-grade teacher) talks about how her mother had asked the teacher to look out for her because she did not have any friends. Nancy goes on to state that if she had been outgoing like other kids, she would have had plenty of friends and the abuse never would have happened.

**Therapist:** (points to the timeline) As you talk about not having friends, I am thinking about the timeline we made. What do you notice about your school years?

**Nancy:** I never spent more than one year in a school. No wonder I never had a lot of friends. So why did the teacher have to look out for me anyway?

**Therapist:** You had started in new schools lots of times and abuse didn't happen. The abuse did not happen because of you or any characteristic about you. It happened because of the teacher and his complete lack of understanding of sexuality and personal privacy.

*Identifying the self before the abuse, during the abuse, and now.* By starting the timeline before the abuse started, the child becomes connected with himself before the abuse. Even with abuse that started in infancy or the early preschool years, there is still a time before the abuse that can be identified and talked about.

What the child was like, as a person, needs to be talked about. What was he like as a little child—what were some of the things he did, what did he play with, was he the type of child who always wanted to be on the go or one who was quieter and played alone. Having the child bring in pictures can help to build a connection between the now child and the little child.

**Doreen** (see pages 98-100) looks at her timeline. The therapist notes that they have left out important parts of Doreen's life—what was she like when she was little, what was school like, what did she do with friends? The therapist asks Doreen what she thinks she was like as a 1-year-old, a 2-year-old, and so on, and writes down on the timeline what Doreen says.

   birth—uneventful
   1 year old—*cried a lot, curious*
   2 years old—beaten by baby-sitter, mo stopped work; *played w mother*
   3 years old—fa & mo fighting, fam moved to grmo's because of lack
      of money, brother born, D ignored; *scared, played by self*
   4 years old—*moved into a house, played w dolls*

5 years old—boy in park pulled down pants; told to suck his penis—
no one knew; sex play w best girlfriend, didn't like but wanted to
keep friend—no one knew; mo caught her masturbating and told
her it was bad; older next-door neighbor said "I can't wait until you
are older," kissed her, didn't like—no one knew; *started school, got
into trouble at school, liked drawing, brought home a stray kitten*

6 years old—brother born; sexual play with 5yo—mo caught and told
her she was bad; *learned to read, liked books*

7 years old—took care of brother; *trouble w math, played w friends, liked
taking care of baby*

8 years old—11-year-old cousin mutual sexual touching—no one
knew; 12yo baby-sitter sexual touching—D told, parents talked to
boy and his parents, mother told D he was just experimenting and
had boy baby-sit again; *best friend lived across the street*

9 years old—*trouble with math, special help, liked reading*

10 years old—2 boys (8yo, 12yo) told her to take clothes off, fun, no
touching—no one knew; *in school choir, liked school*

11 years old—first boyfriend, kissing; *top class in school, school monitor*

12 years old—father in psychiatric ward, father invited roommate at
hospital (Bob, 17yo from an incestuous family) into home; sister
born, D takes over more responsibilities; D started drinking, friend
of Bob sexually abused D, D wrote Bob love letter, Bob sexually
abused D; ? parents knew; D raped by 15yo friend—no one knew;
*new school, hard making friends, talked about B to make kids like me, had
to help mother a lot*

13 years old—Bob's sexual abuse continued; *people called me names at
school, had one friend who had an older boyfriend, boys made passes at
me, more problems with math, barely passing*

14 years old—B's sexual abuse continued, B attempted rape, D told
parents—fa thought okay, mo called her a slut; B moved out; D
assaulted by 5 boys at school, felt good but out of control; *high
school, hung around mostly with boys, fought w parents, hated being at home*

15 years old—heavy drinking, lots of sexual activity, no friends;
*unhappy, still passing in school, lots of parties*

**Therapist:** There's quite a change when you were 12.

**Doreen:** It was an awful year. I was a new kid in the school and people would
say, What does your father do? and what was I supposed to say—"He's in
the nut house"—so I started making up stories.

**Therapist:** (adds "lonely" to age 12) What about the part of you that liked to
read and was able to make friends? What happened to that part?

**Doreen:** I still read a lot, at school and at home. But friends, no, I was too
afraid they would find out about Dad. Then after Bob moved in, I bragged
about him and that he was my boyfriend. The girls thought that was a big
deal, so did I.

**Therapist:** There was a really sensitive part of you when you were little— taking in the kitty, taking care of the baby. What's happening with the sensitive part of you now? (continued on page 104)

## ❏ Messages and Myths

An important part of the discussion around a genogram and a timeline is the identification of the messages, both overt and covert, passed down within a family. Some of these messages have a long history and can be referred to as family myths (Bagarozzi & Anderson, 1989; Ferreira, 1963).

When Ferreira (1963) first introduced the idea of family myths, he talked about a series of well-integrated beliefs shared by family members. These beliefs, which do not necessarily fit reality, serve to maintain the family's homeostatic behavior and to keep the family loyal to the patterns established by parents.

As parents interact with their child, they pass on their view of the child, of interrelationships, of personal and social values, and of the world in general. From this, the child creates her own personal myth (Bagarozzi & Anderson, 1989)—similar to Bowlby's (1971, 1973) internal working model. As the child receives new information from the world, it may agree or disagree with the child's personal myth. When there is dissonance, the child experiences disequilibrium, which requires some shift, either in the new information or in the myth.

Traumatic experiences, such as sexual abuse, shape a child's personal myth. For a child raised in an abusive family, and particularly a multigenerational incestuous family, family messages and myths support the occurrence of sexual abuse and encourage abuse-related internalizations: Children are objects to be used, children are responsible for what happens, children exist to meet the needs of adults. If abuse-related internalizations are to be shifted, distorted messages and myths, both family and personal, need to be identified.

### IDENTIFYING MESSAGES AND MYTHS

The messages a child receives growing up can be identified from events listed on a timeline and from notes included on a genogram. They can also be identified from the attitudes the child shows toward herself and others.

As a therapist asks a child what she would have understood, given the age she was when a particular event occurred, this is noted on the timeline. The accuracy of the message is examined.

Doreen (see pages 98, 100, 101-103) completes her timeline with the therapist. They discuss what her mother's staying home to take care of Doreen meant about family values and concerns and what it meant about her mother's and father's concern for Doreen. They talk about the messages Doreen is getting from her family now and why these messages, ones of disapproval, differ from the early ones. They go back over the messages about sexual behavior that Doreen received when her mother criticized her for masturbating.

**Therapist:** Masturbating by girls has not been well understood. For a long time, people thought there was something wrong with it; sounds like your mother learned that and then put it on you. What do you tell yourself about masturbating?

**Doreen:** Kinda weird, but not bad.

**Therapist:** What did you, as a 5-year-old, think?

**Doreen:** I was bad. But I kept doing it, guess I really was oversexed like Mom said.

**Therapist:** Sounds like that's another message Mom gave you. What would that have been—oversexed?

**Doreen:** Masturbating. I never let her catch me again but I kept doing it even though she said not to.

**Therapist:** That's normal behavior. Masturbating is finding a sensation that feels good and when something feels good, one does it again. It's private because it has to do with your body, not because it's bad.

**Doreen:** But I wrote Bob a love letter. I liked the sex.

**Therapist:** Seems like you have taken in a lot of Mom's messages. Do you remember your friends at 12, do you remember how they "goggled" over rock stars or movie stars? Bob was like that for you. And you had nothing else positive in your life then. Your "loving him" was part of being 12 years old. The sex was attention and it felt good. That's not being oversexed.

**Doreen:** But look at me now!

**Therapist:** Why do you have sex with boys now?

**Doreen:** I want them to like me.

**Therapist:** That's wanting to be liked, not being oversexed. (continued on page 108)

Sexual myths and messages are particularly important to include. Particular attention needs to be given to the societal myths connected with childhood sexual abuse. These myths have not developed in a vacuum but exist because such situations do sometimes occur. They reach the status of myth when they are assumed to occur in *all* situations. "Children who have been abused will grow up to be abusers." "Children who have been abused will have children who are abused." "Children who have been abused will be abused again." "No one will marry someone who has been abused." These scenarios, highlighted in television dramas and discussed on talk shows, are all too often taken in by children as being their future. The therapist needs to point out the discrepancy between myth and reality.[2] The child, together with the therapist, can then list personal characteristics and experiences that will enable her to lead a life less vulnerable to abuse.

The myths that a child holds about sexual abuse may come up in general conversation. "If I did get married, I would never have children. My mother was abused and look what happened to me. I wouldn't want this to happen to my child." In other cases, a therapist may need to ask more directly, "What are your fears as you look at the future?" Discussions about sexual abuse myths, if they have not come up during therapy, can fit easily into the termination phase of therapy. "As you look on from here, what are some of the things that worry you about having been abused?" "There are many misconceptions about abuse that come up on TV. What are the misconceptions you have noticed?"

As a genogram is drawn and notes are jotted about each person, a therapist can start to notice similarities and patterns. There may be similarities in personality characteristics, behaviors, attitudes, and relationship patterns.

Betty (a 15-year-old sexually abused by her stepfather between ages 10 and 13) describes how she likes her ability to keep in how she feels about things, that she has the ability to be patient with other people's foolishness (see Figure 4.10).

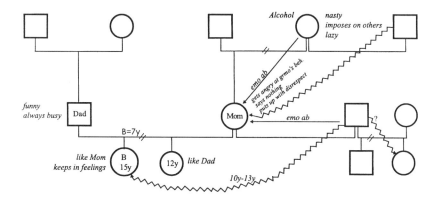

**Figure 4.10.**

**Therapist:** [Notes the similarity between these behaviors and the characteristics Betty had reported about mother.] Your describing that reminds me of the notes we put down about mother. (points to the genogram) "Gets angry at grandmother's behavior"; "Says nothing"; "Puts up with disrespect." It seems that mother has given you the message that this is how you should behave. But when you talked about Mom, you said you thought she should do differently.

**Betty:** I put up with a lot because it's easier that way.

**Therapist:** Yes, you have been taught to, that's what you watched your mother doing. That's been the message, the teaching, in your family. When children are little, they learn what the people around them do. You are older now, you can start choosing which learnings you want to keep and which you don't. "Puts up with disrespect," is that what you want for you?

Messages are also identified as the therapist and child talk about daily experiences, the abuse, or the child's view of herself. When a child reports a self-evaluation that does not fit with reality, the therapist can ask where that evaluation came from, who would have given such an evaluation in the past, whom does it sound like.

> **Maureen** (a 14-year-old sexually abused between the ages of 6 and 10 by a series of her mother's boyfriends) comments that she is really stupid—after all, she is always getting into trouble.

**Therapist:** There are a lot of things that cause trouble. Where did this message of being stupid come from?

**Maureen:** It doesn't come from anywhere. I'm just stupid.

**Therapist:** Listen to that inside your head, the voice saying that you are stupid. Whom does it sound like?

**Maureen:** (startles) Sounds like my mother. (continued on page 109)

Family myths can be queried directly (for instance, "What are the myths in your family about women?") or can be noted from information on the genogram. Patterns in a family often result from an unspoken but strong myth. If these myths are not verbalized and questioned, they are likely to continue for the child.

> **Thea** (a 15-year-old sexually abused between ages 10 and 12 by her mother) and her therapist complete Thea's genogram (see Figure 4.11). The therapist notes that Thea had described her maternal grandmother as having "psychological problems," "spent time in a psychiatric hospital," and as being "strange." Although Thea had described her mother, the only girl in that generation, as "sensitive" and "caring," there was also the notation of alcoholism and of her having abused Thea. In describing herself, Thea, the only girl in this generation, at first says she doesn't know what she is like, and then says she becomes too anxious.

**Therapist:** I'm noticing that the females in your family—your mother and your grandmother—have had psychological problems: grandmother being strange and in a hospital, mother drinking and abusing. I wonder, what are the messages, in your family, about females?

**Thea:** Women are weird, sick. And I feel so depressed, and there was my suicide attempt last spring. Am I going to be like this, like them, all my life?

**Therapist:** What do you suppose it was like for your mother, growing up in her family?

**Thea:** Well, grandmother is really weird and my grandmother and grandfather fought all the time.

**Therapist:** What went on in your mother's life is her issue, not yours. But I was wondering, did she ever have therapy, did she ever have a chance to try to sort it out?

**Thea:** No. Even for the drinking, she never went anywhere. I kept asking her to go. (continued on page 111)

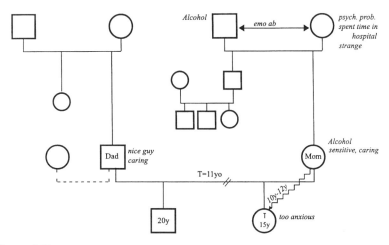

**Figure 4.11.**

Positive messages should also be included on genograms and timelines.

### WORKING WITH MESSAGES AND MYTHS

As messages and myths are identified, they can be looked at and questioned. Therapy provides a time when a child can hear new messages about herself, messages based on reality.

*Questioning messages and myths.* As messages and myths are recognized, it is important to specify where they came from. The reality of a situation can be looked at, further information collected, and then the truth of the message or myth examined.

Adults often give children negative messages to cover up situations adults find distressing.

> **Doreen** (see pages 98-100, 101-103, 104-105) and the therapist continue to talk about the attitudes in Doreen's family toward sex.

**Therapist:** What types of conversation have you and your mother had about sex and sexuality?

**Doreen:** Conversations! None! She thinks I'm a slut.

**Therapist:** When I think back to her yelling at you for masturbating and for playing "I'll show you mine if you show me yours" with a little boy in the neighborhood when you were 5 and 6, it makes me realize that your mom does not know about normal child sexual development and curiosity. Those are normal activities unless they take over all of the child's time and attention, and that was not the situation for you. Your mother calling you a slut when you told about Bob raping you, that means she does not understand about sexual abuse.

**Doreen:** She certainly freaks out if sex is mentioned.

**Therapist:** Your mother's criticism of you seems to be a result of her anxiety over sex and sexuality. What would you tell a child of yours in those situations?

Once a message or myth has been recognized as not true, it is helpful for the child to look at how these beliefs may have affected her life. Recognizing their effect helps the child reexamine past experiences and understand them in a new way.

Maureen (see pages 106-107) talks about how her mother used to call her stupid and razz her each time she made a mistake.

**Therapist:** And are you stupid?

**Maureen:** Teachers think so.

**Therapist:** Do they call you stupid?

**Maureen:** No, but they keep saying I could do better. And my boyfriend, he calls me stupid.

**Therapist:** I am thinking about your coming in here every week. We talk for an hour and you don't have any trouble understanding what we talk about, and then you think about it during the week, and you come back the next week with questions. That's not being stupid. That's being intelligent. If your teachers thought you were stupid, why would they tell you that you could do better? They would be happy with what you were doing. Why do you think your mother called you stupid?

**Maureen:** Mom's parents called her stupid. I've heard them and she's a grown-up. But I feel stupid, so it fits.

**Therapist:** And the feeling comes with the message. Sounds as if being called stupid is a habit in your family. Do you think your mother is stupid?

**Maureen:** Sometimes she does stupid things, like her choice of boyfriends. But she's not stupid. She's managed to make a living.

**Therapist:** You are making a separation between stupid actions and stupidity. Sounds pretty smart.

Therapy, through positive attending to and mirroring of the child's present self, provides positive messages. The conversation examining negative messages and reflecting positive messages needs to include the messages taken in by the child when she was younger for the early negative internalizations to shift.

**Therapist:** Think back to yourself as a little child, what do you see yourself doing?

**Maureen:** I'd line up all of my toys and then they would have conversations together. Other kids wouldn't let me play with them, so I would do this all alone.

**Therapist:** How creative you were. Tell me more about those conversations among the toys. (continued below)

Myths need to be recognized, acknowledged, and then explored to determine their bases (Bagarozzi & Anderson, 1989; Minuchin & Fishman, 1981). A myth may be based on other people's labels and predictions, not on reality. When a child recognizes that the myth is not inevitable, that there are other possible outcomes, then she has the possibility of creating a new story.

*Creating new messages.* Once old messages no longer dictate meaning for present experiences, a child finds it easier to recognize new positive messages. The child is more open to what is actually happening.

For some children, however, negative messages will not shift unless something else is put in their place. New positive messages need to be identified and practiced.

**Maureen** continues to talk with the therapist about feeling stupid.

**Therapist:** Does your foster mother call you stupid?

**Maureen:** No.

**Therapist:** What does she say to you about your intelligence?

**Maureen:** Well, she says that when I stop to think about things, I make good decisions. When I don't think, like when I shaved my head, I do pretty stupid things.

**Therapist:** So, when you stop to think about things, you make good decisions. How often do you say that to yourself?

**Maureen:** What do you mean? Why should I?

**Therapist:** Well, you are telling yourself that you are stupid, which you aren't. So to get rid of that phrase, which isn't true, you need to put a new one, that is true, in its place. The phrase from your foster mother, "When I stop to think about things, I make good decisions," could take the place of "I am stupid."

Let's try an experiment, why don't you, inside your mind, put on a Walkman, a Walkman that has a control for each earphone. Through one earphone, run a tape of what your mother used to say. What would that be? . . . Now through the other earphone, run a tape of what your foster mother says. What would that be? . . . And as the two are playing, which is louder, or are they the same loudness? . . . Now, very slowly turn down the volume from the earphone with your mother's tape and turn up the earphone with your foster mother's tape, just a bit. And when it is just a bit louder, nod your head. . . . All right, let's do that again, down on your mother's, up with your foster mother's. . . .

\*   \*   \*   \*   \*

Thea (see pages 107-108) and the therapist talk about her mother and grandmother, who had both shown psychological problems in the past. Thea notes that her mother never had any therapy despite her problems with drinking and with abusing.

**Therapist:** And you have had some rugged experiences, experiences a child should not have to deal with—your mother's drinking, the sexual abuse, the divorce—experiences that need to be sorted out. And what are you doing about the sorting?

**Thea:** I'm here. I don't like coming, but I'm here.

**Therapist:** So you, as an adolescent, are doing something different from the other women in your family. Strikes me that you are creating a new story. What do you want that story to be?

## ❑ Summary

Family interactions, messages, and myths affect a child's internal view of himself and the abuse. To address these, a therapist needs to explore the dynamics and the events that have occurred in the child's family.

Genograms and timelines help the therapist and child to sort out the child's experience. The diagrams facilitate discussion about messages and myths and help identify the information that needs correcting. The child can become more alert to positive messages in his environment and to the possibility of creating a new story for himself. As the information from the past is sorted out, the responsibility for the abuse is placed more clearly where it belongs, with the perpetrator.

## ❑ Notes

1. My particular thanks to Dr. Sandy Ages for her assistance with some of the examples provided in this section.

2. As noted in Chapter 2, a study of 117 males between ages 18 and 27 who had been sexually abused during their childhoods indicates that a minimum of 63% of these men have not sexually abused children (Bagley, Wood, & Young, 1994).

# PART III

*Issues*

# 5

# Engaging the Parts: Working With Dissociation

A child threatened by extreme abuse or violence seeks a way to keep herself safe, to keep herself away from what is happening. Physically she cannot get away. Psychologically she can.

The child may move herself mentally into the teddy bear on the shelf or up to the corner of the room, from which point she observes things happening to the body that was left behind. Another child may stay present in her body but cut off all emotional or physical feelings. As this space or barrier is placed between her and the abuse, the child's distress and anxiety decrease. She moves behind that space more and more frequently until the movement away, a distortion of reality, becomes a regular pattern of reacting to frightening situations.

Dissociation, which occurs from time to time as a normal phenomenon for both children and adults, is often used as a protective mechanism by individuals who are abused (Putnam, 1996). But even as the child protects herself, this distortion of perception and cognitive integration causes her to lose a part of her feelings, her experience of herself. Although lost to the child's integrated awareness, the feelings, memories, and parts of self continue to exist, separated off, within the child's internal world. The child's internal working model is fragmented.

This chapter discusses the difference between normal and dysfunctional dissociation in children and adolescents and the development of dysfunctional dissociation. The last two sections of the chapter address therapeutic issues: recognizing the dissociation and reassociating what has been cut off.

## ❏ From Normal to Dysfunctional Dissociation

Dissociation is a normal process that occurs from time to time for most people. Fantasy stories and characters created by the preschool child often take on a separate reality. Imaginary playmates may be thought of as both separate and real. These imaginary playmates may be an enjoyable fantasy, an expansion of experience, a way to fill loneliness or boredom, or a process for working out fears and ambivalent feelings (Baum, 1978; Trujillo, Lewis, Yeager, & Gidlow, 1996).

Because the sense of self or ego in the young child has not yet solidified, dissociation occurs easily and does not necessarily indicate trauma or pathology (Putnam, 1991).[1] Trancelike states and blank stares are common (Putnam, 1994) and are particularly likely to happen when a child is scared.

While fantasy dissociation decreases with adolescence, self-consciousness and self-observation increase. For many young people, adolescence becomes a time to "try on" different personas. Adolescents often vary their behaviors or ways of responding depending on whom they are with (Harter, 1983), what novels they have been reading, or how they are feeling. Normal adolescents completing the Dissociation Experience Scale report significantly more dissociative-type experiences than do normal adults (Bernstein & Putnam, 1986).

A normal adolescent, similar to a child or adult, also uses dissociation as a defense mechanism when faced with threatening situations (such as being bitten on the face by a dog) or extremely stressful situations (such as severe teasing). To protect himself from physical or emotional fright, the adolescent "pulls himself away" from the situation and observes what is going on, including himself, from the outside (Spiegel, 1984). This phenomenon, depersonalization, has been reported as having been experienced by almost half of a university student sample (Dixon, 1963).[2] Putnam (1997) notes that for adolescents transient episodes of depersonalization appear relatively common, but that their occurrence decreases with age.

Dissociative experiences, as part of normal development, do not cause a fragmentation of experiences or self. When, however, a child's experiences are such that dissociation (a) occurs repeatedly or (b) fragments significant portions of perceptions, feelings, or information, the child's internal knowledge of self and development of healthy coping mechanisms is disrupted.

The preschool child, whose experience of dissociation has moved beyond normal childhood functioning, may not experience an imaginary companion as separate, but rather as having part of his experiences. A child or adolescent who dissociates has difficulty learning or learns information that he is unable to access in other situations. Dissociation within social situations can leave an adolescent in unwished-for or dangerous positions. As dissociation occurs over and over again, it becomes an automatic or conditioned defense reaction (Peterson, 1991), and alternative ways of coping—for example, talking about things or leaving dangerous situations—are not developed.

For children with dysfunctional dissociation, the affect or information related to traumatic happenings is held separate from the child's conscious awareness. Being split off, these emotions or experiences cannot be (a) moderated by future events and (b) integrated into the child's understanding by normal processing such as play or conversation.

With repeated dissociation, the sense of self becomes fragmented. For the young child, the developmental processes of affect modulation, behavior regulation, cognitive awareness, and increased sense of self are disturbed. For the older child, self-observation and skills at confronting and changing situations are not developed. Although protective of self, dissociation blocks development and hampers a child's effort to make his world understandable and safe.

## DYSFUNCTIONAL DISSOCIATION
## IN CHILDREN AND ADOLESCENTS

During the past 10 years, numerous articles on dissociation in children have appeared, presenting case studies (Dell & Eisenhower, 1990; Fagan & McMahon, 1984; LaPorta, 1992; Malenbaum & Russell, 1987; McElroy, 1992; Riley & Mead, 1988; Silberg, 1996a; Vincent & Pickering, 1988; Weiss, Sutton, & Utrecht, 1985), models of dissociation (Braun & Sachs, 1985; Kluft, 1984; McElroy, 1992; Putnam, 1997), and diagnostic checklists (Evers-Szostak & Sanders, 1992; Fagan & McMahon, 1984; Kluft, 1984; Peterson, 1991; Putnam, Helmers, & Trickett, 1993; Putnam & Peterson, 1994; Reagor, Kasten, & Morelli, 1992; Silberg, 1996c). Studies using larger samples and looking at past histories as well as present symptoms are starting to appear (Atlas & Hiott, 1994; Hornstein & Putnam, 1992; Sanders & Giolas, 1991). Although a number of these articles refer to treatment, only a few detailed descriptions of treatment techniques are available (Kluft, 1996; Shirar, 1996; Waters & Silberg, 1996a, 1996b).

The majority of this literature has centered on the occurrence of dissociative identities, formerly referred to as multiple personalities, rather than dissociation.[3] Because dissociative identities—a disturbance of the integrative functions of identity, memory, and consciousness such that two or more distinct identities exist within an individual— are more dramatic than dissociation, this topic has attracted the attention of the general public, most notably the mass media, and professionals. Recently, Peterson and Putnam (1994) proposed criteria for a "dissociative disorder of childhood" (DDoC) that would encourage identification of children who do not appear to have separate alters but yet show high levels of dissociation. This could be clinically useful in that children with DDoC criteria have been found to exhibit more depression, school problems, thought disorder and cognitive symptoms, aggression, sleep difficulties, and sexual behavior problems than children with more generalized dissociation (Peterson & Putnam, 1994). The internal phenomenon experienced by these children appears to be different from that experienced by children with dissociative identities and different from that experienced by children with generalized dissociation, thus needing a specific therapeutic approach.

Although dissociation can be expected to occur within children who are traumatized, the majority of children who are sexually abused do not develop dissociative identities. Recognizing this, Kluft (1984) has proposed a four-factor theory to explain the development of dissociative identities. The initial factor is described as a biological capacity to dissociate; the second, the occurrence of traumatic experiences that activates the defense mechanism of dissociation; the third, the linking of the dissociative defense with a part of the self-system; and the fourth, the absence of a nurturing or supportive environment during early development.

With regard to the first factor, biological tendency, a recent study indicating a lack of correlation between hypnotizability (understood as a biological factor) and dissociation (Putnam, Helmers, Horowitz, & Trickett, 1995) and preliminary data from twin studies (Waller, as reported in Putnam, 1996) indicate that high levels of dissociation may not be biologically based. Recent discussions have considered the development of dissociation in children of parents with dissociative identities as reflecting a behavioral response (Mann & Sanders, 1994; Peterson, 1991; Putnam, 1997). A child may learn to wall off feelings or to switch ways of feeling and behaving in order to adapt to erratic behavior changes on the part of a parent (Peterson, 1991). In addition, the parent's behavior, dissociating or switching personalities, would provide for the child a model for how to cope with stress (Mann & Sanders, 1994; Peterson, 1991; Shirar, 1996).

The second factor, a traumatizing experience, includes witnessing extreme violence against others as well as experiencing it oneself (Hornstein & Putnam, 1992; Hornstein & Tyson, 1991). Repetitive, sadistic abuse and abuse involving ritualized religious practices, threats of death, or injury are reported by adults and children (Gould & Graham-Costain, 1994; Shirar, 1996) experiencing dissociative identities. Dissociation, as distinct from dissociative identities, has been found in adolescents to correlate with negative home atmosphere as well as with the occurrence of sexual abuse (Sanders & Giolas, 1991).

Kluft's third factor, the linking of the dissociative experience to a part of the self-system, draws attention to research highlighting the relationship between dissociative identities and early onset of abuse (Cole & Putnam, 1992; Putnam et al., 1993). The abuse has occurred before a child's sense of self solidifies. Dissociation without the separation into identities is more likely to occur with later abuse. Albini and Pease (1989) describe severe trauma as interrupting the normal process of integration that occurs through infancy and early childhood. Putnam (1997) describes maltreatment as disrupting the normal developmental tasks related to biological processes, emotional self-regulation, impulse control, and metacognition.

Kluft's fourth factor postulates that it is the lack of "nurturing and healing experiences" during the early years that determines whether dissociation develops to the point of separating individual functions. Several recent studies support the inverse relationship between emotional support in childhood and dissociative characteristics (Irwin, 1996; Mann & Sanders, 1994; Silberg & Waters, 1996).

McElroy (1992) discusses three psychophysiological mechanisms by which dissociation (not necessarily dissociative identities) may occur in children. Dissociation may occur initially as a normal reaction to trauma. As trauma is repeated and dissociation recurs, an internal pattern of compartmentalizing is established and becomes part of the child's internal schema. A second mechanism is parental reinforcement of psychological withdrawal and/or separation of experience (McElroy, 1992). An adult telling a child, after abusing her, that what happened had not hurt or had not even happened creates for the child the sense of a separate self to whom the abuse occurred. The third mechanism discussed by McElroy is similar to that included in Kluft's third factor and relates to children who develop dissociative identities. When a part of the self is split off before the developmental stage of self-integration, it is experienced internally as separate from the core self and may present externally as different in temperament and/or behavior.

Watkins and Watkins's (1992) model, which presents a continuum from normal dissociation to dissociative identity, can also provide a useful framework for work with children. Watkins and Watkins describe each individual as having within the self—that is, as part of the internal working model of self—numerous ego states or personality segments that become activated in different situations. For most people, there is easy communication between and awareness of these ego states. Watkins and Watkins describe three origins for ego states: (a) the natural development of differentiated parts for dealing with different situations; (b) the introjection of significant others, most commonly parents; and (c) the dissociation that occurs when, during trauma, some experience or feeling is too threatening to the self to be taken into the self-experience. For most individuals, the boundaries between ego states are permeable, with the individual moving back and forth as situations require. When distress increases and there is a need to protect the self from reality, the boundaries between ego states become less permeable. Knowledge of each ego state by other ego states becomes limited. With dissociative identities, these boundaries have become rigid and impermeable to the extent that one or more ego states or identities are unknown or denied as part of the self by the other ego states or identities (Watkins & Watkins, 1992).

Putnam (1997) presents a "discrete behavioral states" model to explain dissociative phenomena. An infant is born experiencing discrete behavioral states. Over time, these states increase in number—a result of biological development and environmental experiences—and the linkages between behavioral states increase in number—also a result of both developmental and environmental processes. If abuse occurs during the early developmental phases, when an infant/toddler normally starts to recognize and modulate internal states, this process is disrupted. The development of linkages leading to modulation and the development of modulation within behavioral states is disrupted. If abuse occurs during the early school years, as the development of metacognitive processes enables a child to become more self-aware, the development of integrative linkages and behavioral states of self-awareness is disrupted. In addition, trauma leads to the development of fear-conditioned states and trauma-associated linkages. These disruptions are reflected in a child's developing neurobiological systems. Putnam's discrete behavioral states model provides the clinician with a way of understanding the neurophysiological, cognitive, and emotional disconnections underlying dissociation.

## ❏ Diagnosing Dissociation in Children and Adolescents

The occurrence of dissociative identities and dissociative characteristics in adults can be diagnosed through careful attention to the experiences reported and behaviors exhibited, and from scores on self-report scales. Identifying dissociation in children is more difficult

(Putnam, 1993). Children are unlikely to report dissociative symptoms for several reasons. A child who has, most of his life, heard voices inside his head, lost track of time, or experienced discontinuity of events may have no realization that this is not everyone's reality. Sharing feelings and internal experiences is discouraged and, indeed, often punished in dysfunctional families. When children do become aware that their experience is different, they are often frightened to report it for fear of ridicule or punishment.

Even when a child is aware that something is not as it should be and is in a setting that encourages discussion of internal experiences—for example, situations of adoption or fostering—he may not have the language to explain to others what is happening. In addition, the child, who has dissociated pain or rage, has little motivation for bringing these reactions back to full awareness. He is more aware of what he wants to avoid than he is of anything positive to be gained from talking about these experiences. The child who is in therapy is usually there because some adult has decided the child needs help or needs to change, not because the child is consciously aware that his internal world is distorted. Thus the motivation, as well as the knowledge and language, for reporting internal experiences is far less for a child than for an adult.

The second method of diagnosing dissociation in adults, observing behaviors, also is problematic with children. Behaviors symptomatic of dissociation—appearing to be in a trance, being out of control, exhibiting fluctuating abilities or knowledge, disclaiming knowledge of what one has done—are similar to behaviors seen with daydreaming, behavior problems, attention difficulties, learning problems, and lying (Putnam, 1993). Children identified in recent studies as having dissociative disorders had previously been given a variety of diagnoses, including conduct or oppositional disorders and major affective disorders (Hornstein & Tyson, 1991; Peterson & Putnam, 1994; Sanders & Giolas, 1991). These alternative diagnoses are not necessarily inaccurate—they may indicate coexisting behaviors.

An additional behavioral indicator of dissociation that has often been noted for adults or children in traditional therapy is lack of improvement (Hornstein & Tyson, 1991). Because fewer children than adults have received previous therapy, this observation is usually not available to the clinician.

A third method of diagnosing dissociation in adults, completion of self-rating scales, has also been unavailable for children and adolescents until recently. Although several diagnostic scales for children were developed in the 1980s (Fagan & McMahon, 1984; Kluft, 1984; Putnam et al., 1993; Reagor et al., 1992), only one of these, the Child Dissociative Checklist (CDC), completed by parents, has received adequate reliability and validity testing (Malinosky-Rummell & Hoier, 1992; Putnam et al., 1993; Putnam & Peterson, 1994; Wherry, Jolly, Feldman, Adam, & Manjanatha, 1994).

The CDC includes 20 items measuring confusion and forgetfulness related to time, people, knowledge, or possessions; rapid changes in age, personality, or physical complaints; incidents of extreme anger, blatant lying, sexual precocity, or unexplained injuries; internal experiences related to imaginary companions, voices; and unusual nighttime experiences. Although the CDC is able to discriminate between children who dissociate and children who do not (Putnam et al., 1993) and between children with dissociative identities and children with more general dissociation, discrimination between children with different levels of dissociation is less clear (Peterson & Putnam, 1994; Putnam & Peterson, 1994). Another limitation of the CDC is that it is completed by the parent or teacher (Putnam, 1997), not the child. The external evidence of dissociation, not the internal experience, is measured. This can be misleading in that a dissociative trance-stare and a daydreaming gaze may appear the same to an external observer, although they are completely different internal experiences. Putnam (1997; Putnam and Peterson, 1994) has described the CDC as a screening, not a diagnostic, instrument. Actual diagnosis of dissociation needs to be made by a clinical or structured interview for *DSM-IV* criteria (American Psychiatric Association, 1994; see Hornstein, 1996; Putnam, 1997; Silberg, 1996b). Putnam (1997) emphasizes the importance of considering multiple behavior situations and speaking with different individuals who have observed the child.

The Trauma Symptom Checklist for Children (ages 8-16; Briere, 1996b), which is completed by the child, includes a short dissociation scale with items concerning such symptoms as the mind going away or blank, forgetting things, and feeling outside oneself. The Children's Perceptual Alteration Scale, developed by Sanders and colleagues, is more complete but needs further research (Evers-Szostak & Sanders,

1992; Mann & Sanders, 1994). Some research has been carried out on a selection of items from Achenbach and Edelbrock's (1983) Child Behavior Checklist reflecting dissociative-type behaviors (Malinosky-Rummell & Hoier, 1992; Putnam et al., 1993). Because the Child Behavior Checklist is already used widely in both research and clinical settings, further study of this subscale will be valuable.

Armstrong, Putnam, and Carlson (1996) have adapted the Dissociative Experience Scale used with adults (Bernstein & Putnam, 1986) for preadolescents and adolescents (ages 11 to 17). The A-DES has a young person rate the extent to which she has experienced depersonalization, amnesia, and hallucinatory-type experiences. Preliminary studies indicate good reliability and validity (Putnam, 1997).

Silberg (1996c) has developed the Dissociative Features Profile (DFP), which she applies to behaviors that emerge during completion of a psychological evaluation. This profile includes amnesia, staring episodes, odd movements, behavioral fluctuations, affective reactivity, somatic complaints, and internal dividedness (responses that contradict each other either in content or in level of development). In addition to these behavioral characteristics, Silberg has identified characteristics that emerge during projective testing. These characteristics, referred to as dissociative "markers," include (a) multiplicity (drawings or descriptions including two or more images of something that is usually single), (b) dissociative coping (stories including instances of dissociation), (c) malevolent religiosity (references to Satan, witches, or devils), (d) emotional confusion (contradictory emotions being expressed together), (e) extreme categories (good and bad being expressed in close juxtaposition), (f) violent imagery (examples of torture or mutilation), (g) magical transformation (switching of an object or person from abusive to nurturing or nurturing to abusive), and (h) depersonalized images (humans becoming inanimate or inanimate objects taking on animate characteristics). Although further research is needed, these characteristics can alert a clinician to the possibility that a child is experiencing dissociation.

A child's report of experiences or lack of experiences helps to identify the level of dissociation being experienced. Although children with dissociative identities and those with high dissociation but without the development of separate identities both experience amnesia for traumatic events, children who have developed separate identities are significantly more likely to experience amnesia related to unstressful events (Hornstein & Putnam, 1992; Peterson & Putnam, 1994). Involuntarily initiated body movements (such as a child reporting that his arm would be hitting someone even though he was trying to stop it) is reported significantly more often by children with dissociative identities (Hornstein & Putnam, 1992). Children in both groups heard voices inside, but children with dissociative identities were more likely to hear commands, and especially commands related to violence against self and others (Hornstein & Putnam, 1992).

Because of limited diagnostic tools, the therapist is dependent on her observation of a child for accurate recognition of dissociation. The following section discusses behaviors observed in children with dissociative characteristics. Although these observations are not research based, they can serve as possible indicators for therapists working with children. They do not by themselves indicate dissociation or dissociated identities. They do provide information that can be considered together with information from parents and teachers and observations from therapy sessions.

## CLINICAL OBSERVATIONS WITH THE YOUNG CHILD

The assessment of a young child usually includes drawings, stories, play, and an interview. Because drawings, stories, and play allow the child free use of the environment, these activities usually do not arouse the child's defensive mechanisms. Thus the child's underlying issues emerge in these situations. Although the issues presented through the play, drawings, and stories may differ, a similarity in distress level is evident. In my experience, some preschool children complete pictures and stories showing a high level of internal distress (for example, scribbled drawings despite normal visual-motor capability and demonstrated understanding of the request, or stories with high levels of injury) while their play demonstrates little or no distress. In each case where this has occurred, the child's behavior, as reported by the parent and as later observed in therapy, showed high frequency of dissociation. A lack of correspondence between a child's verbalizations while playing and the play being carried out has also been observed with children experiencing high levels of dissociation.

> Ivy (a 4-year-old placed in foster care at age 3 following a report of severe neglect and abuse by the birth parents) lines the animals up in pairs and then moves the line slowly along the table as she mutters, "They're fighting, fighting, help, help, oh stop that, stop that."

During the assessment, but more likely during therapy sessions, a voice, often only a word or two or just a sound, unlike the child's voice and out of context with the play may be heard. The comments are usually pejorative ("Shut up"; "Fuck off"). The immediate therapist response is likely to be "Did I hear that?" but no more is heard to verify the experience. And the child denies having said anything. Because the therapist is unlikely to create statements or sounds, she can trust her reaction and recognize that the child, or at least some part of the child, has said something.

Sudden shifts in behavior, statements that contradict each other, and vacant stares by the child can also alert a therapist to the possibility of dissociation. A child may refer to a sibling, sometimes a twin, who does not exist and either attribute strong, protective characteristics to the sibling or have scary and hurtful things happen to the sibling. The child may refer to the sibling as good or bad and express a wish to get rid of him. The child may also talk about imaginary playmates as having had scary things happen or as being very strong. The child talks about these imaginary playmates as being the same as the child or as being outside the child's control.

> Adam (a 4-year-old sexually abused over a period of a year by his mother's common-law partner) responds to the therapist's question as to how he felt when Roy (mother's boyfriend) was there: "Not happy, sad, brother felt sad, me and my brother, brother hurted Roy and then I don't know what happened." Adam had a younger sister but no brother.

**Therapist:** Why did brother hurt Roy?

**Adam:** Because we wanted to.

## CLINICAL OBSERVATIONS WITH
## THE SCHOOL-AGE CHILD

Although a clear contrast between the amount of distress expressed in pictures and in play has not been noted with school-aged children, a contrast is often noted between the distress reported by the child during an assessment ("It doesn't bother me anymore"; "I don't think about it") and the distress apparent in the behavior occurring in the home or school. Disjointed themes and verbalizations during a play assessment can alert a therapist to the possibility of above-normal dissociation.

> **Helen** (a 10-year-old sexually and physically abused by her father and witness to considerable violence from father to mother) places the farm animals and dinosaurs at various positions around the fencing. She then asks about a nipple for the bottle. She returns to the animal and dinosaur play and picks up a nipple, commenting that it wouldn't fit because someone had chewed on it, then returns to the animal play, saying that they have to keep guard because they are friends of animals. She then says, "Over my knee; making house for humans now," and starts lining up the dolls.

Reference to switching thoughts on and off can also indicate dissociation beyond normal levels.

> **Jane** (a 12-year-old sexually abused by her stepfather) states that she had been bothered with thinking about the abuse during school so she had just put it out of her mind. She stares for a second and then says, "There," and smiles at the therapist. Jane says she has always been able to shut things away in her mind.

With a child in this age group, the therapist can ask questions about voices inside the child's head, and if there are voices, "What do they say?"; concentration problems at school, and if there are problems, "Where does your mind go?"; and whether the child ever loses track of time or of what he is doing. Silberg (1996b) suggests asking about a child's internal experience when any switch in attention or affect is observed during an assessment. Hornstein and Silberg (1995) suggest asking what the child experiences inside when he is having a tantrum or engaging in some other negative behavior.

During the interview with parent(s), questions are asked about the child's learning and memory. It is not unusual for a child under stress to learn something and then not be able to do it the next day. It is unusual for a child, subsequent to that forgetting and with no additional teaching, to be able to do the task once again.

If parents report out-of-control behavior that seems to erupt for no apparent reason, the therapist can inquire as to what happened before the eruption as well as during the outburst. When a child's behavior is incongruent both with the present situation and with behaviors from the time of the abuse (ruling out trigger responses), dissociation should be considered.

> **George** (a 10-year-old abused sexually and emotionally, including lack of consistent feeding, by both parents up to the age of 6) had, his foster mother reports, started swearing and pounding the table in the middle of dinner. His foster mother told him that if he was going to behave like that he would have to go outside. For the next half hour, George ran around the backyard, yelling about not being fed and calling his foster mother obscene names.
>
> In response to an inquiry as to what had happened right before George's "explosion," the foster mother reports that she had been serving food, but because George was doing something else, she had skipped over him. This had been a trigger. But unlike a trigger response, George did not respond with the 6-year-old behavior he had shown at the time he was denied food. Rather, he responded with rageful behavior, a response apparently split off at age 6. (continued on page 137)

## CLINICAL OBSERVATIONS WITH THE ADOLESCENT

An assessment interview with an adolescent provides an opportunity for the therapist to observe the adolescent's reactions to different types of questions (nontrauma related, trauma related, friend related, family related). Any shifts in manner of reacting as well as shifts in eye gaze are noted. If the adolescent stares off into space or seems to go into herself, the therapist can ask the adolescent where she is now. Typically, an adolescent will respond, "Nowhere," at which point the therapist can ask the adolescent to describe what happened.

> **Jane** (a 14-year-old abused between the ages of 6 and 8 and again at 13 years by her mother's long-term boyfriend) responds to the therapist's request that she describe what had happened just a moment earlier, when she had started to stare into space: "My mind made a bubble, you know, like in the cartoons, and it went out of my ear and left my head empty. But there was nothing in the bubble."

**Therapist:** Is that what happened during the abuse?

**Jane:** No, during the abuse, I would just stare at spots on the wall and so wouldn't feel anything. When Jim said my name, that meant it was all over and I could stop staring and leave the room.

The question as to whether an adolescent hears voices inside or outside her head can be helpful. If the adolescent reports voices inside, the therapist can ask if the voices have said anything since she came into the room and, if so, what they have said.

Terri (a 14-year-old sexually abused as a young child by the next-door neighbor and raised by an emotionally absent and dissociative mother) replies that she does sometimes hear voices inside her head and that she has heard them since she came into the room.

**Therapist:** What have the voices said since you came in?

**Terri:** Well, they told me to tear up the pictures.

**Therapist:** But you didn't tear up the pictures, I am curious about that.

**Terri:** Another voice told me I shouldn't do it.

Questions about early memories and recent memories help clarify whether the adolescent has time gaps either day by day or over her life span. Unexplained illnesses, self-injury, and fluctuations in styles of dressing or doing things can be queried. Further ideas with relation to assessment interviews for dissociation are described by Silberg (1996b) and Putnam (1997).

The objective of an assessment for dissociation is not simply to place a label on a child but to clarify the need for particular techniques in therapy. Dissociation during abuse is a normal defense and does not indicate a dissociative disorder or a need for a special therapeutic approach. For some children, and particularly for young children, dissociative characteristics disappear once the children are in a safe and supportive environment (Putnam, 1997). A therapist needs to determine whether the extent of dissociation is such that the reality of what happened and the feelings from that reality are separated off from the child's awareness. If this is the situation, the child does not have her complete history or a complete range of feelings with which to understand and process future experiences. If the extent of dissociation is such that past experiences and present experiences are held separately, new information cannot be used to process or counter the abuse experiences or internalizations (George, page 127, had not been able to use his experiences of his foster mother feeding him to moderate the meaning of "no food"). The child continues to feel he is living in an abusive world. If the dissociation is such that alternative personalities have developed, new experiences are known by only a part of the child, and the scared or angry parts continue to rage inside. Associating between parts and, eventually, some form of integration or integrated functioning is needed.

## ❏ Treatment of Dissociation in Children and Adolescents

Kluft, in his seminal article "Multiple Personality in Childhood" (1984), proposes that treatment be based on a four-factor model (see page 118). Factors 2, 3, and 4 of this model will be covered in the present discussion. Traumatic experiences, factor 2, need to be terminated. Although this appears straightforward, it is not always easily accomplished. As Hornstein (1991) points out, abuse may be continuing within a home unbeknownst to the therapist. When a child has developed high levels of dissociation, abuse symptoms are more likely to be hidden. If a child's functioning improves and then suddenly falls apart, further abuse should be suspected (Hornstein, 1991; Waters & Silberg, 1996a). Nonabusive stressors that trigger memories of past abuse may also elicit dissociation. To avoid this as much as possible, it is suggested that the child's family be included in the treatment plan. If abuse cannot be eliminated from the child's environment, therapy should not address dissociation—dissociation is still needed as a coping mechanism. In this situation, therapy should center on ego strengthening (Peterson, 1993).

Attention to factor 4, lack of nurturing and healing experiences, also emphasizes the importance of the family. Whether the child remains within the original family, is adopted or fostered, or is placed in a group setting, the adults caring for the child should receive support and counseling. These children need consistent and supportive parenting

(Peterson, 1996; Putnam, 1997; Waters, 1996). Parents often need assistance in how to react in a calm and consistent manner to angry and fearful identities. Although rules and consequences need to be held constant, parents do need to change their manner of responding to fit the shifting developmental levels presented by the child (Putnam, 1997; Shirar, 1996; Waters, 1996). Parents can validate what the child experiences yet at the same time suggest ways of safely expressing feelings, in particular feelings of rage and fear. They need to let children know that what happened before will not happen again. They can provide missing information and links. It is essential for parents, whether birth parents, adoptive parents, or foster parents, to believe in the child and the child's ability to work through the present disconnections and disruptive behaviors. When parents are able to do this, their relationship with the child helps the child connect with the world (Putnam, 1997).

Parents need a place, separate from the child, where they can talk about feelings of anger and helplessness and their concerns regarding the impact this child is having on the family. When possible, this therapy as well as any family therapy is best done by a therapist other than the child's individual therapist.

Kluft (1984) emphasizes the importance of educating the family as well as the child regarding dissociation: why dissociation occurs, what the child is experiencing, and how dissociation can be treated. Information about the dynamics of flashbacks and other posttraumatic behaviors is given to family members, and their help in managing behaviors is requested (Dell & Eisenhower, 1990; Waters, 1996). As with the families of adults with dissociative identities, it is important that parents and siblings *not* encourage dissociation by calling out or paying special attention to particular parts or identities they like (Williams, 1991).

Factor 3, the development of the dissociated self-systems, highlights the need to increase the awareness within a child of all the other parts or feeling states. For the child who has formed dissociative identities, time should be spent getting to know each part—the job that each part performs, why this job was taken on, what the part likes to do, what memories and feelings are held by that part (Peterson, 1993; Waters & Silberg, 1996b). Whenever possible, this should be done through the child and not by calling out a particular part (Putnam, 1997).

The child needs to be educated as to why dissociation happened and the function served by dissociation (Dell & Eisenhower, 1990; James, 1990; Kluft, 1984; Shirar, 1996; Waters & Silberg, 1996b). The extent and phrasing of this explanation will vary depending on the child's age.

James (1990) discusses the importance of identifying, together with the child, the triggers that activate dissociation. Putnam (1997) stresses the importance of children's learning to listen to themselves and track their own behavior. This can be encouraged as the child reports within therapy on his experiences during the week and the therapist inquires about how the child's reactions did or did not fit with the experience. Themes between therapy sessions can be connected together, at first by the therapist and later by the child, to provide a sense of continuity and integration (Putnam, 1997).

Hypnosis has, in the past, been recommended for working with children with dissociative identities. The inclusion of hypnosis in therapy has, however, led to children's testimony being disqualified in court. For this reason, hypnosis is now not generally recommended (Kluft, 1996). Young children easily access internal states, as evidenced in their play, without the use of hypnosis (Waters, 1989; Waters & Silberg, 1996b).

Hornstein and Silberg (1995) have delineated seven tasks to be covered in work with children who dissociate:

1. Establishing a safe, nurturing environment
2. Forming a therapeutic alliance
3. Improving ego functioning and managing negative behaviors
4. Meeting alters
5. Developing alternative coping strategies
6. Decreasing dissociative barriers
7. Working through the trauma

Acceptance by the therapist of the child's inner experience is described as essential for the therapeutic alliance (Hornstein & Tyson, 1991). The child then feels there is space within therapy for all the parts, whether separated-off feeling states or actual separated alters. As tasks 1 and 2 are carried out, task 3 starts to occur. If the child does engage in destructive or assaultive behaviors, consistent and reasonable consequences are used. If the child disclaims responsibility for some action on the basis that another part of him did it, he is told that "all of him" is responsible for things done by any one part (Hornstein & Tyson, 1991; Waters & Silberg, 1996b). It is important that the part that became destructive not go away during the consequence. Hornstein and Tyson (1991) refer to the importance of having the various parts talk together about the behavior. While noting that this may evoke considerable resistance from the child, they emphasize that the therapist must stay with the issue if the child is to learn to bring his parts together. However, these authors do not offer any suggestions for "staying with the issue."

A therapist needs to respond to all parts. Talking about each part as part of a whole, rather than separate, helps a child to grasp the concept of integration (Waters & Silberg, 1996a). Integration is described as a sharing of capabilities; no part is lost.

In their 1995 paper, Hornstein and Silberg emphasize addressing the issues relevant to the child rather than constantly centering on the issues of dissociation. Kluft (1996) notes that this is particularly important with adolescents. Adolescents tend to be particularly difficult to engage in therapy, and adolescents who dissociate are no exception. Putnam (1997) refers to the importance of using "implicit" as opposed to "explicit" interventions. Not only do children and adolescents not have the capabilities for self-observation and monitoring that individuals need in order to be able to utilize standard therapeutic interpretations, maltreatment disrupts the development of metacognitive processes, thus further limiting a child's ability to observe himself. Providing consistency and safety within both the therapeutic setting and the therapist's reactions, accepting and addressing the child's perspective on ongoing events, strengthening the child's self-confidence, and helping the child develop self-observation and self-monitoring skills provide important therapeutic interventions without reference to abuse or dissociation.

For young children, play therapy is recommended (Putnam, 1997; Riley & Mead, 1988; Shirar, 1996; Waldschmidt, Graham-Costain, & Gould, 1991; Waters & Silberg, 1996b). Both the abuse and the internal dissociative system are expressed within the play (Gould, 1993; Shirar, 1996). As dissociative themes are played out, a therapist can inquire as to which part deals with particular issues or feelings. Children who show high dissociation can be encouraged to draw or model from clay the different parts and then identify the characteristics of each different part (Fagan & McMahon, 1984; Graham-Costain, 1993; Waters & Silberg, 1996b). A therapist may tell metaphorical stories about different parts, the conflict between parts, or the trauma experienced (Shirar, 1996; Fagan & McMahon, 1984). It is suggested that metaphors be developed from the child's own interests or experiences (Waters & Silberg, 1996b). Dialogues between parts and role-plays have also been described (Shirar, 1996). A puppet who describes its own "inside family" can be used to provide a model for the child trying to establish links between her dissociated parts (Waters & Silberg, 1996b).

The therapist can encourage communication between parts by addressing a single question to each of the parts in turn (Graham-Costain, 1993). Putnam (1997) has emphasized that therapy is best directed to the child as a whole—for example, the child can be asked how he feels each part of him would respond to the question—unless alter personality states are clearly behaviorally distinct and identifiable across different settings.

In some cases, gradual integration appears to occur as therapy progresses (Putnam, 1997; Waters & Silberg, 1996a). Some therapists describe specific imaging related to integration—rainbows (James, 1990), *Star Trek* (Kluft, 1984), and parts hugging each other until they merge (Shirar, 1996). Kluft (1996) emphasizes integration as essential for healthy development.

Little attention has been given within the dissociation literature to how therapy can address the physiological dysregulation that occurs with abuse (Friedrich, 1995; Putnam, 1997) and is, most likely, an underlying component of extreme dissociation. Both Friedrich (1995) and Putnam (1997) stress the importance of consistency and stability within the child's environment and within the therapeutic setting as a way of stabilizing the child and of providing a model for behavior control. Whether this will actually decrease the hyperresponsivity of the biological systems caused by abuse is not currently known.

Although medications have been an important adjunct to therapy with adults with dissociative identities, little research has been carried out with children. In a review of psychopharmacological interventions for children experiencing dissociation, Nemzer (1996) emphasizes that medication should not be used for dissociation. Medication can be used, and can provide very important relief, for specific symptoms (such as attention problems, sleeplessness) or comorbid conditions (for example, depression). Kluft (1996) suggests that medication be used only when the targeted behavior exists across identities, not within a dissociated state. Putnam (1997) stresses the importance of baseline and follow-up assessments to monitor both positive and possible negative effects. If medications are used, drug holidays are recommended to minimize any cumulative dosage effects.

In 1994, the International Society for the Study of Dissociation published guidelines for the treatment of dissociative identities. Although these guidelines do not address the treatment of children, they are instructive for therapists working with children. Integration is identified as the overall treatment goal. Interventions are to be directed toward increasing a sense of "connectedness" or relatedness among the personalities. "Psychodynamically aware psychotherapy, often eclectically incorporating other techniques," is suggested as a treatment orientation (International Society for the Study of Dissociation, 1994). Whereas cognitive therapy is seen as helpful in addressing dysfunctional trauma-based beliefs, behavior therapy is not recommended. Aversive conditioning is contraindicated, as it might resemble abusive experiences. Hypnosis is recommended for calming, soothing, containment, and ego strengthening. At present, guidelines for treatment of dissociation in children are being developed (Silberg, 1997). They are similar to the above, with the additional guideline of recognizing the role of parents as crucial for successful therapy.

For a child to move toward integration or a decrease in dissociation, the child's internal experience of his environment and of himself needs to change. The following section will supplement the preceding literature review by discussing some specific ideas and techniques from clinical work with children and adolescents who dissociate. This section is divided into three parts: working with the environment, explaining dissociation, and helping the child explore the dynamics of dissociation.

### WORKING WITH THE ENVIRONMENT

As the therapist works with the family, he can help the family support and validate the child, minimize stressors, provide clear boundaries, model new ways of coping, and, most important, nurture the child. The therapist needs also to be a support to the parent and, particularly with adolescents, to provide a separate therapist for the parent.

As discussed above, the environment needs to be free of abusive situations. In addition, the environment needs to avoid situations with dynamics parallel to those that occurred during the original abuse.

> **Kelly** (a 16-year-old sexually and emotionally abused by her father in a family where the father would attack and manipulate the close attachments between siblings as a way of keeping the children vulnerable) establishes, after many months, a trusting and close relationship with her key worker in the group home. While the worker is away on vacation, the supervisor of the home mentions to Kelly that she feels Kelly has become too dependent on the key worker and that she, rather than the key worker, will start accompanying Kelly to important appointments.
>
> Kelly's behavior explodes (she runs around the neighborhood, sets off "cherry bombs") in a way not seen for a considerable period of time.

By alerting parents, or parent figures, to dynamics that occurred in the original abuse setting, the therapist can help to avoid similar dynamics.

The natural desire of parents and other adults is for a child to be happy. They respond with pleasure and become more involved with the child when the child is happy. For most children, this is a positive experience. For the child who dissociates, however, this parental response, and the accompanying response of ignoring negative events and thoughts, can reinforce dissociation.

> **Tara** (a 4-year-old adopted at 15 months out of a chaotic war-torn environment in which she had experienced neglect as well as sexual and physical abuse) tells her adoptive mother about her imaginary friend, who got hit and had a gun stuck in her mouth. Her mother, in an effort to decrease Tara's fears, replies that things like that do not happen to little children. The parents do not talk with Tara about her first year of life. Although Tara knows she is adopted, any reference to violence or distress is avoided.
>
> The therapist encourages Tara's parents to respond to Tara's questions about her birth and first year with honesty. They acknowledge that she had been frightened by guns and that that had been very scary. They also state that her world now is different and is safe.
>
> With time, Tara starts to worry about guns and fire coming into her house but no longer talks about things happening to imaginary friends.

After more time, she is able to say, "That happened but I'm with Mommy and Daddy now and it doesn't happen here." Her interactions with others become more relaxed and her extreme swings in behavior disappear.

\*   \*   \*   \*   \*

Cindy (a 12-year-old sexually abused and neglected by her birth parents) tells her adoptive father she is lonely. He replies by telling her that isn't possible—she now has four brothers and sisters and a mother and father who love her, and that's a happy situation. Cindy becomes increasingly withdrawn.

When her father mentions this episode in a session with the therapist, the therapist explains that the "lonely Cindy" is a part from Cindy's early experience that was pushed away because it was too frightening to acknowledge. He suggests the father ask Cindy how he and the others in the family could help the "lonely Cindy" to feel at home in the family.

A therapist can encourage parents to recognize the reality of a child's past experience and of the child's present inner world. As parents recognize that reality, the child comes to know that she, too, can survive recognizing it and can include it inside herself—that is, integrate it.

Amy (a 5-year-old severely sexually abused by her father and witness to violence against her mother) is on a rampage around the foster home, attacking the foster mother, the other children, and her own possessions. When the foster father has to restrain her, Amy states that she will get rid of that Amy and will be good. The foster parents respond that that would be wonderful.

Over the next few days, as Amy helps her foster mother and plays and giggles with the other children, the mother tells her how much better she likes this Amy and how she hopes the other Amy is gone for good.

When the foster parents and therapist meet, they discuss the importance of recognizing and including all aspects of Amy when interacting with her. Over the next months, the foster parents note to Amy, when she is really good, that they appreciate the part of her that is trying so hard, but that they know the scared and angry part of Amy is still there and needs a lot of caretaking too. They ask how the angry part is feeling and what that part wants them to know.

At first, Amy says little, but with time she starts to talk some about angry feelings and, as this happens, her outbursts decrease.

The child's environment needs to be supportive and nurturing to the negative as well as the positive parts. This does not mean that negative behavior is to be condoned. Aggressive and destructive behavior by children who dissociate needs to be responded to with clear, consistent consequences in the same manner as it is with children who do not dissociate. The discussion, however, would be different. Forcing a child to admit to something that she is not aware she has done encourages internal manipulation. Angry alters of adults with dissociative identities talk about getting the good or, as they often put it, "the wimpy part" of them in trouble. It is important that the outside world not, even without meaning to, collude with internal manipulation. While clearly stating responsibility and consequences for negative behavior, parents can recognize that all parts of the child may not be aware of that behavior. If they notice the child dissociating, they can ask the child to "come back" before continuing a discussion about the behavior. If they realize that the child has already switched, they can ask what triggered the switch and how they can help the child feel safer. When a flashback occurs, parents can provide grounding by staying with the child and reminding the child where she is and that although frightening things happened in the past, those things are not happening now. Although parents are not, and should not be, therapists, their appropriate responses at the time of dissociating can help stabilize a child's world.

Therapists can help parents recognize what is happening. They can explain that the most destructive part or identity was created when the child was most scared (Putnam, 1989). With this information, a parent is often able to see the child and the child's behavior differently. Therapists can encourage parents to notice what happened right before an outburst and to listen to what the child says during an outburst.

> **George** (a 10-year-old; see page 127) and his foster mother talk with the therapist about George's "explosion" at the dinner table. His foster mother comments that George knows she is going to feed him. The therapist points out that although one part of George knows he is going to be fed, there seems to be another part that doesn't know that. The therapist asks George to draw a picture of the part of him that knows he is going to be fed and the part of him that does not know that. She then asks what the two parts might say to each other.
>
> George draws a large 10-year-old part and a little 6-year-old part. The 10-year-old says to the 6-year-old, "You know you are going to get fed, so you shouldn't scream!"

**Therapist:** George, the problem is that the 6-year-old George doesn't know that. He hasn't been around while Mom has been feeding you, the part of you that is here now has been around. [Realizes that this conversation may be too abstract for a 10-year-old.] Why don't you close your eyes and picture the 6-year-old inside of you—where is he?

**George:** He's in the corner. Everyone else is at the table, but he is in the corner.

**Therapist:** Who is at the table?

**George:** My sister is there, Mom and Dad too, hey, I'm there too.

**Therapist:** Tell me about the "you" at the table.

**George:** Well, it's me.

**Therapist:** All right, can you take "you," the 10-year-old, over to the corner where the 6-year-old is and ask him to come to the table so he can find out about the feeding that is going on?

**George:** He doesn't want to come, he thinks he is going to get hurt.

**Therapist:** How can you let him know he is not going to get hurt?

**George:** I could tell him.

**Therapist:** All right, go ahead and let me know what happens.

**George:** He is coming.

As parents recognize that underlying fears can still exist, the child feels validated—an important step toward integration.

A therapist can encourage parents and group home workers to model new coping mechanisms. The child, who has used dissociation as a way of dealing with stress and fear, cannot be expected to stop dissociating unless she learns new ways of coping. It is likely that, within the child's original home, feelings such as fear and anger occurred only in extreme form. Not only would these experiences have been scary, and possibly have led to dissociation, they also would have been the child's only model for handling feelings.

Within foster environments, parent figures tend either to handle their anger and fear in ways not apparent to the child or, when pushed too far, to explode. Therapists can encourage parents to verbalize the way they problem solve or work through emotions. Talking, taking a walk, and writing down or drawing feelings are some of the coping responses parents can be encouraged to use in front of a child.

While encouraging the parent(s) in new ways of responding, the therapist needs also to be sensitive to the discouragement often felt by foster and adoptive parents. The child who has been abused by an early attachment figure is going to have difficulty forming future attachments (Friedrich, 1995; Putnam, 1997). Parents are going to need a support system and ways to take care of themselves as they work with these children (Waters, 1996). Most of all, they need to have small changes in their interactions with the child noticed and praised if they are to be able to notice and praise their child. The therapist may wish to include a foster, adoptive, or biological parent together with the child in fun activities. Many parents are so anxious to teach a child positive behaviors they forget that the relationship is more important than correcting and teaching.

### EXPLAINING DISSOCIATION

The reasons for dissociation, the dissociative process, and the way in which dissociation can be resolved need to be explained to parents, in some instances to teachers, and, most important, to the child. Dissociation can be explained to an adolescent or an adult as a process that all people experience to some extent. Watkins and Watkins's (1992) description of a continuum ranging from normal ego state differentiation to dissociative identity segmentation can be helpful. The segmenting of traumatic experiences or feelings can be described as a creative process the child used to protect himself from a world that was too frightening to know. This explanation encourages the child and parent to recognize the original process as a healthy one, not something bizarre and crazy. Conceptualizing differentiation-dissociation as a continuum establishes for both the child and the parent the possibility of moving from severe dissociation back to normal ego state differentiation.[4]

Parents need to be educated as to the different parts or identities the child may have formed. Although parents need to recognize these different parts and adapt their responses to the developmental levels of particular parts, their interactions should be with the child as a whole.

Sara (a 16-year-old sexually abused as a young child by several family members and stressed by ongoing dysfunction in the family) switches between personalities when interacting with her parents. Her parents try to accommodate each personality but become increasingly frustrated and angry as they feel continually manipulated. Interactions lead to constant explosions in the home.

The parents then change their approach and interact only with Sara. When Sara says that Sara isn't there, it is "Darkness," they reply that they know Darkness is an important part with important feelings, but they wish to interact with Darkness through Sara and will Sara let her know of their concern. The chaotic interactions at home start to settle a bit.

Teachers may also become involved in chaotic interactions with an adolescent with dissociative identities. A therapist can be helpful in working with the adolescent to determine which part is going to turn in assignments and take tests. If several parts have taken on these responsibilities, the therapist and child can contract for one part to turn in assignments and sign tests at school. The therapist needs to have the child check with all the parts of himself for a contract such as this to be successful. The therapist may then, together with the adolescent, meet with the teachers. The importance of a consistent response to the adolescent, despite variation within the adolescent's behavior, is emphasized. Chaotic situations may also occur if friends give a great deal of attention, thereby providing secondary gain, to the adolescent's switching. The school can be encouraged to react calmly, with only one staff member, no students, being involved with the adolescent if extreme switching, such as regression, occurs.

A therapist can explain the effects of dissociation on a child's learning: For mild dissociation, if the child is not aware of the teaching he will not learn; for severe dissociation, if only one part of the child has learned the information, another part of the child will not know that information. The child's behavior does not need to be pathologized.

When, during a session, an adolescent wonders why he does not feel anything about the abuse or states that he cannot remember something that has happened, the therapist has an opportunity to explain dissociation. As the therapist talks about the process of dissociation, she tries to engage the adolescent in the description. This not only helps the therapist understand that particular adolescent's dissociative structure, but also assures that the explanation is relevant for the adolescent.

Emily (a 15-year-old with unknown early abuse history and later sadistic and manipulative sexual abuse by her adoptive grandfather) listens to the therapist describe how a child may take a part of herself away inside her mind when a situation is terrifying and how, after this happens several times, the child may experience the part that was abused/terrified as separate from the rest of her. The therapist explains that when something else frightening happens, like her grandfather abusing her, another split can happen.

**Emily:** And then each part splits again, just like a tree.

**Therapist:** Why don't we make a picture of this tree. (hands Emily paper and a pencil)

Emily draws a tree with the trunk dividing into two branches and labels this division "Whatever happened when I was little." She then draws splits in one of the branches and labels these "Grandfather started abusing me" and "Mom and Dad fought."

**Therapist:** [Notes that this picture is very different from the one she had pictured in her mind—many splits from the base of the tree.]

Emily draws more splits and labels some of them. She explains that others happened for reasons she doesn't even know.

When discussing dissociation with school-age children, therapists need to use more concrete questions and explanations.

Kim (a 9-year-old who witnessed, at age 4, her younger sister being stabbed to death by her father and was sexually abused by neighborhood boys) talks about not remembering the stabbing even though she knows she saw it. When the therapist asks about other frightening things that happened in the home, Kim says she doesn't remember anything.

**Therapist:** Some children close frightening things off behind a door or in a box. Other children take themselves away from frightening things.

**Kim:** Away in a car or a plane or a train or a bus or a truck.

**Therapist:** How smart and creative it is to find a way to go away and feel safe. What happened to the part or parts that went away? (Kim shakes her head.) Do you ever hear voices? (Kim nods.) When a part goes away by car or plane, or however it goes away, the part keeps on existing. That part may be the part with the memory and feelings from what happened. And sometimes parts talk inside a child's head. Do the parts have names?

**Kim:** They used to. One was Kimmy, that's what I was called when I was little, and Kimberly, that's what I was called when I was bad, and Kit.

**Therapist:** Do they have names now?

**Kim:** No, and I only hear the voices sometimes now.

**Therapist:** I'm thinking about how important those parts of you were in helping you when things were really frightening. As we get to know the voices that are still sometimes there, we can understand more of what happened back then and more of how all these parts can get along together now. (Kim's foster mother's completion of the CDC based on Kim's behavior when she first came into care 18 months earlier is 19—high dissociative—and based on present behaviors is 11—above normal, but not extreme dissociative.)

Some school-age children express dissociation through their drawings or play.

**George** (a 10-year-old; see pages 127, 137) sets up fencing down the middle of the sand tray. On one side he writes "good" and on the other he writes "bad." Then, looking at the therapist, he states that that is he—part of him is good and part of him is bad. George explains that he has to get rid of the bad, he doesn't like it, and starts to wipe out the word "bad."

**Therapist:** (gently places her hand in front of George's hand to stop him from wiping out the word) It is going to be really important for us to find out more about this part, not just get rid of it. It is there for some reason and we need to understand that reason. (writes "scared" in the sand under "bad") When frightening things happen to a child, like they happened to you, a child gets really scared. But since it is frightening to be scared, sometimes a child will take that part away, put a fence between that part and the other part of himself. But feeling scared may feel dangerous, so the scared part gets angry and behaves like an angry or "bad" child. Tell me what it is like for this part of you.

A young child may bring the topic of dissociation into therapy by drawing a picture of a child with a smile and then putting a small figure with tears behind that child, by talking about a twin who was bad so he was sent away, or by lining up pieces of paper on the floor and then saying that that is he. The therapist can talk about the different parts, how the child had moved one part away from the others to keep them safe, and how it will be important to find out more about the parts that were moved away or cut off.

Linda (a 6-year-old abused by three different individuals and then, after being taken to the police station to disclose, pressured by her mother to recant) makes a puppet out of Kleenex and draws three faces on the head of the puppet.

Therapist: Tell me about the faces of the puppet.

Linda: Three faces—the happy face is okay but the other faces are bad.

Therapist: I'm noticing how one face has a smiling mouth, one has a sad mouth and tears, and the third has an angry mouth. Tell me about them.

Linda: The happy face is good and the others are bad.

Therapist: I'm thinking about how scary it would have been for you when you were touched on your vagina and how, when that happens for some children, they take a part of themselves away so the other part can still be happy. And then other things happen, more touching or being told not to tell, and you might get really angry but want that anger to stay away from the part of you that wants to be happy.

## EXPLORING THE INTERNAL DYNAMICS OF DISSOCIATION

With children of all ages who have dissociated identities or who simply dissociate from time to time, a therapist needs to stay alert for moments of dissociation, acknowledge the dissociation, work with the child toward understanding what is happening inside, and encourage reconnection. For the young child, a concrete form of connection often helps.

Tessy (a 5-year-old sexually and physically abused in her birth home and in a foster home) messes the plasticine around and around in her hand. "Fuck."

Therapist: [Realizes, even though the voice she heard was very gruff, that it was Tessy who spoke.] The "fuck" sounded like a hurt or angry part of you. Tell me about the "fuck" part.

Tessy: I didn't say anything.

Therapist: I guess the part of you that is playing here didn't say anything. But another part of you, maybe the angry part, seems to have. You have lots of reason to be angry with all the touching and hitting that happened to you. It's all right for you to be angry—not all right to hurt people, but all right to be angry. What does the angry part of you want to say?

**Tessy:** Stop that!

**Therapist:** Could the part of you that is playing here help the angry part say that? Maybe the two parts of you could hold hands to say it.

A therapist needs to think through responses carefully to ensure that dissociation is not reinforced.

> **Bobby** (a 6-year-old sexually abused by his mother) mentions during a play therapy session that he had a bad brother who had died.

**Therapist:** [Knows that Bobby did not have a brother.] It seems as if you feel a part of you is bad, the brother part, perhaps because of the abuse. The abuse was bad, not you. It is going to be really important to let the brother part of you come work together with you to give the "bad" back to the abuse. [Knows that Bobby is still very attached to his mother and that telling him to give the "bad" back to mother might have brought out and strengthened part of him that doesn't want to be angry at his mother.]

When a child suddenly takes on the behavior of an animal, the therapist should neither treat the child like an animal nor try to coax the child out of "being" the animal. Rather, the therapist should try to understand the role of the animal in the child's internal system, reflect this role to the child, and then ask what the child and the animal part/feeling could do together. Telling a child to get rid of a part is likely to reinforce dissociation.

The school-age child can make a sand tray picture of his internal world or draw the different parts/feelings with what each part/feeling would say. This can help the child recognize and come to some understanding of what is going on inside. Listing what each part/feeling needs from the other parts/feelings helps to establish a sense of interrelating. Intrusive voices may occur during play and should be responded to and discussed.

> **Betsy** (a 10-year-old sexually abused by her father and neglected by her mother) sets up a scenario in which the therapist is the child in school who is having to write lines about talking in class, while Betsy is the French teacher standing over the child. As the therapist completes the lines, Betsy says, "She was groaning, groaning."

**Therapist:** [Notices that the comment is out of context.] It would be really scary to hear the groaning.

**Betsy:** What groaning?

**Therapist:** A part of you told me, just now, about some groaning. Who do you think made that groaning, the groaning that was really scary?

**Betsy:** My mother.

**Therapist:** What do you remember from that time when mother was groaning?

**Betsy:** It came from the other room, he was hurting her. I wanted to go stop him but I was too scared to go. I just stayed there and whispered, "Stop! Stop! Stop!" but he didn't stop.

**Therapist:** How were you feeling inside when your father and mother were in the other room and your mother was groaning?

**Betsy:** Okay.

**Therapist:** It would have been really scary to be there and to hear that. It seems as if you had to send the scared feeling away so you could feel okay. What could you say now to the scared feeling?

In other situations, dissociation during therapy may be more blatant. Although blatant dissociation is easier to discuss, it can be so surprising that it can catch a therapist unaware, and the therapist may initially respond inappropriately. Any inappropriate response should always be corrected. The experience or feeling behind the dissociation should be discussed.

**Emma** (a 12-year-old severely sexually abused by her father for many years) starts swearing, picks up a chair, and throws it against the wall. The noise startles her and she dashes from the therapy room. After a minute Emma returns with an apologetic smile on her face, says she is sorry, and asks the therapist for a hug.

**Therapist:** (Startled by the request and without thinking, gives Emma a hug.) [Realizes that she has reinforced the dissociation by not recognizing the angry part of Emma and by giving a positive experience to the quiet, smiling Emma.] And here is a hug for the angry part of Emma. Throwing the chair is not all right—I shall bring in some plaster next week so we can fix the wall—but being angry is all right. How could the angry part of you let me know, without breaking things, about some of the feelings inside? Could the angry part of you tell me, draw a picture of, or show me with the toys how that part of you is feeling?

An important part of the work with a school-age child is identifying the types of situations that trigger parts of the child. Doing this with the child and parent together can be helpful. New ways of coping with stressful or scary situations can be discussed and practiced.

Children are not necessarily receptive to the idea of dissociated parts or feelings. When this happens, the therapist can continue to identify any dissociation observed, perhaps being curious as to what is going on for the child, but should not pressure the child into specific dissociative work. Pressuring a child raises the possibility that the child may create a part to deal with the therapist or may become antagonistic to therapy. Therapy addressing other areas—supportive interventions within the environment, making connections between events inside therapy and events outside therapy, problem solving, developing self-esteem—facilitates integration.

As Hornstein and Putnam (1992; Putnam, 1997) note, dissociative identities are more likely to be evident in adolescents than in young children. It may be that the internal system loses some of the flexibility that exists in children, or continuing negative situations may further solidify the boundaries between dissociated parts. Within Putnam's (1997) developmental framework, the increased evidence of dissociative identities in adolescence may reflect the lack of metacognitive processes that usually develop by adolescence. The dissociation being more evident does not, however, mean that it is easier to work with. Therapy with adolescents is often difficult and problematic (Kluft, 1996; Putnam, 1997). Adolescents tend to swing between being willing to discuss dissociative experiences and refusing to have anything to do with such a discussion.

> Emily (a 15-year-old; see page 141) sits on the couch looking at the therapist with no interest. She responds to the therapist's comments by saying that the week has gone as usual and she doesn't need to be here.

Therapist: It seems as if the part of you that does not like therapy has come today.

Emily: I'm the one who is here and I am me. There's just one of me. Your talking about parts is stupid.

Therapist: You're right, you are you. It's all the different feelings and reactions inside. Those feelings and reactions—like not wanting to be here—need attention. Those feelings did not get noticed when you were little, so it is really important that we notice them now. What was the week like?

Even when an adolescent refuses to discuss dissociation, the therapist needs to stay alert to changes in the way the adolescent presents herself and to any contradiction between ideas and feelings. The therapist can then comment on these changes and contradictions—not the dissociation behind the behavior—and talk about the protection they represent. Focusing specifically on the dissociation when the adolescent does not wish to do so is likely to lead to the adolescent leaving therapy.

The therapeutic interactions discussed above are also helpful for adolescents: establishing safety and support, noticing and explaining dissociation, recognizing and accepting negative emotions and/or parts, recovering and working through memories, encouraging interaction between parts, identifying triggers, and learning coping skills. Techniques used with adults can often also be helpful (Kluft & Fine, 1993; Putnam, 1989, 1997). The use of the dissociative table (Fraser, 1991) can be introduced as a way to understand changes that occur or confusions inside.

Betty (a 14-year-old from a very conflictive and manipulative background where sexual abuse was suspected) is often antagonistic to the therapist, comparing the therapist to her stepfather. She does agree to do some looking inside. While keeping her eyes open, Betty responds to the therapist's request that she find a safe place where she can put a table and then gather the parts of her around the table.

Betty:   The table is a rectangle and there is a figure at each end and three empty chairs on each side. This is weird, at one end is a plastic shell of my body that has nothing inside, at the other end there is an invisible version of me. Along the side no one is in the chairs but there is an object on the table in front of each chair. In front of the first chair is a picture of my mother, in front of the second chair is a picture of my stepfather, and in front of the third chair there is a vase of flowers. The invisible part of me moves around the table sitting in the different chairs. As I sit in each of those chairs, I pick up and hold in front of my face whatever is the object in front of the chair. The other side of the table is empty.

Therapist:   Can I speak with the plastic shell?

**Betty:** That's not possible because there is nothing inside to do the speaking. And the invisible part can't talk because she doesn't exist. If the invisible part moves to a chair with an object, she then becomes the object—my mother, my stepfather, or the happy, springlike child.

**Therapist:** [Notes that this describes the types of responses Betty had made in therapy over the past several months and that it fits the theory of introjected and trauma-created ego states or parts.] That fits with what happens here in the sessions. Sometimes you are like your mother, very stand-offish, and other times like your stepfather, twisting around things that are said, and still other times, in a good mood. (Betty nods.) That would be really hard for you, not having a sense of who you are. The invisible part of you has worked so hard to find yourself and the plastic shell has worked over the years to protect you. What is happening at the table?

**Betty:** Nothing.

**Therapist:** Look around the room and see if you notice anything else.

**Betty:** Nothing.

**Therapist:** I really appreciate the view you have given me of what it is like inside you—the being invisible, the taking on others' faces, and the nothing. It will be important for us to look for other aspects of you—perhaps the little you before your parents separated, perhaps the scared you who was so often alone.

Along with discussions of dissociation, therapy needs to address the feelings and internalizations related to the sexual abuse experience and related to present experiences. As the child works through this distress, there is less need for dissociation, and therefore more possibility for integration.

## ❏ Summary

Dissociation is a normal phenomenon and defense experienced by children, adolescents, and adults. For a child who is repeatedly traumatized, this defense becomes repetitive and, in time, automatic. For some children, dissociation occurs only with stressful situations or when distressing events are recalled. Other children dissociate repeatedly as a way of dealing with daily situations. With severe early trauma, a child may develop separate identities to handle different facets of the child's life.

Because dissociation appears similar to other childhood behavior, it has often been overlooked in the past. With increased recognition that dissociation begins early in life and the development of the Child Dissociative Checklist and other instruments, the study and treatment of childhood dissociation is increasing.

Therapy requires first and foremost the establishment of safety. The therapist explains to the child the dynamics of dissociation, describing dissociation as a creative coping mechanism that is no longer needed. The child is encouraged to look at and understand her internal parts—whether feelings or function ego states or alters—and to increase communication between these parts. The child is encouraged to become more aware and observant of herself and her behavior and to learn new and positive ways of coping and of moderating her behavior. The role of the family as a support and as a source of observations and connections for the child is extremely important. The trauma that necessitated the dissociation is then addressed. Integration of feelings, functions, or parts is encouraged.

## ❏ Notes

1. Professionals trained within a psychodynamic framework speak of the child's ego as having not yet fully developed, whereas professionals trained within a cognitive framework speak of the lack of metacognitive processes in young children.

2. Depersonalization should not be confused with situations in which an individual thinks about how she looks from the outside but is still consciously within herself.

3. The term *dissociative identities* is used in place of *multiple personalities* in the present discussion. Where studies or articles published before the change in terminology are discussed, the term *dissociative identity* is substituted for *multiple personality.*

4. There is considerable debate as to whether dissociation is a spectrum ranging from normal to pathological or whether there are distinct types of dissociation. Putnam (1997) states that each model accounts for some of the research findings. Using the continuum model when talking with families or children does not imply that the typological model is inaccurate, rather the continuum conceptualization provides for them a more supportive, less stigmatizing, framework.

# 6

# *Reconnecting to the Body: Sexuality*

The infant, child, adolescent—from his own exploring and curiosity, from his parents' teaching and modeling, and from his interaction with peers and watching of television—learns about sexuality, his own and that of others. As his body grows and hormonal changes occur, he observes and experiments. This is part of normal psychosexual development.

For a child who is sexually abused, the developmental flow is disrupted. Sexual activity at a developmental level beyond that of the child is imposed on the child. The child witnesses a sexual reaction in the abuser that does not fit the child's cognitive understanding. The child may have a sexual response that does not fit his knowledge of his body or his wish for his body.

A child experiences his body being used by another person and internalizes a sense of himself as an object used by others. Depending on the context of the abuse, the severity and extent of abuse, this internalization may become part of the child's internal working model of himself within sexual relationships, himself within family relationships, or himself within all relationships.

In situations of abuse, sexualized behavior by a child may lead to special attention, the avoidance of punishment, or pleasurable physical sensations. In this way, sexualized behaviors are reinforced and the child internalizes a connection between being sexual and having good things happen.

For a child who experiences physical responding during abuse, there is little or no understandable context into which to place this responding. The sexual reactions are connected by the child with the atmosphere (gamelike, manipulative, threatening), the sensations (pleasure, pain, numbing), and the emotions (anxiety, excitement, anger, fear) that occurred within the abuse scenario. The child's internal sense of sexuality takes on these characteristics.

Finkelhor and Browne (1985) refer to these effects as traumatic sexualization. If a child is to develop healthy and enjoyable sexuality, therapy needs to address the negative internalizations related to sexuality. The child needs an opportunity to move on with normal sexual development.

In order to recognize the therapeutic needs of a child who has been sexually abused, a therapist needs to understand healthy sexual development and the ways in which abuse can distort this development. This chapter briefly reviews research on normal sexual development as well as research on the effects of abuse on sexual development. The child's therapeutic needs are then considered, and a process for addressing these needs is described.

## ❏ Children and Sexuality

### NORMAL SEXUAL DEVELOPMENT

A child who is not abused moves through numerous stages of awareness with regard to her body, her genitals, sensations related to her genitals, other people's bodies, sensations related to their genitals, reproductivity, and sexual intercourse. Rutter (1971), in his discussion of normal psychosexual development, describes the first year of life as being one of genital reflex reaction, self-exploration of parts of the body—the genitals being one part—and, for some infants, a connection between the touching of the genitals and pleasant sensations. Close and comforting holding is part of the infant's learning about body comfort, safety, and sensations. A relationship between the amount of early holding and healthy adult sexual responding has been hypothesized (Yates, 1991).

During the toddler and preschool years, masturbation, exhibitionism, and peer sex play are common (Rutter, 1971; Yates, 1991). It is during this period that the first two components of sexual identity, recognition of self as a particular gender and gender role behavior, appear (Green, 1994).

During the early elementary school years, referred to as latency, masturbation may continue. This is a time when children are more likely to engage in same-gender sex play (Yates, 1991). Sexual jokes are told in the school yard, and teasing often takes on a sexual connotation. Although not examined through research, this appears to be a time when curiosity about sexual characteristics and sexual activity increases. Crushes on older adolescents and adults frequently occur. Overt sexual behavior decreases through the elementary school years (Friedrich, Grambsch, Broughton, Kuipers, & Beilke, 1991).

With puberty, both girls and boys become increasingly involved with the changes and physical responses of their bodies and with establishing dating relationships. The third component of sexual identity, sexual orientation, usually emerges during this time. Social mores, particularly adolescent mores, are influential in determining the progression of dating, courtship, and marriage (Rutter, 1971).

One study of children ages 2 to 7 found an increase in sexual knowledge with age that reflected environment as well as age (Gordon, Schroeder, & Abrams, 1990a). Children from lower, compared with higher, social classes had less information about sexual body parts and pregnancy. All children in this sample showed very limited knowledge of sexual behavior. Experiences such as bathing with parents, sex play with peers, exposure to sexually explicit material, and discussion with parents were reported less often by parents from lower social classes.

After age 7, outside influences, including the school, peers, and the media, have increasing influence on a child's sexual knowledge. Although many schools include courses in sex education, these tend to focus on the mechanics or risky aspects of sexual development and interaction. Through the mass media, children are exposed to increasingly explicit scenes of adult sexual activity that may or may not be related to caring relationships. Adolescents are, for the most part, left on their own to transpose whatever learning they have regarding caring and loving to the area of sexuality.

## EFFECTS OF ABUSE ON SEXUAL DEVELOPMENT

For the child who has been abused, this progression of self-learning and learning from parents, school, peers, and media is interrupted. Sexual activity at a level beyond the child's cognitive, emotional, and physiological understanding is imposed on the child. The learning imposed is distorted and is discordant with the child's developmental stage. For the child who experiences neglect or emotional abuse or who experiences sexual abuse from someone important to him, learning related to caring and loving is also distorted.

The behavior most consistently shown to distinguish between children who have been sexually abused and children who have not been sexually abused is increased sexualized behavior (Beitchman, Zucker, Hood, daCosta, & Akman, 1991; Eibender & Friedrich, 1989; Friedrich, 1993; Friedrich et al., 1992; Friedrich, Urquiza, & Beilke, 1986; Gomez-Schwartz, Horowitz, & Cardarelli, 1990). Adolescent boys who had been sexually abused as children report significantly higher levels of sexual dysfunction than nonabused adolescents as well as a higher prevalence of homosexual behavior (Johnson & Shrier, 1987). Higher levels of prostitution and sexual promiscuity have been reported by adolescent girls who had been sexually abused compared with non-abused adolescents (Cavaiola & Schiff, 1988; Goldston, Turnquist, & Knutson, 1989; Kendall-Tackett, Williams, & Finkelhor, 1993; Van Gijseghem & Gauthier, 1994). In a study of adolescent female behavior with an unknown male, girls who had been sexually abused showed significantly more flirtatious behaviors and submissive behaviors than did girls who had not been abused (Mausert-Mooney, as reported in Putnam, 1997). Greater gender identity confusion has also been reported (Aiosa-Karpas, Karpas, Pelcovitz, & Kaplan, 1991). Studies of children who molest other children indicate that a high proportion of these children (in some cases 100%) were themselves sexually abused (Johnson, 1993). Gil and Johnson (1993) have described the sexually intrusive behaviors of children who have been abused as ranging from normal sexual exploration to sexually reactive to extensive mutual sexual behaviors to molestation. Sexual molestation by children has been variously described as a learned response, a reenactment of the trauma, an effort to avoid powerlessness (sometimes referred to as identification with the aggressor), and an effort to avoid feelings of anger, confusion, anxiety (Gil & Johnson, 1993), or loneliness (Friedrich, 1995). Friedrich (1995) highlights the role of behavior dys-regulation in extreme sexualized behavior. Sexual molesting by children, in that it reflects issues other than sexuality, is not covered in the present discussion.

Studies with adults, similarly, indicate higher levels of sexual dys-function and dissatisfaction for both males and females sexually abused as children or adolescents (Beitchman et al., 1992). Clinical studies have found sexual compulsions, confusion around sexual orientation, and dysfunctional relationships to be characteristics of males who were sexually abused in childhood (Bruckner & Johnson, 1987; Dimock, 1988). Dichotomous responses—withdrawal from sexual contact or sexuality without intimacy—are reported.

Abuse of boys by a male has been found to be a particularly strong predictor of poor sexual satisfaction and sexual maladjustment (Mendel, 1995). Abuse of boys by a female is a strong predictor of adult sexual assault toward adult women (Mendel, 1995). Because victimization does not fit into society's concept of masculinity, boys who have been abused often feel their masculinity is threatened. Mendel (1995) concludes from his national survey of males that "men who have been sexually abused appear to live in a state of dissonance, struggling to find congruence between these conflicting aspects [victim/male] of their lives" (p. 205). Concerns around becoming sexually abusive occur frequently (Bruckner & Johnson, 1987). The experience of childhood sexual abuse has been found at twice the incidence in a population of male sex offenders as in the general male population (Groth, 1979).

For women, dysfunctional sexual behavior, defined as use of sexual interactions for other than intimacy and pleasure, has been found to correlate with childhood sexual abuse (Briere & Runtz, 1990). Within both clinical and nonclinical samples, women sexually abused as children have reported more orgasmic dysfunction and compulsive sexualized behaviors than have nonabused women (Goodwin, Cheeves, & Connell, 1989; Meiselman, 1978). Disruption of sexuality within relationships—for example, being orgasmic with new partners but not following marriage—has been reported (Gelinas, 1983).

## ❏ Therapy

Reconnecting to the process of normal sexual development and to sexuality as a personal and meaningful expression of self is an important part of therapy for a child who has been sexually abused. Reactions to the sexual aspect of the abuse need to be sorted out.

### RECONNECTING TO HEALTHY DEVELOPMENT

When children are abused and internalize a sense of themselves as altered or damaged, they no longer are able to trust the reactions and changes in their bodies. Therapy can provide an opportunity for children to reconnect to their sexual development, to their bodies as important parts of them, to appropriate sexual behavior, and to themselves as sexual beings.

*Sexual development.* Children who have been sexually abused all too often interpret both previous and subsequent nonabusive sexual experiences as negative, and therefore as indicating something negative about them. A therapist has an opportunity to help a child place both past and future sexual experiences within a healthy context. The giggliness and curiosity of normal early sexual experiences and the suspense and somewhat titillating aspect of thinking ahead to future experiences can be evoked by the therapist.

> **Samantha** (a 15-year-old sexually abused between ages 11 and 13 and approached again at 14 by her mother's boyfriend) looks back over her timeline.

**Therapist:** When you were little, maybe 4 or 5 or maybe younger or older, did you ever play doctor games or "I'll show you mine if you show me yours"?

**Samantha:** I did that with my cousin.

**Therapist:** That can be lots of fun. Did you get all giggly over it or what happened? Did your parents ever find out?

**Samantha:** Yes, my mother, and did she ever get mad.

**Therapist:** That's too bad, because that may have taken the fun out of it. I guess your mother didn't know about normal child development. That is something a lot of kids do. Kids can learn about each other's bodies that way. Do you remember what it was like before your mother found you?

**Samantha:** I remember that we were in the closet and there wasn't much light. Yeah, it was pretty funny.

**Therapist:** How did you first learn about boys having penises?

**Samantha:** Well, when we were all little we used to take baths together. Then when we were older, my brothers would try to peek on me and I didn't like that.

**Therapist:** Baths together when kids are young are normal and can be fun. But you are right, when you got older and wanted privacy, your mother should have put tighter restrictions on your brothers. Curiosity is normal, but, at the same time, there has to be a learning of each person's right to privacy. What were some of the things you were curious about about sex?

**Samantha:** Oh, I don't know. Mom was pretty open. She would answer my questions.

**Therapist:** What about looking at or touching friends as you and they started to develop breasts and pubic hair?

**Samantha:** Yeah, I did that with a friend when we were about 11. She had gotten some hair and I hadn't.

**Therapist:** It is really fascinating to an 11-year-old. And that's the age kids get crushes on adults or older teens. You may have had a crush on David.

**Samantha:** I thought he was wonderful. Mom said I flirted with him. Maybe that's why the abuse happened.

**Therapist:** No. Flirting is not asking for abuse. Kids have a right to try out feelings and behaviors and adults have the responsibility of putting in guidelines.

**Samantha:** He told me he was educating me but he wasn't. I didn't need his education.

**Therapist:** You're right. You did find out, as a kid, about sex in a really normal way. David touching you and having you touch him was not fair. It's nice that you did and still can do your own educating.

A lot of kids learn that if they rub their genitals it feels good and so they do it, masturbating, when they want that good feeling. Did you masturbate when you were little or do you do it now?

**Samantha:** (pulls back in the chair) Ugh, that's dirty.

**Therapist:** Sometimes people talk about it that way or sometimes, if you first get physical sensations from your vagina or clitoris during the abuse, you start to connect the feelings with the abuse and that can make it seem dirty. But the sensations are part of the way a person's body works and they are really special. It can be sort of an alive feeling. What do you suppose it would be like to have those sensations when you rub yourself or when you are with someone you really care for and they touch you?

**Samantha:** As far as I am concerned, I think sex is all overrated. I can take it or leave it.

**Therapist:** Sounds as if maybe you would like to give yourself some space from it right now. But I know you have told me that you are sexual with your boyfriend. What is that like for you?

**Samantha:** Oh, sometimes it is okay but other times I just go along with it to keep him, you know if I didn't he wouldn't keep going with me.

**Therapist:** Puts you in a real quandary. What would you like the sexual contact between the two of you to be like?

A therapist needs to be relaxed with the topic of sex and with normal developmental stages of sexuality if he is to be able to provide, for the child, a sense of normality and comfort around sexuality. Asking about and providing an opportunity for the child to smile at previous experiences can be helpful. If a child has not had early sexual experiences, this also can be normalized. In the case of experiences that have not yet occurred, therapy can establish anticipation. Positive anticipation helps an adolescent be more open to future sexual activity and, thus, better able to experience it as positive.

By talking about normal physiological and emotional changes, a therapist can help a child link experiences, even those that occurred within an abusive event, to part of the process of growing up. Talking about an orgasm as the discovery of one's own sexual response helps to shift this experience away from being swallowed up in the negativity of abuse to part of the child's process of becoming sexually aware. An orgasm can be talked about as an experience that has many aspects. A child can be encouraged to look forward to the mutual caring and positive aspects of orgasms she will be able to discover in the future.

It is important for boys to understand about penile response. When abuse interrupts a boy's sexual self-discovery, he may not have a chance to learn that a penis becomes erect for many reasons. Physical jolting, touch, being excited, or thinking about something sexual or something dangerous may cause an erection. A boy may not know that an erection does *not* mean that he wants something sexual.

> **David** (a developmentally delayed 12-year-old sexually abused by his mother from a young age to age 8) explains to the therapist that the abuse occurred because he wanted it. As a baby he used to get erections and the erections let his mother know he wanted to be touched.

> **Therapist:** David, all baby boys have erections. Penises in little boys work that way, sometimes they get stiff when they get bumped or they get stiff when the baby is thrown up in the air. All sorts of different reasons. And then when boys get older and they think about something—it could even be the abuse they think about—their penis will start to go hard. That doesn't mean they want to be touched.

> **David:** But it felt good when she tickled me there.

> **Therapist:** Of course it did. Your penis is made so that it will feel good when touched. And you can touch your own penis and have that good feeling. It is your right, it is every kid's right, to find out about their own good feelings. And you can do that when you touch and rub yourself. But no one has the right to touch a child sexually. Nor should an adult touch another adult unless that adult wants to be touched. (continued on page 163)

Information about physical responding is particularly important for children who were told by their abusers that the children's physical responses to the abuse proved they wanted it.

Children often find it helpful to read about sexual development, either on their own or together with a parent or therapist.[1] Gordon, Schroeder, and Abrams (1990b) found that although young children (ages 2-7) who had been abused demonstrated a similar level of sexual knowledge to that of children who had not been abused, they showed a higher level of emotional reactivity to sexual content. Clinical observation indicates that as these children become older they often acquire less accurate sexual information than do other children. High emotional reactivity can lead to conscious avoidance or unconscious dissociation during sex education classes and kibitzing about sex between peers. Children who have been sexually abused are all too likely to label normal body changes and normal sexual responding as abnormal or perverted.

It can be helpful for the therapist to find out how a child first learned about intercourse. If the initial learning was within the context of abuse, the therapist will want, at some point, to talk about the aspect of intercourse that provides an intimate connection between two people who care for each other. Intercourse can be described as a way that two adults can be close and provide pleasure for themselves and each other. The fact that the child's knowledge or experience of intercourse contradicts this allows the therapist to highlight the distinction between sexual abuse and sexual intimacy. The therapist can talk about the discovery of sexual intimacy as an experience the child has ahead of him.

Discussing normal age-appropriate sexual behavior within a family session helps to educate parents as well as the child. The topics of sexuality and sexual behavior are opened up for discussion within the family.

*The body as an important and healthy part of self.* For many individuals sexually abused as children, the body becomes a hated part of the self. The child experiences the body as the part of herself to which the abuse occurred. In some cases, the child may blame her body for the abuse having happened. Although for some children this negative response starts at the time of the abuse, for others abused at a young age, when body-consciousness is not as strong, the negative response develops when the child reaches puberty.

For a child abused at a young age, therapy and future physical activities can help the child build a positive awareness of her body. This creates for the child a relationship with her body totally separate from the abuse. Activities such as ballet, judo, and gymnastics that emphasize body awareness and body control are suggested for children who have been abused. Sports such as swimming or track, during which a child becomes more attuned to her body, can be helpful. Within therapy, a child can be engaged in conversations about body changes and how it will feel to start developing breasts or pubic hair.

**Tanya** (a 9-year-old sexually abused at ages 5 and 6 by an older brother) talks with the therapist about her upcoming birthday.

**Therapist:** It is really exciting to get older. I guess one of the changes is having your body start to develop. Are you finding that your breasts have started to grow? (Tanya grins and nods.) Do you touch them sometimes to see if they are getting bigger? (Tanya nods.) Kinda neat, isn't it? Some kids find that they like having their body change and some kids don't—what's it like for you?

**Tanya:** I don't like the idea of boys looking at me.

**Therapist:** They get really curious, don't they? I guess some of that has to do with their bodies being so different and some of it has to do with their thinking that looking at girls is a way of being a big shot. But what is important is how it feels to you, because bodies are special and each of us has a right to our own body privacy.

**Tanya:** Sure didn't feel that way with creepy Dick.

**Therapist:** No, Dick didn't know about bodies being private. That was what was so good about your telling Mom when she asked what was going on. Your body is yours and you can make decisions about it. Not about how fast or how much it grows—that just goes on, doesn't it—but about what you wear and how you move and who can sit close to you and who can touch you.

For children abused at an older age, the negativity from the abuse is more likely to pervade the body concept. For these children, particularly adolescents, it is often a long process to regain a positive sense of self and body. Acknowledging negative feelings can be an important first step in moving the feelings to a more cognitive level. A child can then become aware of why the negative body feelings are there. As this occurs, the therapist can introduce more positive aspects of the body.

> **Cindy** (a 17-year-old sexually abused between ages 12 and 15 by her father, who was highly manipulative and controlling) talks with the therapist about her dislike of her body. She explains that her father used to compare her breasts to her mother's breasts.

> **Therapist:** How unfair, he didn't let you have a chance to get to know your own body and appreciate your body. When you think about your breasts now, what do you notice about them?

> **Cindy:** I don't.

> **Therapist:** If you gave yourself a chance to think about them, what do you think you would notice? (no response) When you have children, do you think you will choose to breast-feed or bottle-feed?

> **Cindy:** Oh, I want to breast-feed.

> **Therapist:** And that's a special connection you have with your breasts. A connection that allows you to be really close to your future babies and close to your body. [If Cindy had indicated that she would bottle-feed, the therapist could have highlighted Cindy's having control over what happens with her breasts, her body.]

An adolescent can be encouraged to participate in activities such as tae kwon do, tai chi chuan, or yoga to increase awareness of each body part and to gain a sense of control over her body. A therapist can also help an adolescent center on whatever part of the body or body movement he does like and encourage discussion about that.

> **James** (a 13-year-old sexually abused at age 8 by his mother's boyfriend and at 12 by an older neighborhood boy) talks with the therapist about his favorite activities. He describes his passion for skateboarding.

> **Therapist:** What are the tricks that you do on the skateboard?

> **James:** Well, I can run up this ramp and then flip the board out from under me and it flips and then I come down on it.

> **Therapist:** That must take a lot of muscle strength in your legs, but also, how is it you move your upper body to make it all happen?

**James:** I never thought about it. (stands up and starts leaning in different directions) Okay, when I lean like this, that leg pushes. See, you can feel it straight through your body.

Awareness can, with time and encouragement, lead to appreciation. Older adolescents may be able to use some of the self-exploration exercises suggested by Wendy Maltz (1991).

*Age-appropriate behaviors.* An abuser, by providing rewards for sexualized behaviors or by telling a child that he is teaching her what she should do when dating, creates a distorted understanding of interpersonal behavior. The young child, following what she has been taught, rubs up against adults in order to please them. The school-age child, thinking it is expected, French-kisses a boy she has just met. An adolescent, wanting boys to like her, has intercourse indiscriminately.

With a young child, the therapist learns of inappropriate behavior either through the child's behavior in the session or through the parents' description of behavior in the home. When a child becomes sexually inappropriate during a session, the therapist needs to (a) identify the behavior as something learned from the abuse, (b) explain that the behavior is not what the therapist or other people want, (c) suggest an appropriate behavior, and then (d) reward the child for the new behavior.

**Amy** (a 6-year-old sexually abused by several boarders living in the home and possibly by her stepfather) announces that she is going to take her shirt off.

**Therapist:** You were taught by the men living in your house that people want to look at your body, that people like you when you show them your body. But no, your body is yours, and because it is private for you, I don't want to look at it. I like it when you show me the way you make things or the way you play.

**Amy:** I'm going to take it off. (starts pulling off shirt)

**Therapist:** I'll turn my chair around while your shirt is off because your body is private. (turns chair around) Let me know when your shirt is back on so I can watch you making things or playing. I like to do those things with you. . . . Seems like it is really hard for you to believe that I don't want to see your body. Let's see, what could you show me—I remember the airplane you made. I liked it when you showed me that.

Sexualized behavior should not be allowed to continue within a therapy session. Although sexualized behavior during therapy may be a reenacting of the abuse in order to understand better what happened, it also indicates that the child either does not understand social mores or does not have adequate impulsivity control.[2] Allowing this behavior is viewed by some therapists as providing an opportunity to work through the abuse. However, because therapy is a generally accepting and supporting environment, the ignoring of sexualized behavior may be misunderstood by a child as acceptance or approval of the behavior. The sexualized aspects of the abuse can be worked through using play objects or talking. Ignoring the behavior would mean that the child would lose an important opportunity for learning social mores and personal control.

> David (see page 158) passes by the therapist on his way out of the session. The back of his hand rubs against the therapist's leg. At first the therapist thinks this happened by mistake, and then, recalling the abuse scenario (being rubbed on his legs and genitals and having to rub his mother on her legs and genitals), realizes that it was a sexualized action. By the time the therapist realizes all of this, David is out of the room.
>
> When reviewing her notes before the beginning of the next session, the therapist reminds herself that the "leg rub" on the way out the week before is going to need to be discussed. Although she would generally wait for an issue to reappear in therapy, the therapist also realizes that not having drawn guidelines last week around the rubbing may have inadvertently reinforced for David the idea that women like to be rubbed. She will need to bring up what happened.
>
> During the session, the therapist asks David if he remembers what he did as he left the previous week.

David: Yeah, I said good-bye. It was fun last week.

Therapist: Yes, and you rubbed your hand against my leg. Maybe an old habit from what your mother taught you, but I do not like to have my legs touched or rubbed, women and girls do not like to have their legs touched or rubbed. When you are older and you care very much for someone and that person wants to be touched, then rubbing, in private, is all right.

I like it when you say good-bye when you leave and tell me if it has been a good session. Let's pretend it is the end of the session and practice your leaving without any touching.

Helping a child become aware of his behavior and, in time, monitor his own behavior is an important part of therapy for the older child with sexualized behavior.

Family therapy or parent therapy can provide support to parents in responding clearly and promptly when children behave sexually.

The **foster mother of Robbie** (a 6-year-old sexually abused from infancy to age 5 by his mother) reports that when Robbie is sitting next to her, he starts to rub her leg in a sensual manner. She tells him to stop and he will, for a moment, but then he starts again. She says it has reached the point that she simply tells him not to sit next to her anymore.

**Therapist:** Sounds as if Robbie is repeating with you something his mother taught him. Rather than avoiding it, let's use it as a chance to teach Robbie new behaviors, new ways to sit close to someone.

When he starts to rub your leg, make a comment about the rubbing he is doing. Be sure you state exactly what he is doing that is inappropriate. Children often have a hard time knowing exactly what it is they are supposed to be stopping. Tell Robbie that you know that the rubbing is something his mother taught him. Then tell him you don't like to be touched like that or rubbed by children and that other women don't want to be touched and rubbed by children. Then suggest something the two of you can do together. When Robbie does it, that will give you a chance to praise him.

You may have to do this several times before he unlearns the old behavior and learns a new behavior. Remember how long the abuse went on. This is really important for Robbie, and you can give him a chance to learn new behaviors.

With older children and adolescents, it can be helpful for the therapist to ask about the types of sexual activities they are involved in with their peers. Asking how they decide how much touching to do and when to do it provides the child with a chance to sort out what is appropriate and to identify behaviors that need changing.

Adolescents who have been abused often report that they either physically leave or dissociate when peers start talking about dating and dating activities. Because of this, they have no way to learn normative behavior. Therapy can provide such a time. Any questions asked by the therapist need to be respectful, not voyeuristic, and the adolescent can choose to answer or not to answer.

Some adolescents who have been abused will use sex as a way of being popular. This may result from their not knowing other ways of interacting with peers. A therapist can help an adolescent learn new ways to interact. At other times, adolescents continue in sexual situations even though they do not want to be sexual, because they lose their assertiveness once a sexual activity starts. The sexual activity can trigger the adolescent back to the time of the abuse and, thus, to herself at a younger age, with the more limited capabilities of that age. The therapist can help the adolescent figure out what is happening and then how to become grounded to herself now and her present capabilities (see page 66). For the adolescent who describes herself as enjoying being promiscuous, the therapist can wonder aloud about the part of her who likes to be close to another person. How does that part feel when the promiscuous behavior is going on?

Adolescents can be encouraged to think about how other people understand their behavior and whether this is the understanding that they want others to have of them.

*Sexuality as a positive aspect of self.* Being involved in a sexual interaction without any understanding of what is happening, with an experience of pain or fear or within an atmosphere of manipulation, creates for the child a link between sexuality and negative experiences. If this link is internalized, it becomes part of the child's internal sense of herself as a sexual being.

Talking about sexuality and what sexuality is can help a child differentiate between sexual abuse and sexuality. The negative experiences need to be placed with the abuse, not the child's sexuality. This can be particularly hard for a child who, having become engaged in the sexual activities, looked forward to them or sought them out and may have come to identify herself as sexually abnormal. In such a case, the therapist can encourage the adolescent to think about the situation from another perspective.

Susan (a 17-year-old sexually abused between ages 8 and 15 by an older brother) talks about when she would be at home alone with her brother after school. She comments that the abuse would occur in her brother's room.

**Therapist:** What would take you into his room?

**Susan:** At first he would bribe me, offer me candy and that sort of thing. Then he would just call me in and sometimes I would just go in.

**Therapist:** And when you went in, tell me about that.

**Susan:** It was for the sex. I'm really a sicko to have wanted that.

**Therapist:** It sounds as though you experienced normal arousal that feels good. But that you are thinking that it is wrong to have felt that.

**Susan:** I hated it, hated that I enjoyed it. And now when I have sex with my boyfriend, afterwards I just wash and wash and wash.

**Therapist:** Sounds like the situation in which the sexual sensations happened, a situation first created by your brother and a situation that never should have been created, has become mixed up with normal, good sexual sensations.

**Susan:** Just feels dirty.

**Therapist:** It's our job to separate out the dirt—the dirt that belongs with what shouldn't have happened—your brother abusing you, getting you entangled in a sexual activity—and does not belong with your own body feelings. We need to separate the feeling of dirt from feelings of sexuality.

**Susan:** Good luck.

**Therapist:** What would you tell an 8-year-old who asked you what sexuality was all about?

**Susan:** Well, if an 8-year-old asked me, it would mean she respected me. I'd probably say nothing, I wouldn't want to say something wrong.

**Therapist:** Sounds like you would want her to be able to find out on her own. Like you should have had a chance to do! And if you had, if you had had a chance to discover sexual sensations by yourself, what do you think you would have felt, thought about them?

**Susan:** Would have been kinda surprising, I guess.

In *The Sexual Healing Journey* (1991), Maltz talks about changing an individual's attitudes toward sex. She emphasizes the importance of recognizing the false ideas and myths that sexual abuse attaches to sex and then identifying the healthy components of sex. Because a child's life often does not provide opportunities for observing and learning about healthy sexuality, this needs to be brought up during therapy. Discussions of sexuality during group therapy are very helpful.

A child's unique experience needs to be considered. Was there pain involved, were there threats, did the child have to have an orgasm before the abuse would stop? If so, these characteristics probably became associated with that child's understanding of sexuality. Therapy provides a time when these experiences can be identified and then defined as distinct and separate from sexuality. Did the child cut off physical sensations or emotional reactions? If so, the possibility of experiencing sensations and reactions when choosing to be sexually intimate in the future can be discussed.

## SORTING THROUGH REACTIONS

Research and clinical work with adults who were sexually abused as children has helped therapists understand the effects of abuse on sexuality. Compulsive sexual thoughts and behaviors, confusion with regard to sexual orientation, dysfunctional relationships, sexual dissatisfaction, and sexually abusive behaviors have been reported (Beitchman et al., 1992; Bruckner & Johnson, 1987; Dimock, 1988; Goodwin et al., 1989; Meiselman, 1978). These behaviors, reflecting a child's abuse-related internal sense of self, indicate to therapists topics that need to be discussed.

*Compulsive behaviors.* Children may exhibit compulsive behaviors at home or in therapy or may report the occurrence of such behaviors. These behaviors may be connected to a child's wanting attention or arousal sensations, to a reenactment of memories of abuse, or to arousal occurring at that moment. They may also reflect poor regulation of behavior (Friedrich, 1995). By noting what is happening and talking with the child about it or reviewing what happened in consultation with a colleague, a therapist tries to identify the dynamics behind the behavior. These dynamics will need to be addressed for the compulsivity to decrease.

As the therapist identifies an internalization and then develops and provides a new interpersonal experience, the child's behavior may shift. If no shift or reaction occurs, the therapist continues to try to understand what is happening for the child. Inquiring about the behavior, when it happens, what it is like for the child, how it is similar to the abuse, how it is different from the abuse, where else the child may have seen it, or how it connects with early family messages can help the child and therapist understand the behavior. The possibility that the behavior is connected to a dissociated part also needs to be considered.

> **Jennie** (a 17-year-old multiply sexually abused as a child, diagnosed in the mentally retarded range, and referred for therapy because of concerns around her obsessive masturbation with objects) comes into the first therapy session wearing a string that has skipping rope handles on it. When the therapist inquires about the handles, Jennie smiles, makes a masturbatory gesture, and asks if the therapist is going to take them away.

> **Therapist:** [Realizes that removing the objects before understanding the meaning for Jennie will not be helpful.] No, our job here is to talk about and understand what is happening for you.

> **Jennie:** My worker has told me I have to get rid of the handles.

> **Therapist:** Tell me about the handles.

> **Jennie:** They look like a penis, like Tom's. I don't want to talk about that. Are the handles safe? (shows the handles to the therapist)

> **Therapist:** [Wonders whether the handles represent a concrete memory for Jennie, whether they connect to her sense of sexuality or whether they represent her wanting to feel physical stimulation.] Seems that it is really important to you that the handles be safe. You noticed that they look like a penis but you want them to be safe. [As she centers more on Jennie's concern with safety, the therapist realizes that Jennie may be using the handles to feel in more control of herself and her sexual responding. Perhaps the compulsive masturbating with objects is a response to her internalization of powerlessness or of no control over sexual responding.] With the handles, you are in charge; with the abuse, someone else was in charge.

> At the next therapy session, Jennie comes in with handles that she has decorated like faces and uses them like puppets to ask questions about Tom touching her. The therapist notes that Jennie is now in charge of learning about what happened, about her body, about keeping her body privacy safe.
>
> At the next therapy session, Jennie is not wearing the handles but has strung a plastic cover on elastic and is wearing it over her genitals. The

therapist notes her taking control over her genitals, her sexuality, and what touches her or does not touch her.

With other children, and particularly adolescents, compulsive sexual behaviors may not be mentioned during therapy. A therapist can ask a child what comes into his mind when he thinks of sex. If there appears to be any aberrant quality to the thought, the therapist and the child together can try to trace the thought. Was it something the abuser said or did, was it something that happened during the abuse, was it something separate from abuse that somehow became connected with the abuse?

> **Carl** (an 18-year-old sexually abused between ages 8 and 15 by a male neighbor), in reply to a question as to what comes to his mind when he thinks of sex, says, "Women, lots of women, lots of different women."

**Therapist:** That's interesting, because you have told me that you like one girl and that your relationship with her is really important to you. Where do you think the idea that sex means many females comes from? (Carl shrugs.) What did Mark tell you about sex?

**Carl:** Well, he used to say that a man had to have it with a lot of women, that's what made it good. He would tell me about all his different affairs.

**Therapist:** And what do you think?

**Carl:** I'd rather just be with my girlfriend, but I can't stop my thoughts about having sex all over the place. We have sex but it doesn't feel like enough— first it's great, then it just feels empty. I start fantasizing about other females.

**Therapist:** Do you know that you can use your girlfriend in your fantasies, that when it starts to feel empty you can take your mind back to the feelings you had with her just a moment before and really concentrate on them, that you can think of other places and times you would like to be with her?

Through discussion of the behavior, as well as possible reasons for the behavior, the process becomes more cognitive, and the child will experience himself as having more control. The internalizations of powerlessness and of sexuality as a negative experience may start to shift. When a child's behaviors are extreme and hurtful to the child or others, more direct external controls may be needed (Friedrich, 1995). Placing clear guidelines around extreme behaviors is important in providing the child with protection both from being hurt and from becoming abusive.

Children who have been sexually abused are aware of the general impression that children who have been abused will become abusers. Clarifying that there is not a direct line from being abused to being sexually abusive is important in separating the child from past abuse and future sexuality from sexual abuse.[3]

*Sexual orientation.* Research with both males and females has indicated a higher incidence of homosexuality among adults who experienced childhood sexual abuse than among nonabused adults (see reviews in Beitchman et al., 1992; Mendel, 1995). Mendel (1995) clarifies that concern related to sexual orientation is experienced by both heterosexual and homosexual males and most particularly by males who were severely abused.

A therapist can help an adolescent talk about sexual orientation, or, for those who cannot talk about it, can describe as normal the confusion around orientation (Pearce & Pezzot-Pearce, 1997).

> **Mark** (a 13-year-old sexually abused by his older brother between ages 5 and 8) talks about girlfriends and how they are always hanging around him.
>
> **Therapist:** [Remembers that the group home workers had told her that Mark avoids all girls and wonders what the present conversation means. She remembers negative comments Mark has made about homosexuality and wonders if Mark's conversation may reflect an anxiety that the abuse from his brother means he is homosexual.] You seem really anxious that I know about all these girls, and I am kind of wondering if you are worried as to whether girls like you or you like girls.
>
> **Mark:** Sure I like girls.
>
> **Therapist:** [Noting that Mark centered on his reaction, not the reaction of girls to him.] And if you like girls, that's fine, and if you don't like girls, that's fine. And if you feel attracted to boys, that's fine, and if you don't feel attracted to boys, that's fine. Some boys who were abused by older boys or men start to wonder if the abuse means they are homosexual. What John did was not homosexuality. Homosexuality occurs between two adult males or two adult females who want to have a sexual relationship. An older male, like your brother, sexually touching a boy is sexual abuse, not homosexuality.
>
> **Mark:** I don't know why you are making all this fuss.

**Therapist:** Some boys think that if they had an erection during the abuse that means they are homosexual or that they wanted the touching. Boys' penises become hard and erect when something sexual occurs or even when they think about sexual things, that's simply the way penises respond.

**Mark:** Sex between males is weird.

**Therapist:** It may seem that way, but sex between two adults who care for each other and who want to be sexual is special and not weird. A lot of boys who were abused by a male struggle with their reactions toward other boys or men—both positive reactions and negative reactions. That's a normal struggle. What's the struggle like for you?

*Dysfunctional relationships.* When a child is abused by someone close to her, she experiences distorted personal relationships. The abuser, who should have been the nurturer, imposed his needs on the child. Not only the child's needs but also the child's personal boundaries were not respected. The child internalizes an absence of boundaries as well as the necessity of meeting other people's needs. As the child forms relationships, these internalizations influence her expectations and, thus, her behavior toward other people.

Future relationships are also affected by the many sexual myths in our society. Therapy can provide an opportunity, particularly for the adolescent, to explore these myths.

> Jane (a 17-year-old sexually abused as a child by her father, a domineering and frightening man, and raped recently following an evening at a dance club) reports that she finally has told her boyfriend about the abuse. She explains that since then she has started to feel more relaxed with him.

**Therapist:** What is that like, feeling more relaxed?

**Jane:** Well, I have to be careful. I certainly don't want to neck with him because maybe then he would get aroused and I would say no and that wouldn't be fair to him. And I would be at fault.

**Therapist:** Wait, each person is responsible for handling their own arousal. You're responsible for handling your arousal and Tim is responsible for handling his arousal. Being aroused doesn't mean you have to be sexual.

**Jane:** Well, for boys, it is all the same thing. If they get aroused, they need sex.

**Therapist:** They may or may not want to be sexual, but they don't *need* to be. Boys can become "unaroused" and if the person they are with doesn't want to be sexual, then they have a responsibility not to be sexual.

**Jane:** I wonder if Tim knows that.

**Therapist:** What would happen if you talked with him about it? What do you want in your relationship with Tim or with some other boy in the future?

The therapeutic relationship in itself can provide a model of open, respectful conversation. For some adolescents, this will be the first time they have been listened to carefully and with respect.

*Sexual dissatisfaction.* Sexual abuse and, indeed, sometimes the therapy following abuse can cause a child to feel that sexual touching is bad. Sexual touching as a positive experience and as a way two adults who love each other can give each other pleasure needs to discussed. The possibility of the child's being able to enjoy sexual touching when he reaches adulthood needs to be reaffirmed. This is particularly important for a child who does not have, within his family, an example of a positive sexual relationship.

**Timmy** (a 5-year-old sexually abused at age 4 by his grandfather) draws on the blackboard a picture of a penis and a hand. He then takes his finger and rubs at his picture of the penis.

**Therapist:** Tell me about the rubbing.

**Timmy:** Getting rid of it.

**Therapist:** It's not fair for Grandpa to have touched your penis. But penises are okay and really important. They don't need to be gotten rid of. You can rub your own penis to get a good feeling and, when you are grown-up and you love someone, that person can touch and rub your penis because it is a way of showing special loving. But, because it is special, people save it until they are older.

*Replay of abuse.* Children who have been abused may at times within the therapy act out the role of the abuser, or may tell the therapist to act out the abuser role. This can put the therapist in a dilemma. Should the therapist follow the child's lead and permit a replaying of the abuse, which could retraumatize the child, could reinforce abuse-related internalizations, or could, by being allowed, imply that the behavior is acceptable? Or should the therapist not follow the child's lead and risk having the child feel nonvalidated or losing an opportunity for the child to explore an important issue? The danger of the first alternative is far greater than the danger of the second.[4]

Work with traumatized children has indicated that a replay of trauma, without some change, does not resolve the trauma (Pynoos & Nader, 1993; Terr, 1990) and may indeed retraumatize the child (Terr, 1990). In addition, given that abuse of a child can cause a chronic neurological effect leading to higher levels of system arousal (Everly, 1993; van der Kolk, 1996b) and impulsivity (Perry, 1996), clear guidelines around behavior, and in particular aggressive or sexualized behavior, are important.

Working within the framework of the internalization model, the therapist can consider whether a reenactment reflects the child's internalization of herself as powerless, the child's internalization of herself as an object to be used, or the child's acting out of an internalized memory of being abused or not protected. The therapist can review what has happened previously in the session and the feeling within the session and within himself to determine which internalization is being acted out.[5]

**Therapist:** It may be that you are feeling lost or powerless and that it feels as though the only way to be in control is to be like M. How else could you be in control now?

**Therapist:** It seems that you are feeling you should be abused. No, you are you, a special person whom no one else should hurt.

**Therapist:** You may be remembering the abuse and how M did that to you. It is my job here to protect you from being hurt.

**Therapist:** You may be letting me know what it was like when M abused you.

The child may be trying to work out her confusion as to why the abuse happened or why the perpetrator acted in a particular way. The child may be playing out her rage and, because of the modeling she experienced within the abuse or within her family, chooses abusive behavior to express rage.

**Therapist:** You may be wondering what it would be like to abuse someone, why someone abuses? What do you think?

**Therapist:** A lot of anger, and it makes sense that you are angry, but it's not fair to hurt someone, not fair for M to have hurt you. What else could you do with your anger?

In most cases, when this type of play emerges, the pace of the session is such that the therapist has little time to think. Most important for the therapist to remember is that reenacting trauma is not reparative. The child, the therapist, or the doll needs to be protected. The child needs to know that her world now is different from her world at the time of the abuse, that she will be protected from hurt and from hurting. Although limiting behavior may indeed close out exploration of certain feelings or reactions, it provides important behavior guidelines and safety for the child. The child needs to know she can control herself in a way that her rageful or abusive feelings do not hurt people or animals.

If a child becomes aroused during a therapy session, the therapist should comment on the child's reaction. The arousal can be talked about as (a) normal responding to the topic with which they are dealing and (b) a response that can decrease on its own. Children who have been abused have all too often learned the myth that arousal necessitates sexual behavior.

## ❑ Therapeutic Process

Children, and particularly adolescents, are surrounded by sexual behavior—in television, books, and peers' jokes and innuendo. For children who have been abused, this behavior also exists within their memories and, for some, within flashbacks. Yet sexual behavior and sexuality is seldom discussed in families. Even among peers, it may be talked about only through exaggerated stories or giggled comments. Some therapists may find discussions of sexuality to be awkward or contrived, and therefore may avoid them. Without the opportunity to discuss sexual issues during therapy, however, many children are left with an abuse-laden understanding of sexuality and an abuse-related sense of their own sexuality.

A therapist needs to think through her own reactions to and comfort with sexual topics. She needs to be open to different forms of sexual expression and to think through carefully the differentiation between sexuality and sexual abuse. If the therapist was herself abused, she needs to have worked through that experience and to have sorted out her own internalizations of herself as a sexual person (Wieland, 1997).

Within the therapy, it will, for the most part, be the therapist's job to clarify and pursue topics related to sex and sexuality. And it will be the therapist's job to be sure that, within the play or the conversation, the child has a sense of control over the session. The therapist needs to take care that the child does not feel abused and is not left feeling vulnerable.

## INTRODUCING THE TOPIC

A therapist cannot wait for a child to bring up topics related to sex, because most children learn that sex is not to be discussed with adults. Therapists themselves, because of early learning and experiences or lack of learning and experiences, may find it difficult to notice issues related to sex and sexuality and, when they do notice such issues, may find it difficult to talk about them. Therapists have the responsibility to work through their own reluctance around sexual topics. Once a therapist has done that, she will be more alert to play patterns, behaviors, and conversations that indicate a child's concern, at some level, with sex or sexuality.

Sexualized behaviors or reactions that occur during therapy can be noted and explored.

> **Alice** (a 10-year-old sexually abused between ages 7 and 9 by an uncle) starts to become tense and somewhat flushed while she is describing an abuse scenario.

> **Therapist:** It seems that you may be feeling some physical response, perhaps some tingling between your legs or in your body now as we talk about what happened. And that may be a feeling you experienced when the abuse happened. That would make sense, because our bodies do react when

certain parts of the body, like the genitals, are touched; that's the way bodies are.

A child talking about boyfriends or girlfriends or the wish to have a boyfriend or girlfriend may indicate concerns related to sexual interactions. A therapist should not, however, automatically assume sexual content, because the conversation may also indicate a fear of betrayal. Play that includes sexualized actions by toys or by the child usually indicates that sexual issues or memories are relevant at that point for the child.

Talking about early childhood provides an opportunity to explore and normalize early sexual experiences. Completing a genogram or timeline provides a therapist with an opportunity to ask about family messages related to sexuality or sexual behaviors.

> Trish (a 16-year-old sexually abused between ages 9 and 11 by her mother) completes a genogram with the therapist. The therapist asks what messages were passed down through Trish's father's family about sex.
>
> Trish: Well, until I told last spring about the abuse, my dad never said anything to me about sex. Now, after all this, he has started telling me that I better not sleep around.
>
> Therapist: Why do you think he is saying that?
>
> Trish: He seems to think that I'll use sex to get friends.
>
> Therapist: What do you think?
>
> Trish: I don't know. I mean, what does he think I am? Does he think I can't get friends or does he suddenly think I am all sex? He never said it before.
>
> Therapist: Sounds as if he has confused sexual abuse and sexual behavior. Sometimes the two get mixed up in people's minds, but they are *not* the same thing. How might you explain the difference to him? (continued on p. 177)

## ESTABLISHING THE CHILD AS IN CONTROL OF THE CONVERSATION

Because the child was not in control while the abuse was occurring, it is important that the child be in control of conversations during therapy. This can, however, place the therapist in a difficult position. When a topic has been raised that a child does not want to pursue, the child's wish needs to be respected. At the same time, having a topic, such as sexuality, not discussed can reinforce for the child that the topic is too "disgusting" or awkward to be discussed. This would increase the child's vulnerability.

A therapist needs to respect a child's wish to stop talking about something, yet, at the same time, clarify that the topic does not imply anything negative about the child. The therapist needs to be sure that the child is comforted in some way.

> Trish (see p. 176) and the therapist talk about some of Trish's early sexual experiences and then some of her experiences with her boyfriend. Trish comments on how weird this is.

> **Therapist:** Talking about sexuality or the sexuality?

> **Trish:** Talking about it.

> **Therapist:** It's not just normal everyday conversation, is it. And if you want to stop, just let me know. I think it is important to talk about because sometimes sexuality and sexual abuse get mixed up even though they are very different.
>   The reason I was asking about sexual activity with your boyfriend is that sometimes young people find that some parts of sexual intimacy are not enjoyable.

> **Trish:** Well, I don't like it when, you know, he comes down on me.

> **Therapist:** Can you tell him that?

> **Trish:** Yes.

> **Therapist:** And what does he do?

> **Trish:** He stops. I don't want to talk about this anymore.

> **Therapist:** [Feels in an awkward spot—she has to respect Trish's wish not to talk, but it is also clear that this is a topic that needs to be addressed.] All right. We don't need to talk about it, but I do want to let you know why I asked. Sometimes a sexual activity will remind you of something that happened during the abuse and it takes your mind back, and that's not fair to you.

> **Trish:** My mother did something like that.

**Therapist:** We can go back now, or some other time, and let the younger Trish know that Mom never should have done that but that the "now you," the older Trish, can decide herself whether she wants to experience something and get enjoyment from it.

**Trish:** Okay.

**Therapist:** Where is the younger Trish right now?

**Trish:** In her room. (starts to look distressed)

**Therapist:** [Realizes that she should not have continued to pursue this but concerned about leaving Trish in a distressing memory.] What does the younger Trish need?

**Trish:** I don't want to do this.

**Therapist:** I hear how scary this is and that you don't want to look at it anymore, but I am also concerned about the younger Trish and that we mustn't just leave her there. Could you take the "now Trish," the 16-year-old Trish into the picture, maybe all the way in or maybe just to the edge? If you can see her, nod your head to let me know.

**Trish:** (nods) She is in the doorway. It's the first time, mother had me take my clothes off and she took her clothes off.

**Therapist:** [Aware of Trish's wish not to go through the memory.] And the 16-year-old in the doorway, what does she notice?

**Trish:** The little Trish is frightened.

**Therapist:** And the 16-year-old who noticed what mother did not notice, what can she do for the little frightened Trish? Just watch and let me know.

**Trish:** She went over and hugged her.

Creating safety and comfort around the topic of sex and sexuality is important. Although it is important that these discussions not be initiated until the child has gained a sense of safety in therapy and with the therapist, it is essential that they do occur at some point.

## ❏ Summary

Sexuality is an important part of each child's internal sense of self. When sexual abuse occurs, a child loses part of normal self-exploration and self-development. Therapy can provide an opportunity for the child to regain healthy development and to sort through distorted experiences and internalizations.

Discussions of sexuality, however, often do not occur during therapy. A therapist needs to be comfortable with the topic of sexuality and with talking about it. As a therapist's comfort level increases, she becomes more alert to play, behavior, and conversation that indicate concerns around sexuality. A therapist can ask about early experiences and present experiences. A therapist can ask about the messages and behaviors in the family around sex. Concerns can be explored, normalizing information given, the possibility of positive experiences raised, and appropriate behavior guidelines established.

## ❏ Notes

1. Books such as *Growing Up Feeling Good* (Rosenberg, 1995) can be helpful.

2. Because of the chronic arousal effect trauma can have on the brain stem and midbrain, together with the decreased development of cortical brain areas occurring with neglect (Perry, 1996), a child who has been sexually abused may have less control over impulsivity than do other children (see also Friedrich, 1995). Initial research indicates alteration within numerous neurobiological systems as a result of trauma (Putnam, 1997) and maltreatment (DeBellis & Putnam, 1994).

3. As noted previously, it may be helpful for a therapist to tell a child about research showing that only a minority of males (I have found no research related to females) who were sexually abused as children later sexually abuse children themselves. Bagley, Wood, and Young (1994) found in a study of 117 males ages 18-27 that 87% of the men who had been sexually abused on one occasion and 63% of the men who had been sexually abused on multiple occasions had *not* as adults abused children.

4. Prior (1996), in his discussion of the therapeutic value of violent play for experiencing mastery and new positive relationships, notes that the child and therapist together need to walk a fine line for the play not to be retraumatizing. He does not, however, discuss the dangers involved if they stray from that fine line.

5. Davies and Frawley (1994) discuss the replay of the abuse scenario through transference and countertransference. I have discussed this in my own work in relation to therapy with children and adolescents (Wieland, 1997).

# 7

## *Avoiding the Thoughts: Resistance*

When a child is sexually abused, she has few ways to resist what is happening. When a child enters therapy, there are many ways for her to resist. Resisting and, in time, moving beyond the resistance are important parts of therapy for the child or adolescent who has been sexually abused. Resisting is important and positive in that the child asserts herself and does not accommodate to the needs of the parent or therapist. Similarly, choosing to move beyond the resistance is important. The child is taking control of her future.

Resistance, however, places the therapist in a dilemma. The healthy aspect of resistance needs to be respected and, indeed, encouraged for a child who has few skills for asserting herself. Yet, at the same time, the therapist knows that if resistance does not shift, therapy may be of limited help to the child. By observing the resistance, the therapist can become more sensitive to the child's needs. By identifying within resistance other dynamics, the therapist can develop more appropriate interventions. By looking for the reasons behind resistance, the therapist can address the child's issues.

Within the psychoanalytic literature, resistance has been defined as anything that blocks the emergence of the unconscious or the working through of the conscious (Chethik, 1989; Pearson, 1968). Within therapeutic discussions, the term resistance is often used to describe behaviors that frustrate a therapist. For purposes of the present discussion, resistance is defined as an avoidance of therapy. This may be an avoidance of the topic of abuse or other early experiences, an avoidance of the emotional and physical feelings related to the abuse, or an avoidance of a relationship within therapy. Resistance may occur on the part of the child, the parent, or the therapist.

The present chapter discusses resistance by the child, the parent, and the therapist. The discussion of child resistance considers a variety of dynamics that may be present and, if so, need to be addressed directly. The reasons behind resistance and ways to help a child through resistance are explored.

## ❏ The Child's Resistance

### RECOGNIZING RESISTANCE

Children have many ways of avoiding therapy. The young child can refuse to come into the room or, once in the room, to play. Play may center on methodical games. The older child can become disengaged by replying "I don't know" repeatedly or by not replying at all. The adolescent can forget appointments or come late. He may talk continuously and thereby leave no space for the therapist, or he may discount each thing the therapist says.

These behaviors may indicate more than just a wish to avoid therapy. They may indicate (a) transference, a portrayal of earlier relationships; (b) dissociation, a coping style that allows the child to separate himself from what is going on; (c) regression, an anxiety response that blocks more developed capabilities; or (d) "time-out," a time simply to integrate all that has been going on. It is important that the therapist recognize these additional meanings, when they occur, and address the reasons behind the behaviors.

*Recognizing transference.* Davies and Frawley (1994) describe eight transference-countertransference positions that are likely to occur between a therapist and an individual who has been sexually abused: uninvolved parent and unseen child, impulsive abuser and helpless victim, idealized rescuer and entitled child, and seducer and seduced. At different points in therapy, a child may take on any one of the eight roles.[1] In addition, there will be transference-countertransference positions resulting from early attachment experiences. Secure relating, clinging relating, avoidant relating, or disorganized relating (Karen, 1994; Main & Solomon, 1990) will occur within the therapy setting.

As the child takes on a role, she explores the dynamics experienced earlier in her home or in other important relationships, including, for most children, the abuse relationship. This exploration is an important step in (a) helping the therapist understand the child's early experiences and (b) providing for the child the experience of a new response. It may, however, create a movement away from the therapeutic or working alliance.

If this movement away is experienced solely as resistance—that is, the transference is not recognized—the therapist is likely to miss the dynamics being played out and may react in a manner similar to the early negative pattern of the child's family (emotional countertransference; Klein, 1989; Littner, 1960; Wieland, 1997).

> **Nina** (an 8-year-old neglected and abused sexually by both parents from infancy to age 5) comes into the therapy room, picks up the stuffed bear, and lies on the sofa with her back to the therapist. This continues for quite a while.
>
> **Therapist:** [Feels confused  why this resistance? She has been so careful to move slowly in working with Nina. Why are they back at square one? Perhaps she should just give Nina some time or she should try to move Nina through this resistance by starting some play activity. . . . Then she realizes that she is feeling excluded and hurt—she has put so much energy into the therapy with Nina. This feeling of being neglected may be similar to what Nina felt as a child. Nina, by being self-involved, may be portraying her parents.] Your being with the bear leaves me alone and lonely. And how lonely that must have been for you when no one paid attention to you when you were little.

\* \* \* \* \*

**Nina** later curls up in the space behind the file cabinet. She is quiet and nothing seems to be happening.

**Therapist:** [Waits for something to happen but nothing happens. Why is Nina avoiding at this point? It gets so tiring, after all the child has to have some responsibility for therapy working. What needs to be covered at the business meeting tonight? . . . Then she realizes that her mind has gone off on other thoughts; she recognizes that something is happening, she is neglecting Nina.] It may feel as if you are being neglected here, my not noticing you and your quietness. It is my job to notice you. I notice . . .

If the therapist does not recognize the transference and sees only resistance, the therapist loses the opportunity to explore early dynamics. Of even greater negative consequence, the therapist's reaction may reinforce the child's early negative experience. A new relationship experience—for example, having her loneliness recognized and of being attended to—is missed.

Being aware of transference-countertransference dynamics can help a therapist differentiate these dynamics from straight resistance. Before assuming that a child is simply resisting, the therapist needs to check his own reaction to a situation. Does his reaction fit transference-countertransference positions?

*Recognizing dissociation.* Dissociation is a common coping pattern for children who have been abused or have witnessed severe abuse (Hornstein & Tyson, 1991; Kluft, 1985). By removing themselves mentally from an abusive situation, children avoid the terror and the pain of abuse. Because therapy brings up this terror and pain, a child who has developed a pattern of dissociating is likely to dissociate during therapy.

Although dissociation can often be noticed from an eye shift or a sudden change in mannerisms, other instances of dissociation are more difficult to recognize. A child whose experience of dissociation includes dissociated identities may, during the session, switch to another aspect or part of himself. When the part switched to is the "not knowing," the "depressed," or the "watchful" part, the therapist may encounter a child who just sits and watches him. The child shows little, if any, reaction to the therapist's observations or questions. The therapist, understandably, becomes frustrated. Why the resistance now?

Mislabeling dissociation as resistance may lead a therapist toward trying to reengage the child rather than working with the relevant dynamics.

> **Tim** (a 12-year-old raised in a physically, emotionally, and sexually abusive home for the first 6 years of his life) sits and watches the therapist. They had been talking about his early memory of watching through "a window" as his parents fought. Tim had said that he would hear nothing as he watched.
> Tim continues to sit quietly. The therapist makes a few observations about Tim sitting and watching, but Tim does not respond. The therapist wonders about the thoughts going on inside Tim's head; Tim does not respond.

> **Therapist:** [Feels back at the beginning of therapy, when it had been so hard to engage Tim. Why now, why this sudden resistance? Was it a resistance to recognizing the dissociated aspects of himself or a resistance to remembering the abuse? In either case, the therapist feels increasingly uncomfortable and incompetent. Maybe she should suggest an activity in order to reengage Tim in some way. . . . Then the therapist becomes more aware of the watchfulness going on. Is this the watching part of Tim?] I am noticing how you are watching me, not answering or even necessarily hearing me, but watching me. I am wondering if this is the part of you that watched your parents? (Tim nods.)

When the therapist does not identify dissociation, she loses an opportunity to address and work with the child's dissociative processes. Identifying the child's response simply as resistance or trying to reengage the child can trigger a switch to another part of the child, thereby reinforcing the dissociative process.

Careful assessment of a child will help to alert the therapist to possible alternative dynamics. If a child has shown dissociative characteristics, the therapist should check out this possibility each time the child exhibits what appears to be resistance.

*Recognizing regression.* In therapy, a child often returns to earlier patterns of behavior, either at home or during the therapy session. Whereas this may represent a child's anxiety around the abuse and an avoidance of therapy, at other times it may reflect anxiety regarding events happening in the child's present life.

**Sally** (a 10-year-old sexually abused and neglected by her birth parents from infancy to 5 years) dips markers into cups of water and then pours glue into the water. This is the same play pattern she had engaged in a year ago. At that point it had been a movement forward from the aimless messing that had been occurring. Now it is a contrast to Sally's usual craft play.

**Therapist:** [Thinks about the picture of the nightmare Sally had brought in, scrunched up, and thrown into the wastebasket before starting on the water play. How could she help Sally through this resistance and to the point of being able to talk about the nightmare?] I'm noticing that you are playing with the water and markers and glue in a way that you did last year. Maybe the play helps keep away the scary feelings from the nightmare. What else could we do for the scary feeling? (Sally continues the water play.)

[Remembers that Sally's foster mother is going to be away at the end of the month. Perhaps this is not avoidance, but anxiety around Mom leaving.] I'm remembering that Mom, in a few weeks, is going away for a week. That can be scary for a child. What will it be like when Mom is away and what will it be like when she comes back? (Sally looks up at the therapist.)

If the therapist does not identify regression, and therefore the underlying anxiety, he may try to move a child away from an activity that, at that point, the child needs.

Failure to recognize regression is most likely to occur when a therapist is not adequately aware of what is going on in a child's life outside of therapy. With a young child in particular, a therapist needs to encourage ongoing communication with parents.

*Recognizing "time-out."* A therapist experiencing resistance from a child during a therapy session should think through whether transference, dissociation, or regression may be happening. If he does not recognize any of these dynamics, he should not immediately assume that a negative form of resistance is occurring. Just as children tend to develop intellectually and physically in spurts, they often respond to therapy in the same way. What appears as avoidance or resistance may be time-out to integrate a new experiencing of self.

When therapy starts to feel like a process of treading water and the therapist wonders about resistance, he can check with the child's parents. If the parents report positive changes at home, the therapist may wish to allow some "treading water space," some space to process positive internalizations.

The therapist also needs to remember that sexual abuse is not always traumatizing. A child with a clear sense of self and a stable supportive environment may have few questions or issues to be worked through. For this child, abuse-related internalizations are minimal and can be worked through within the family context. Lack of presentation of issues may be an indication of health, not resistance.

## PATTERNS OF RESISTANCE

Negative resistance can take many forms. An adolescent may not come to an appointment or may arrive late. The young child may tell her mother she hates therapy or the therapist and may throw a tantrum when it is time to go to therapy. Once within the therapy session, not talking or talking so much that there is no space for thinking are common ways to resist. A young child may choose toys or games that limit representative play. Practicing the alphabet or making lists on a blackboard can block both the child's and the therapist's thinking.

A more subtle form of resistance occurs with the child who tries to please the therapist. Some children resist the therapeutic situation by centering on the therapist. They ask questions of the therapist and worry aloud about how the therapist is doing. This may reflect transference and may be a replay of these children's early experience of being valued only if they take care of adults, and should be discussed as such, with the therapist providing for the child an experience of being taken care of. Or this may be an avoidance of a relationship with the therapist.

## UNDERSTANDING RESISTANCE

Resistance among individuals who have been abused often reflects a wish to forget or put the experience behind them. For others, resistance occurs because the child is uncomfortable or unable to talk about feelings and internal experiences or wants to protect the family. Resistance may result from inappropriate therapist interventions or may occur when a child is gaining something from the distress being experienced. Resistance may, on the other hand, not indicate anything negative. Not wanting therapy, for a child, may be not wanting to be labeled or teased when he has to leave school. For the adolescent, it may reflect an age-appropriate response to adult direction.

*Wanting to forget or put the experience behind.* Sexual abuse brings emotional and physical pain; it brings cognitive confusion. The logical response to such a situation is avoidance. If it were not for the impact of abuse on a child's internal world and, in some situations, on the child's physiological system, and, thus, on present and future experiences, forgetting would, indeed, be recommended.

Therapists can, from their vantage point of reading and working with other children, recognize the importance of therapy. Children have no such vantage point. They know what it has felt like and that they do not like it. They know how it makes them feel about themselves, and they want to avoid that. They are afraid of nightmares and flashbacks starting again. Those who have had suicidal feelings may be afraid that therapy will bring those feelings back. Resistance of therapy makes sense.

> **Cynthia** (a 15-year-old sexually abused by a teenage baby-sitter at ages 7 and 8 but unable to disclose until age 12) says she doesn't want to come to therapy. She states that she has handled what happened back then; it is her mother who feels there is something wrong and that Cynthia needs therapy.
> When asked by the therapist how often she thinks about it, Cynthia says she thinks about it about once a day. But that's okay because she used to think about it all the time. When asked what she thinks about her body, she says she hates it. But that makes sense because she is fat.

Wishing to avoid old events and feelings may occur only at the beginning of therapy or may occur each time a new part of the abuse or a new feeling related to the abuse emerges. At those times, keeping away the old distress becomes the child's focus.

Children who have been threatened with harm to themselves or to someone important to them if they tell often experience intense fear during therapy. This fear comes from their having done what was forbidden. To avoid the fear, they become silent in therapy. Indeed, silence was a way of coping during the abuse and, thus, a behavior that feels a great deal safer than talking.

*Discomfort with feelings or a wish to protect the family.* Families in which sexual abuse occurs tend to be families with poor communication skills (Alexander, 1985; Trepper & Barrett, 1989). Feelings are not recognized and even events, particularly negative events, are seldom discussed. A child coming into therapy from such a home is more skilled at ignoring emotions than at talking about them. She may have no vocabulary for expressing feelings or may feel that talking represents a weakness. Incestuous families often give either overt or covert messages to a child not to talk about anything that goes on inside the family.

For the young child, play provides an alternative for expression. For the prepuberty child, a sand tray is helpful. The adolescent has a more difficult time. Boys, in particular, have seldom been encouraged to identify or express how they feel.

Discomfort may also come from having had early negative attachment experiences. For these children, the intimacy of therapy can feel threatening and, therefore, is something to be avoided. Many of the children coming into therapy were abused by someone close to them. The abuse-related internalization "I am betrayed by people close to me" increases resistance.

Resistance to therapy may also occur when the child is protecting her family. Particularly if family stability is based on abuse not having happened or not having been distressing, a child may resist becoming involved in therapy. Becoming involved in therapy would contradict the family myth that abuse is acceptable.

*Inappropriate therapist interventions.* The therapist needs to remember where the child is within the experiencing of therapy, the experiencing of the abuse, and the experiencing of his own strengths. As therapy starts, it is helpful for the therapist to respond to the child's here-and-now experience and to provide interventions that allow the child some distance from the subject of abuse.[2] Although the reality of the abuse and the internal distress needs to be recognized, exploring the trauma or the internal dynamics too soon can be frightening. An individual can feel overwhelmed and out of control (Davies & Frawley, 1994; Pearce & Pezzot-Pearce, 1997). A child may respond by pulling back and protecting himself (Rosenfeld, 1981). He may state that he is bored or that he is not bothered by the abuse, or may simply refuse to discuss it (Pearce & Pezzot-Pearce, 1997).

As therapy progresses, the child's play, behavior, and conversation let the therapist know which issues are paramount at any particular moment (this has been discussed in more detail in Chapter 1). If a child is smearing black paint or crayon on a piece of paper, that is not the time to talk about distance in the family, just as when a child is placing the colts far away from the horses it is not the time to talk about feeling black or damaged inside. When an adolescent talks about not trusting a teacher, it is not the time for the therapist to talk about the chaotic feelings that result from ambivalent attachments, just as when an adolescent talks about his feelings seeming to swing out of control, it is not the time to talk about the experience of being betrayed by someone close. A therapist's talking about issues not related to the child's play or conversation is not only not helpful, it is intrusive. Intrusion on the part of the therapist leads to resistance on the part of the child.

Briere (1996a) talks about the importance of the therapist's staying within the therapeutic window, the space in which the individual can be challenged and motivated toward "psychological growth, accommodation, and desensitization [without] overwhelm[ing] internal protective systems" (p. 146). As Briere points out, when the therapist's interventions are outside the therapeutic window, avoidance is an appropriate response on the part of the individual. Although a therapist often needs to push a child to think and to talk about internal experiencing, this needs to be done in a manner and at a level that feels safe for the child.

Some therapeutic approaches that may be appropriate in other situations can create resistance when used with someone who has been abused. A therapist who does not actively respond to the child (therapist as blank screen) runs the danger of replaying the neglecting parent, whereas a therapist who tells the child what to do (therapist as adviser) runs the danger of neglecting the child's experience. Both can trigger, within the child, a feeling of danger. A therapist who does not address abuse issues and internalizations as they are presented in the play or conversation can also create resistance. The child is all too likely to understand from the therapist's lack of response that the abuse is too awful to talk about and should be avoided.

Therapeutic errors also occur when a therapist does not attend carefully to time, location, and relationship boundaries. A child will often try to move the therapeutic relationship into a friendship or into a relationship in which he takes care of the therapist. When the therapist allows this to happen, the child loses the safety and structure of the therapeutic relationship—the child is again the one tending to the adult. The child may become either disappointed or frightened and may back out of therapy.

*Secondary gain.* A child who has been placed in the position of "the special child" for whom the rest of the family must care is unlikely to want to give this up. A child who gets to sleep in her parent's bed because of nightmares may not want to get rid of nightmares. It is not the effects of abuse that the child wishes to hold on to, but rather the favored position or treatment that has resulted from those effects. This child may resist therapy.

When a child becomes involved with drugs and alcohol and, through this, gains a sense of community or importance along with avoidance of pain, it is unlikely the child will want to pursue therapy. For children who dissociate, the part whose identity revolves around abusive behaviors will likely resist therapy.

*Normal responding.* Children who leave school for therapy are often labeled by other children as "strange" or "sick." Teasing may occur in the school yard or in the child's imagination. It is normal and healthy for a child not to want to be labeled or teased and to resist situations, such as therapy, that can lead to this.

For an adolescent, there is an added dimension. Adolescents are at the normal stage of moving away from dependency on parent figures, of resisting listening to and following adult dictates. They are searching out more control over their own lives. Therapy may feel, to the adolescent, like someone else trying to shape them. Resisting therapy, for this adolescent, could indicate a healthy response.

## HELPING CHILDREN THROUGH THE RESISTANCE

A therapist who is aware of a child's difficulty in talking about the abuse and expressing himself leaves space for the child to resist therapy. By being sensitive to this resistance and trying to understand the reasons behind the resistance, the therapist starts the work toward engaging or reengaging the child in the therapy process.


*When the child wants to forget.* Children and adolescents struggling to forget the abuse need time to play or talk about their lives now. They need a chance to connect to their present-day strengths. This helps stabilize their lives, at which point thinking about the abuse will not be as frightening.

For young children, the ability to play is a strength, and providing an opportunity for play connects them with this strength. For older children and adolescents, connecting to strengths can be more difficult. For some, deciding what they want from therapy and how many times they want to meet gives them a sense of being in control, and that provides strength. For others, especially preadolescents who do not know what they want, such questions can feel frightening. These children need help finding a safe topic to talk about (for example, "Fill me in on what has been happening this week") and acceptance of their wish to avoid the past ("Seems like you would rather not be here, that makes sense. What would it be like not to be coming here?"). Drawing the family genogram or making a timeline of the events in his life can provide the young person with an activity that feels less threatening, an opportunity to observe the therapist taking and using the information he is giving, and a safe experience of looking at relationships and past events.

When a young child pulls away from issues, the therapist can talk about the abuse and abuse-related internalizations through the metaphor of play. Ekstein (1966) describes the metaphor as allowing the child greater distance from conscious processing of the conflict while reducing the distance between the child and the therapist. Older children and adolescents reflect their abuse-related internalizations through their discussion of present-day events. These events can then provide a metaphor for talking about the earlier hurt and pain and for starting to look at the adolescent's internalizations of self and world. A therapist's labeling and normalizing of abuse-related internalizations and emotions can provide a sense of stability. When the therapist's comments are in the form of general observations, rather than personal interpretations, the child is less likely to be frightened.

The therapist needs to be alert to the child's reluctance to talk about the abuse and to check with the child as to which types of questions are feeling all right at a particular time. The phrase *this particular time* is important. It sets the expectation that there will be a time when such a discussion will be possible. Without it, the child may feel a given discussion is closed, and when the therapist later goes back to the topic or question, the child feels betrayed. The therapist's checking as to how questions feel places the child in more control of the discussion.

> **Alison** (a 16-year-old sexually abused at ages 7 and 8 by a teenage baby-sitter) pulls back when the therapist asks about what happened during the abuse.

> **Therapist:** Seems as if that question feels like too much *right now.* (Alison nods.) That's fine. Really important that you let me know when something I ask feels like too much at that particular moment.

> Later in the session, Alison talks about her family when she was 7 years old and how she and her brother used to have fun playing with the baby-sitter. The therapist asks what would happen then and Alison starts talking about how the baby-sitter would come into her room after he put her brother to bed. The therapist asks what happened then and Alison talks about the abuse.

> **Therapist:** [Realizes that she has repeated the question that Alison had earlier said felt too uncomfortable.] I just realized that I've asked what you said you didn't want to talk about earlier.

> **Alison:** (smiling slightly) It's okay, I know I need pushing.

> **Therapist:** And we need to keep track of when and what pushing feels all right.

At times during therapy a child may become frightened and want to stop a discussion or an imaging. This is particularly likely to happen when a flashback occurs. The therapist needs to respond to this wish, but at the same time not leave the child feeling vulnerable. The therapist can explain why a particular question was asked, can explain why flooding sometimes occurs, can bring the "now self" into an image to care for the "younger self," or can help the child put the distressing image away (see Chapter 6, pages 177-178).

It can be helpful, at the beginning of therapy or when the child starts talking directly about the abuse, for the therapist to let the child know that nightmares or intrusive thoughts may increase for a time. The child will then be able to recognize what happens as normal and is likely to be less frightened.

Time at the end of a session for moving away from distressing content is also important. Play therapists, as part of the process, tell children when 5 minutes are left in a session. It can be helpful for a therapist to let an older child or adolescent know, when a session has been particularly difficult, that the time is almost over.

For some children, none of this seems to be enough. Changing to another format of therapy—for example, parent-child dyad therapy, family therapy, or group therapy—and thereby taking the focus off the child may help a child feel safer and more comfortable with the therapeutic process.

*When a child is uncomfortable talking about feelings.* Young children often resist talking about the past or about feelings by playing board games, doing schoolwork on the blackboard, or engaging in repetitive methodical play, such as building blocks. Games and toys that do not engage a child's imagination can be eliminated from the play area and time limits can be set for repetitive activities (Chethik, 1989). Although activities such as making lists or doing homework may help a child gain a sense of control, they also can take over the session and block out process thinking. The child's discomfort could be discussed, drawn, or acted out.

For older children and adolescents who are not used to talking about feelings and distressing events, completing a genogram or timeline at the beginning of therapy is helpful. Writing things down, rather than just talking about them, is helpful for some children.[3] Some older children and adolescents find drawing or depicting their world in the sand tray an easier mode of expression than talking. Sand tray activity can be particularly valuable for older children who, as young children, had little opportunity to play or to be noticed and appreciated as they played.

The therapist's talking about normal reactions to experiences of abuse—sense of damage and blaming of self, intrusive thoughts or flashbacks, feelings of responsibility, and feelings of confusion, anger, and grief—can be reassuring. The therapist's use of the word *sorting* rather than *going back to* or *working through* when talking about feelings and past experiences can feel safer. An explanation of confidentiality may also help a child feel more comfortable.

A therapist can explore with a child how people in the child's family communicate with each other, how they express negative and positive feelings, and how they get attention from each other. Discussion of which of these patterns the child wants to keep, which he wants to change, and how he wants to change them gives him an experience in talking and a sense of being able to change things. Talking at the end of a session about which part of a session, if any, felt comfortable and which part was difficult can help a child gain confidence in his ability to articulate feelings. Talking about ways in which the therapist and child can, together, increase the sense of safety within a session can also be helpful.

When discomfort results from lack of experience with or fear of attachment, the therapist needs to be particularly careful to respect boundaries. The therapist's accepting the child the way he is and being consistently available to the child within the established boundaries can provide the space and security the child needs to start forming a positive attachment (Friedrich, 1995).

Young children sometimes become frightened of the therapy session and want their parents to be there. Although this is not an ideal situation for therapy, it may be a necessary step in helping a child feel safe. The parent can be encouraged to sit at the far end of the room and read a book, thus allowing the child space to separate and to become engaged in therapy. At times, even this is not possible, and the therapist may need to do the therapy through the parent. By noticing both the child's and the parent's responses, and the abuse-related internalizations reflected in these responses, the therapist can gently address the fright and confusion that stem from the abuse.

As mentioned above, switching to dyad, family, or group therapy can provide for some children or adolescents a more comfortable setting for exploring issues. If the child feels that by talking she will betray family loyalties—and this may occur with extrafamilial as well as intrafamilial abuse—individual therapy prior to dyad or family therapy may be counterproductive.

*When the therapist makes an error.* When the therapist is aware in a session of moving too fast or too far, he can acknowledge his error and apologize. Even if the therapist does not become aware of his mistake until after the session, it can be discussed at the next session.

When a child who previously was engaged in the therapy misses an appointment, is late, or is particularly avoidant, the therapist should review the previous session for possible therapeutic errors. Whereas such a shift may be a result of some event in the child's environment, the therapist should always be open to the possibility that resistance is occurring because the therapist has moved outside the therapeutic window.

**Judy** (an 18-year-old emotionally and physically abused along with her siblings by her father and sexually abused between ages 10 and 15 by her father) talks on and on so quickly that the therapist has little chance to say anything.

**Therapist:** [Recognizes that Judy is blocking his comments. He goes back over the beginning of the session and then last week's session in his mind to try to understand why this is happening. He remembers that last week Judy had said she was feeling funny whenever she saw a young child on a father's lap. When he had tried to explore this, she said that if anything happened before age 10 she did not want to remember it. Later in the session, Judy had talked about how her father had made all of them, as young children, walk around the house nude.] I'm noticing how much you are talking today and that there is no chance for me to say anything. I'm wondering if you are angry or distressed from last week when you said you did not want to think about anything sexual happening before you were 10 and then we ended up talking about your father forcing you and your brothers to walk around nude.

**Judy:** I was so upset when I got home. I never talked about that before because I felt it was betraying them. So many things happened when we were little. Maybe someday they will be ready to talk about it. When my brothers swore, like my parents swore all the time, they were just copying them . . . (looks off in the distance).

**Therapist:** You seem to have gone a long way away. What is going through your mind now?

**Judy:** Last night I decided all the things I wanted to talk about today. I really fought with myself that I had to talk about these things, but now I can't do it.

**Therapist:** You started talking just now about your brothers, which was what you said you didn't want to do. Maybe you are afraid that once you start talking about some things, you will get into things you don't want to talk about yet or I will push you into talking about other things. (Judy nods.) We are going to need to work together to find a way to talk and yet keep the limits you want. I need to stay aware of areas you do not want to talk about *at this particular time* and let you know when you move into them so you can choose what you want to do at any particular moment.

Consultation and further reading in the area of sexual abuse can help a therapist identify therapeutic mistakes that may have occurred in a session. Respect for the child and the therapist's awareness of his limited ability to understand are essential.

*When a child is experiencing secondary gain.* Meeting with parents to gather information on the child's development, the types of interactions occurring at home, and the family's response to the child's disclosure is part of an initial assessment procedure. A therapist can sometimes, from this interview, recognize and help the family identify patterns that may be reinforcing a child's dysfunctional behavior. Talking with the parents from time to time during the therapy process, about the child's behavior at home and the family dynamics, will also help the therapist to identify any secondary gains occurring for the child.

A therapist's meeting separately with parents of an adolescent can be problematic. Family sessions may be more useful for identifying secondary gains and for helping the adolescent's family restructure boundaries and interactions. For an adolescent who is extensively involved in drugs and alcohol, this choice needs to be looked at and dealt with before therapy related to sexual abuse experiences is likely to be helpful.

*When resisting is an appropriate response.* Scheduling therapy appointments at times least disruptive to a child's day can relieve stress on the child and remove a cause of resistance. Recognizing the normal role of arguing and disagreement within adolescent growth can help a therapist to be patient with these behaviors. With an adolescent who resists through silence, the therapist may want to talk about this as a normal wish not to be involved in the process that is going on. Sometimes the adolescent can be involved in a discussion of the options open to her at that point—for example, individual therapy, group therapy, dyad therapy with the nonperpetrating parent, family therapy, no therapy—and the possible outcomes of each one. Discussion may then be able to move on to what the adolescent might be able to get out of therapy.

*When the child is not ready.* For some children, the timing of therapy may not be right. They may need a chance to come and go from therapy several times before they are able to become engaged in the process. By helping a child not to feel bad about not pursuing therapy, and by leaving space for the child to come back, a therapist can enable a child to do his own working through of the resistance.

## ❏  The Parent's Resistance

A therapist may, unfortunately, overlook a parent's resistance to a child's therapy. After all, the parent is not there in the session. The parent is, however, important, not only to the maintenance of therapy—paying fees, providing transportation—but to the success of therapy. If a child is discouraged from working within therapy, little benefit will result. A parent's resistance needs to be recognized, understood, and discussed.

### RECOGNIZING RESISTANCE

A parent who is providing transportation for a child may schedule activities that make it impossible for the child to get to therapy, may bring the child late, or may forget appointments. Other parents, who are conscientious about appointments, may block the child's therapy by talking to the therapist during the child's time or by asking the child multiple questions about the therapy. If the child feels she is going to need to tell her parent what went on in therapy, she will be reluctant to talk about issues important to her. A parent who is critical of therapy, either to the child or to the therapist, sets up emotional blocks within the child or the therapist.

## UNDERSTANDING RESISTANCE

Many parents, even though they recognize that abuse occurred, do not want to admit their children were abused or were hurt by the abuse. They feel that if their children will just forget the abuse, it will be as though it never happened. Taking a child to therapy forces a parent to acknowledge the abuse as detrimental, to acknowledge him- or herself as not protecting the child, and to acknowledge that the world the family lives in is dangerous. A parent may avoid therapy for a child in order to avoid feelings of guilt, inadequacy, loss, and despair.

Parents go through times of being angry at a child for being where the abuse happened, for "allowing" the abuse to happen, for not telling, for telling, for not forgetting, for wanting attention, for being avoidant, for "causing" problems. For the parent who was sexually abused herself during childhood and never received therapy, there may be anger at the child for not "getting on with life," as she did. Even when a parent knows that this anger should not exist, it is there and it blocks the parent's support of therapy.

Some parents, particularly mothers, find it difficult to watch therapists help their children and be close to their children in a way these parents are not able to do. This can create jealousy and bitterness that leads, without any conscious thought, to resistance. A parent may also become jealous of the close relationship and special time her child is experiencing.

A few parents resist therapy for their children because their own self-images are based on their having children or foster children who need help. When their children gain new competencies, this threatens the present parent-child relationship and may raise questions about the parents' style of parenting

## ADDRESSING THE RESISTANCE

Mothers of children who have been sexually abused experience significant psychological distress (Deblinger, Hathaway, Lippmann, & Steer, 1993; Manion et al., 1996; Williamson, Borduin, & Howe, 1991) and question their own ability to judge the world and to protect their children (Hooper, 1992). For a mother to be able to provide support for her child, including obtaining and following a therapy plan, she needs to regain a sense of herself as competent (Hooper, 1992).

During the initial parent interview and throughout the time the child is in therapy, the therapist can acknowledge the parent's losses and distress. The therapist can help the parent talk about her feelings of guilt. As the parent's own distress is recognized, she becomes better able to acknowledge the impact of the abuse on herself, her family, and her child. Where possible, the therapist will want to arrange therapy for the parent(s) with a separate therapist.

At the same time the therapist talks with the parent about the impact of abuse, the therapist can reassure the parent. The parent needs to know that her child, as a person, is not damaged, and that the distress from the abuse can be worked through and the child can grow up with a healthy concept of self. As the parent becomes reassured, her need to deny the impact of abuse and the necessity of therapy often decreases.

A parent's individual therapy, or supportive contact from the child's therapist, can provide a space for the parent to express her anger at what has happened, at the child, and, if it is there, at the therapist. The anger can be normalized and then discussed. If the therapist has not already explained the role of therapy and the importance of contact between the therapist and parent, or if the parent has not understood these issues adequately, the therapist can explain them now. The role of the parent as the most important adult in the child's life needs to be emphasized. Indeed, it is *because* parenting is so important and so demanding that therapy is better done by someone else.

The establishment of a partnership between the parent and the therapist is important. Foster parents, in particular, are more support-ive of therapy when they experience themselves as important to the therapy. The therapist needs to explain and demonstrate this by phon-ing and meeting with the parents. When the therapist will be working with foster parents or when another agency is involved, clear guide-lines need to be discussed and followed carefully with regard to the roles of the therapist and the caseworker. If a parent's distrust of the therapist continues, some dyad sessions with the parent and child together in which the parent-child relationship is emphasized may be helpful.

A parent who resists her child's therapy because of her own wish to have a close therapeutic relationship can be encouraged to pursue individual therapy. Therapy is particularly important for parents who have themselves experienced childhood abuse.

Parents for whom a distressed child has provided special prestige or attention need a chance to look at this and at their attitude toward the child. Parents need considerable support to examine and shift parenting styles and to allow their child to become less dependent on them. The therapist's recognition and praise of the efforts parents are making can help lower the parents' resistance.

## ❏  The Therapist's Resistance

The definition of resistance—avoidance of the topic of abuse, of feelings related to the abuse, and of the therapeutic relationship—applies equally well to the issue of the therapist's resistance, or what is often referred to as counterresistance. Here, too, the therapist needs to recognize what is happening and to take time to understand her own behavior. The therapist needs to determine what can help her respond more appropriately with a particular child.

### RECOGNIZING RESISTANCE

As a therapist reviews a particular child's therapy and realizes that the abuse has not been adequately addressed or emotions have not been discussed, the therapist should not automatically label this as resistance on the part of the child. The therapist may not have been open to these topics or to abuse-related internalizations. Indeed, this should be the therapist's first question.

Feelings of discouragement and a wish to terminate therapy that cannot be explained by transference-countertransference dynamics related to the session dynamics may indicate resistance by the therapist. A therapist's labeling of a child as untreatable usually reflects the therapist's resistance to looking at her limitations as a therapist and her need for further consultation or training. It may reflect a personal reaction to the subject of abuse or a lack of knowledge regarding the dynamics of abuse (Wieland, 1997).

Resistance behaviors that may be easier for therapists to recognize are errors of management—misscheduling of appointments, being late, switching therapy times, talking to a parent or teacher without speaking first to the child, breaching confidentiality. When a therapist consistently starts a particular child's therapy session late or consistently puts off calling a particular parent, she is resisting some part of that child's therapy. Not paying attention during a session, when this is not a countertransference response, also indicates resistance. Feeling that the child is not bringing any content to therapy, not that she is not understanding the content, indicates resistance. The therapist needs to look at each of these reactions.

## UNDERSTANDING RESISTANCE

Resistance is likely to occur for a therapist when the content of therapy either threatens the therapist's worldview or triggers the therapist's own early experiences. A therapist's unresolved conflicts related to children or to issues of sexual abuse create a blocking of what the child is playing or saying in therapy (Pearson, 1968). Therapist biases and prejudices that are not recognized and separated out block the therapist's awareness of the child's issues (Wieland, 1997). As the therapist blocks information or reacts in an overly emotional or detached way, the child stops bringing those issues to therapy. This is not, however, the child's resistance. The child is reacting to the therapist's resistance.

Resistance may occur because of an area of incompetence a therapist has not addressed. Resistance can also occur if a therapist starts to feel incompetent and gets caught in that feeling. Fatigue and outside pressures may also increase a therapist's resistance to content presented in a therapy session.

## WORKING THROUGH THE RESISTANCE

Because a therapist's resistance arises out of her own internal issues, it is often difficult for her to work through resistance on her own. Supervision or consultation encourages a therapist to look at her reactions to a particular child or a particular type of abuse. What in her own experience is she reminded of? How is her experience similar to or different from that of the child? How does this experience get in the way of her understanding and responding to the child? Why is she feeling discouraged or incompetent at this particular time? Is this an area beyond her competence and, if so, what changes can be made? Does she have enough time away from work and abuse issues?

When a therapist is not able to arrange supervision or consultation, free association writing related to a child and the child's story can help the therapist be aware of what is personally triggered during sessions. Once the therapist is aware of these triggers, she can do some personal work around her issues. For some therapists, personal therapy can help remove sources of resistance. For others, personal reflection on their reactions to abuse in general or to a particular child can be helpful.

It can be beneficial to the therapist to undertake further reading in the area of sexual abuse, particularly when the stories she is hearing feel overwhelming and threatening. Reading case studies and books on therapy with children who have been traumatized can help the therapist gather ideas and, therefore, feel less threatened by a child's distress.

When a therapist recognizes resistance related to a particular child, she needs to spend more time and effort as she reviews the previous sessions' notes, listens to and watches the child in session, attends to transference and countertransference dynamics, considers the internalizations that may be expressed, decides on interventions, and, following the session, writes up notes and marks the next appointment. Between sessions, the therapist can let the events of the session float through her mind. Without trying to push this information into any sort of frame, the therapist can attend to her own thought wanderings and make note of any connections and ideas that come. The therapist's being open when thinking about a child outside of a session can lead to greater openness and less resistance when she is in a session with the child.

❑ **Summary**

When therapy feels stuck, the therapist needs to consider whether the resistance belongs to the child, the parent, or himself. Although avoidance of therapy, emotions, or the topic of abuse by a child is resistance, it also may reflect transference, dissociation, regression, or simply time-out for assimilating the work that has been done. It is important that these issues be addressed directly and not dismissed as solely resistance. Resistance may also reflect a child's wanting to forget, being uncomfortable talking about feelings, gaining something from negative experiences, expressing normal dislike of adult decisions, or protecting herself from therapeutic errors. A parent's resistance may reflect the parent's distress resulting from the abuse or more personal dynamics related to the parent's own experiences. As the therapist recognizes and then seeks to understand these resistances, he can refocus the therapeutic process to the needs of the child or parent at that particular point.

Whenever resistance occurs, the therapist needs also to examine his own attitudes and reactions, both toward the child and toward the topic of abuse. The therapist needs to be open to recognizing that he may have caused the resistance or that the resistance belongs to him, not the child. Careful attending to a child with emphasis on addressing the abuse-related internalizations can help both the therapist and the child move through feelings of resistance.

## ❑ Notes

1. See Wieland (1997) for a discussion and examples of the manner in which these positions occur with children and adolescents.

2. A therapist can create a distance between an intervention and the child by talking within the metaphor of the play, by referring to experiences of other children, or by making general observations.

3. Ways in which a foster mother and birth mother are the same and different, intrusive thoughts and replies to those thoughts, and things to do when frightened are just a few of the many things that can be written down.

# PART IV

*The Adolescent's Experience*

# 8

# Therapy: The Adolescent Comments

"Hopping, therapist to therapist." "Dark, hard." "A beautiful picture—a tunnel with dark areas but opening at the end." Each experience of therapy is unique. Not all experiences are helpful, and some are harmful. As adolescents and young adults describe their adolescent experiences of therapy, particular characteristics emerge as being positive and healing, whereas other characteristics often create problems.

"They were like night and day, the therapies." Adolescents and young adults are clear on what they have found not helpful, what has made them feel worse—not just momentarily but in the long term—what has been supportive but not able to resolve anything, and what has been helpful. As we come to the end of this volume on addressing the internal trauma, it is appropriate to give some attention to the comments of adolescents who have experienced therapy.

This chapter summarizes the interview responses of 15 adolescents and young adults who, during their childhood and/or adolescence, experienced sexual abuse and who received therapy as adolescents. The numbers of therapists with whom these individuals had been in contact range from one to seven. Most had also met with school counselors or protection agency workers. All reported both positive and negative experiences. The negative experiences are summarized in the following section, and then the positive experiences are described. Listening to these young people—indeed, listening to all the children and adolescents with whom they work—can help therapists learn how to create a healing space and a therapeutic experience.

❑  **Therapy as a Negative Experience**

The adolescents and young adults interviewed described therapy that included physical touch or sexually provocative comments or behavior as detrimental. Sexual comments or behaviors by therapists, even when the adolescents recognized them as wrong, created confusion and reinforced abuse-related internalizations. Therapy described as desensitization for physical touch felt intrusive, and the adolescent experienced increased anxiety and a repeat of the out-of-control feelings experienced during the abuse.

Being forced or pushed into therapy was also described as detrimental. When control over what they did—attending or not attending therapy—was taken away, the young adults noted that they, as adolescents, became angrier and acted out, either in or out of therapy. They stated that although they often needed a great deal of outside encouragement and even needed to be taken to therapy, that was different from being forced. Inclusion of a parent at the beginning of therapy, when the adolescent did not ask for the parent to be involved, was described as creating resentment and causing the adolescent to close down. Some adolescents did mention that they appreciated it when their parents had their own therapy. Meetings in which caseworkers were included were described as very negative by an adolescent who came from a family in which there was considerable talking behind people's backs, but as positive by adolescents without such experiences.

Therapy with a "blank slate" was described as not helpful. Adolescents reported feeling closed out and unable to talk about the abuse or to expose their feelings. "Lack of feedback left me empty and lonely. It was like talking to a wall." "Empathy and support was not enough." The long silences were described as increasing the adolescents' feelings of inadequacy and their sense that people were blaming them. Diagnostic labeling was described as somewhat helpful in that it provided the adolescents with a new way of talking about the internal distress, but several stated that it created a feeling of being crazy. Note taking by the therapist during the session was described as scary by an adolescent who had been threatened by her father that no matter where she was he would find out what she told.

Advice and direct confrontation were described not only as not helpful, but, in many cases, as detrimental. Interviewees explained that after these experiences, they would either avoid therapy or avoid bringing up particular topics even though these continued to present problems for them. This happened even within a positive therapeutic relationship. Being pushed to talk about abuse incidents when they did not want to was described as intrusive and often led to the adolescent stopping therapy. Other adolescents felt they were not pushed enough or that the all-important question—Why did the abuse happen?—was not discussed sufficiently.

Not being asked about experiences other than the abuse, similar to not being asked about the abuse, felt restrictive and as if the therapist was not interested in them. Playing games and talking about surface issues were considered unhelpful and, in one case, described as detrimental in that the adolescent felt she was encouraged to avoid the abuse. Some adolescents described becoming angry and defensive when asked questions they did not expect. It was not the depth of the question but the unexpectedness that was upsetting and caused them to close down. Intense work around memories or flashbacks without an adequate support system was described as upsetting and leading to suicidal feelings.

Being given exercises to complete between sessions was also problematic. Several adolescents found they could not complete the exercises and, for some of them, this led to feelings of failure. For some, the exercises brought up deep feelings and they felt caught, once again, alone with fear and panic. For others, the exercises worked well.

Adolescents reported that when a therapist complimented them on how well they were coping, the false front they had been presenting was reinforced and they were less able to talk about the not-coping feelings inside. When the conversations in therapy included discussions about the therapist and his activities, adolescents reported feeling good in that they enjoyed the interaction but reported that afterward their sense of loneliness was even greater.

Therapy with someone not knowledgeable or comfortable in the field of sexual abuse was described as being of limited help. Adolescents who had the experience of having a therapist express surprise or shock regarding what had happened reported feeling stigmatized and uncomfortable and found that they talked less about the abuse.

The setting of the therapy room also sometimes caused problems. For an adolescent who had been abused on a couch, sitting on a couch in the therapist's office triggered feelings of fear. Adolescents who had experienced therapies that did not give them a sense of structure and safety reported that they either withdrew from the process or experienced an increase of internal chaos.

❏   **Therapy as a Positive Experience**

Descriptions of positive adolescent therapy experiences included comments about the room, the therapist's demeanor, and therapy interventions. As therapists work with children and adolescents, they need to be aware of each of these dimensions.

THE ROOM

Several young adults commented on the importance of the atmosphere in the therapy room—comfortable furniture, calming colors. Feeling free to sit in different places was important for them. Having toys in the room and knowing that children used the room as well was important to several adolescents and made them feel more welcome, even though they themselves did not use the toys. Having a clock on the table was also mentioned as a help for pacing themselves and for avoiding having a therapist constantly looking at her watch.

The adolescents interviewed expressed a preference for a therapy room outside a hospital setting. They described feeling less stigmatized when going to a houselike setting for an appointment. For the adolescents who had previously been hospital inpatients, seeing a therapist in a hospital felt threatening. Privacy within the setting—no phone calls or people knocking at the door—was emphasized as important. Although a comfortable room was described by most of the adolescents as important, the possibility that this setting may itself be a trigger—for example, the adolescent who was abused on a couch—needs to be kept in mind.

## THERAPIST DEMEANOR

The therapist's manner had been particularly important for each of these adolescents. They talked about the importance of the therapist's being calm and relaxed and yet attentive to each subject the adolescent raised. One individual mentioned that she remembered that her therapist did not always respond immediately, but would take some time as she thought through what had been said. This time was different from when the therapist was waiting for the adolescent to say more. The adolescent stated that she felt a sense of value and that there was, as she and the therapist worked together, a way for things to be worked out.

Self-confidence and a presentation by the therapist as not having problems was noted by several individuals as being important. They recalled that they felt they were able to rely on the therapist rather than moving into the familiar role of taking care of an adult. The therapist's not talking about himself was described as important.

The therapist's making eye contact and sitting at a comfortable distance from the adolescent was also mentioned. The therapist's leaning forward was noted by one adolescent as feeling intrusive and as giving a sense of sensationalism or awfulness to what the adolescent was discussing. At the same time, a therapist seeming uninvolved or yawning was described by several adolescents as detrimental to the therapy process. Being talked to as a young adult, not a child, was described as important.

## THERAPIST INTERVENTIONS

The young adults and adolescents described the content, as well as the process, of therapy as being important. "Being told my reactions were normal, what a difference that made." "Getting information about what was happening, about abuse, that helped." "I started to get a framework for understanding what had been happening inside me." "I wasn't crazy, I was normal." Having what was happening now linked to what happened in the past was described by several adolescents as important in helping them make sense of their world.

Flexibility in the therapist's approach was mentioned by several young adults as having been important to them when they were adolescents. "I could talk about a lot of different things. She paid attention to everything, not just the abuse." "Sometimes she would give me ideas for marking on a calendar how often I was doing something and sometimes she would wonder what was the feeling when I did it. Sometimes we just talked and sometimes we did imaging. I didn't feel that everything would be handled the same way, like by rote, but that each thing would be handled in a way that could work for that particular problem. That helped me to talk about more things." "I couldn't talk. There was nothing to talk about. So she saw the whole family and I heard them talking about emotions. My mother even confronted my father; she had never done that. I wasn't the only problem."

Flexibility in scheduling was important. Being able to stop and restart therapy was described by several adolescents as giving them control and taking the pressure off.

The ways in which therapists phrased their comments were described as making a difference. The adolescents remembered liking it when ideas were given as tentative and they were asked what they felt was happening. Several noted that not being told how to solve something but rather being helped to think things through was important. One adolescent described as particularly helpful having been told she needed to work at changing situations rather than sitting back and waiting for a situation to change.

Remembering, finding out why they did certain things but could not do other things, controlling the panic, and comforting their younger self were listed as the most important parts of therapy. Reconnecting with feelings and dealing with day-to-day upsets were also mentioned. Several adolescents noted how much they appreciated learning techniques for leaving issues in the therapy room. Some adolescents found drawing particularly helpful and, in certain cases, tearing up the drawings.

The genogram was described as helpful. Some adolescents noted that although the genogram did not include any new information, having it laid out that way was helpful. The therapist's noting similarities and differences was described as helping them understand what was happening.

All of the young adults who had used imaging as part of their therapy mentioned the imaging as the most helpful experience during therapy. One young adult talked about how the imaging enabled her to recognize the younger part of her and realize the needs the "little me" has. "I use that all the time now, I take really good care of the little me." Another individual described the process of taking in the now self with the younger self within the imaging as most important. She had always thought that she was "all screwed up" and this helped her connect with a part that was stronger and could help the other part.

Having a safe place within the imaging was noted as important. One young adult said that during the imaging she had "always looked back to see how she could get back." Therapist comments such as "knowing that you are here now and in a safe place," the calmness of the therapist's voice, and a sense that the therapist was with them had been important during the imaging. Support for what they did in the imaging was also important. "Like when I started beating him up in my imaging. I was so scared of all the anger, but she kept saying that I was doing a good job so it started to feel okay and I felt I wasn't going out of control."

Adolescents who dissociated during therapy described the question "What was happening when you were away?" as extremely helpful. The question helped them to become aware of what was happening inside.

## THERAPY PROCESS

The interviewees' experiences of starting therapy varied considerably. "It was awful. I had nothing to talk about and we just sat." "I didn't want to go. I was afraid everything would get worse, but I knew I had to do something." "I worried about her, would she be strong enough, would it help." Some individuals who began therapy with an assessment procedure in which they had specific things to do described that as being helpful. Others who had been asked to complete drawings as part of the assessment reported that they hated doing the drawings and described the process as making them feel like little kids.

The adolescents reported that they kept going to therapy because (a) they did not want to feel the way they did and (b) they felt some help from the therapy. One individual described herself as often feeling a sudden blank when coming to a session—nothing to talk about, so why go. She also described a part of her that realized therapy could help and that, as a result, she would end up going. Another adolescent described butterflies before coming and then a frozen feeling once in the room. This adolescent explained that she kept going to therapy because she experienced a sense of caring by the therapist and hoped that in time the frozen feeling might decrease.

Specific comments or questions about the abuse were described as raising a great deal of anxiety. The young adults and adolescents, thinking back on their therapies, noted that when this occurred within a positive therapy relationship, it was all right. "I knew they were being asked for a reason." "In the back of my head, I knew they were good." Direct questions about feelings or the abuse were described as being disconcerting at the beginning of a session but helpful in the middle of sessions. Becoming angry with the therapist was a problem for several adolescents in that it caused them to stop discussing particular topics, but they did learn that their anger did not stop the relationship.

The problem of limited time was reported by a majority of the adolescents. Adolescents who had had the experience of being provided a time at the end of a session to put some closure on the issues being discussed, to move away from any frightening feelings, and to chat about what they were going to do next reported less concern about the time limitation and described feeling better when they left. When the therapy time had been used for processing right until the end, adolescents reported feeling cut off and more upset as they left.

The worst part of the process was having earlier symptoms—panic attacks, flashbacks, suicidal thoughts, depression—come back. "It was hard to keep believing in therapy, I'm glad she did." Several adolescents reported that this return of earlier symptoms was less scary because their therapists had predicted them as something that happens when new areas of the abuse are looked at.

## THERAPY APPROACHES

As the adolescents and young adults talked about the therapies they had experienced, they expressed appreciation for different types of therapy. They appreciated the behavioral work that helped to slow down the chaos and gave them a sense of control. This they described as helping them keep going. They appreciated the cognitive work that gave them a framework for understanding what had happened and what they were experiencing. This helped them develop better methods of coping. They appreciated the internal work that enabled them to connect with themselves, both the "now" self and the "little" self. This seemed to help them move the cognitive understanding from something they knew to something they felt.

As I listened to these adolescents and young adults talk about their therapy experiences, I was struck, once again, by the importance of both the content of therapy and the relationship of therapy. Within the content, the abuse needs to be addressed. Although ideally this will include a discussion of the abuse scenario, even if the child is not ready to talk about the abuse itself, the dynamics surrounding the abuse are addressed. The centering of blame on the child, the threats and lack of protection, the juxtaposition of love and hate, closeness and betrayal, the wish for attention and pleasure, the distortion of sexuality and of reality, and the sense of damage are talked about, as are the dynamics within the child's family and particularly the child's early experiences of attachment.

The question of why the abuse happened needs to be addressed in therapy. Therapists are often reluctant to discuss the why question for fear of providing excuses for perpetrators. Pursuing the why question, however, helps to shift the abuse—the reason for the abuse and the emotional weight of the abuse—from the child back to where it belongs, with the abuser.

The context within which the abuse happened and, for some, within which the abuse was kept secret needs to be explored. The therapist needs to consider carefully the details of the context—abuse happening on a couch, people talking about others behind their backs—in order to prevent the therapy setting or process from inadvertently repeating these details. The feelings and experiences from the time of the abuse need to be recognized and talked about.

The therapy relationship is also important and needs to be discussed. This is particularly critical for children who have experienced an insecure or disorganized early attachment. Because the early attachment experiences are where a child learns how to behave with an adult, these early experiences are replayed within the therapy (transference). The therapist is placed in the role of the negligent, critical, or disorganized parent and may, if not careful, take on that role. By keeping track of the abuse scenario and the early relationship dynamics, the therapist can recognize transference reactions within the therapy setting. By keeping track of her own experiences and biases, the therapist can recognize countertransference reactions (Wieland, 1997). Once the therapist recognizes and separates out the countertransference reactions belonging to herself from the countertransference belonging to the therapy situation, she can learn more about the child's early experience and can then promote a more positive now experience. It is this experience that will help provide new and more positive internalizations for the child.

## ❑ Summary

Sexual abuse in childhood or adolescence may create confusion or may create trauma. In either case, abuse-related internalizations become part of the child or adolescent's internal working model. The child/adolescent and therapist need to work together to understand not just the present experiencing of the abuse but also the experience at the time of the abuse, not just the behavior symptoms but also the internal trauma.

The therapist needs to read and discuss with colleagues the literature on trauma, child development, and sexual abuse. The therapist needs to attend to the play, the conversation, and the behavior of the child or adolescent and to "hear" the internal trauma. The therapist needs to become aware of the types of reactions and interventions that are helpful and reactions and responses that are not helpful. The therapist then can, together with the child, address the internal trauma.

The child and therapist move together through the work of therapy. Situations and internalizations are talked about and are played out.

Imaging can help the child recognize what the experience was like at the time it occurred and can help the child accept and comfort himself. Drawing genograms, timelines, and identifying messages passed down to the child can help clarify how it was that abusive situations occurred and what the child understood from these situations. The therapist needs to consider the possibility of the child's experiencing a dysfunctional level of dissociation. For all children, issues related to sexuality need to be addressed. At times, through all of this, resistance may occur on the part of the child or the therapist. Recognizing, leaving space for, and then addressing the resistance allows the therapy to move forward.

The therapist also needs to know when to stop addressing the trauma, when it is time for the child or adolescent to move on. For some children, because the trauma is limited or because the child is feeling particularly anxious or vulnerable, a set number of sessions can be established at the beginning of therapy, so that there is a clear-cut ending point for therapy or for that particular piece of therapy. For others, a decrease in posttraumatic symptoms and the child's increased sense of self as someone who is whole and capable can indicate the time for therapy to draw to a close. Awareness of feelings, both positive and negative, together with fewer situations in which the child feels out of control or dissociates would similarly indicate the time for therapy to stop. When the child returns to his earlier healthy patterns of interrelating and exploring, the adult knows that the abuse-related internalizations are shifting. When a child who experienced neglect and abuse during early life shows less tension and less vigilance, together with more positive patterns of relating, the child is ready to move on without the support of therapy.

For all these children and adolescents, coming to the end of a piece of therapeutic work should not be defined as everything being solved. With older children and adolescents and with the parents of young children, future times of difficulty can be discussed. When a child starts to develop physically and becomes aware of sexual sensations, when he becomes sexually active, when he marries, when he has a child, when his child becomes the age he was when the abuse started, new issues or even the old issues and feelings may resurface. The 11-year-old, 16-year-old, or 30-year-old will have different reactions and questions from the 5-year-old. Knowing this ahead of time makes it easier for the child, adolescent, or adult to seek out therapy again. This is not the old trauma recurring; rather, it is new issues that similarly can be addressed and worked through.

Working with children and adolescents who have been sexually abused is both challenging and rewarding. Learning about the dynamics of child development, sexual abuse, and psychotherapy is demanding and time-consuming. Hearing each child's internal trauma is challenging, intellectually and emotionally. Addressing the child's internal trauma takes stamina and skill. Watching as a child shifts the blame to the right place, learns to trust, places boundaries where they should be, identifies with a positive sense of sexuality, reconnects to feelings, and starts to feel a positive sense of self is rewarding.

# References

Achenbach, T. M., & Edelbrock, C. (1983). *Manual for the Child Behavior Checklist and Revised Child Behavior Profile.* Burlington: University of Vermont, Department of Psychiatry.

Adams-Tucker, C. (1982). Proximate effects of sexual abuse in childhood: A report on 28 children. *American Journal of Psychiatry, 139,* 1252-1256.

Aiosa-Karpas, C., Karpas, R., Pelcovitz, D., & Kaplan, S. (1991). Gender identification and sex role attribution in sexually abused adolescent females. *Journal of the American Academy of Child and Adolescent Psychiatry, 30,* 266-271.

Albini, T. K., & Pease, T. E. (1989). Normal and pathological dissociations of early childhood. *Dissociation, 2,* 144-149.

Alexander, P. (1985). A systems theory conceptualization of incest. *Family Process, 24,* 79-88.

Alexander, P. (1992). Application of attachment theory to the study of sexual abuse. *Journal of Consulting and Clinical Psychology, 60,* 185-195.

American Psychiatric Association. (1994). *Diagnostic and statistical manual of mental disorders* (4th ed.). Washington, DC: Author.

Armstrong, J., Putnam, F., & Carlson, E. (1996). Appendix A: A-DES (version 1.0). In J. L. Silberg (Ed.), *The dissociative child: Diagnosis, treatment, and management.* Lutherville, MD: Sidran.

Atlas, J. A., & Hiott, J. (1994). Dissociative experience in a group of adolescents with history of abuse. *Perceptual and Motor Skills, 78,* 121-122.

Bagarozzi, D. A., & Anderson, S. A. (1989). *Personal, marital, and family myths: Theoretical formulations and clinical strategies.* New York: W. W. Norton.

217

Bagley, C., Wood, M., & Young, L. (1994). Victim to abuser: Mental health and behavioral sequels of child sexual abuse in a community survey of young adult males. *Child Abuse & Neglect, 18,* 683-697.

Barnett, E. (1981). *Analytical hypnotherapy: Principles and practice.* Kingston, ON: Junica.

Barnett, E. (1991). *Hypnoanalysis with survivors of childhood sexual abuse.* Paper presented at the annual meeting of the Ottawa Society of Clinical Hypnosis, Ottawa, ON.

Baum, E. A. (1978). Imaginary companions of two children. *Journal of the American Academy of Child Psychiatry, 17,* 324-330.

Beitchman, J. H., Zucker, K. J., Hood, J. E., daCosta, G. A., & Akman, D. (1991). A review of the short-term effects of child sexual abuse. *Child Abuse & Neglect, 15,* 537-556.

Beitchman, J. H., Zucker, K. J., Hood, J. E., daCosta, G. A., Akman, D., & Cassavia, E. (1992). A review of the long-term effects of child sexual abuse. *Child Abuse & Neglect, 16,* 101-118.

Bernstein, E. M., & Putnam, F. W. (1986). Development, reliability and validity of a dissociation scale. *Journal of Nervous and Mental Disease, 86,* 727-735.

Bowen, M. (1978). *Family therapy in clinical practice.* New York: Jason Aronson.

Bowlby, J. (1971). *Attachment and loss: Vol. 1. Attachment.* London: Pelican.

Bowlby, J. (1973). *Attachment and loss: Vol. 2. Separation.* London: Pelican.

Braun, B. G., & Sachs, R. G. (1985). The development of multiple personality disorder: Predisposing, precipitating, and perpetuating factors. In R. P. Kluft (Ed.), *Childhood antecedents of multiple personality.* Washington, DC: American Psychiatric Press.

Briere, J. (1992). *Child abuse trauma: Theory and treatment of the lasting effects.* Newbury Park, CA: Sage.

Briere, J. (1996a). A self-trauma model for treating adult survivors of severe child abuse. In J. Briere, L. Berliner, J. A. Bulkley, C. Jenny, & T. Reid (Eds.), *The APSAC handbook on child maltreatment* (pp. 140-157). Thousand Oaks, CA: Sage.

Briere, J. (1996b). *Trauma Symptom Checklist for Children.* Odessa, FL: Psychological Assessment Resources.

Briere, J., & Conte, J. R. (1993). Self-reported amnesia for abuse in adults molested as children. *Journal of Traumatic Stress, 6,* 21-31.

Briere, J., & Runtz, M. (1990). Differential adult symptomatology associated with three types of child abuse histories. *Child Abuse & Neglect, 14,* 357-364.

Bruckner, D., & Johnson, P. (1987). Treatment for adult male victims of childhood sexual abuse. *Social Casework, 68,* 81-87.

Burgess, A. W., Hartman, C. R., McCausland, M. P., & Powers, P. (1984). Response patterns in children and adolescents exploited through sex rings and pornography. *American Journal of Psychiatry, 141,* 656-662.

Cavaiola, A., & Schiff, M. (1988). Behavioral sequelae of physical and/or sexual abuse in adolescents. *Child Abuse & Neglect, 12,* 181-188.

Ceci, S. J., & Bruck, M. (1993). Suggestibility of the child witness: A historical review and synthesis. *Psychological Bulletin, 113,* 403-439.

Ceci, S. J., & Bruck, M. (1995). *Jeopardy in the courtroom: A scientific analysis of children's testimony.* Washington, DC: American Psychological Association.

Chaffin, M., Bonner, B., Worley, K., & Lawson, L. (1996). Treating abused adolescents. In J. Briere, L. Berliner, J. A. Bulkley, C. Jenny, & T. Reid (Eds.), *The APSAC handbook on child maltreatment.* Thousand Oaks, CA: Sage.

Chethik, M. (1989). *Techniques of child therapy: Psychodynamic strategies.* New York: Guilford.

Cole, P. M., & Putnam, F. (1992). Effect of incest on self and social functioning: A developmental psychopathology perspective. *Journal of Consulting and Clinical Psychology, 60,* 174-184.

Courtois, C. A. (1988). *Healing the incest wound: Adult survivors in therapy.* New York: W. W. Norton.

Courtois, C. A. (1996). Informed clinical practice and the delayed memory controversy. In K. Pezdek & W. Banks (Eds.), *The recovered memory/false memory debate.* New York: Academic Press.

Davies, J. M., & Frawley, M. G. (1994). *Treating the adult survivor of childhood sexual abuse: A psychoanalytic perspective.* New York: Basic Books.

DeBellis, M. D., & Putnam, F. W. (1994). The psychobiology of childhood maltreatment. *Child and Adolescent Psychiatric Clinics of North America, 3,* 1-16.

Deblinger, E., Hathaway, C. R., Lippmann, J., & Steer, R. (1993). Psychosocial characteristics and correlates of symptom distress in nonoffending mothers of sexually abused children. *Journal of Interpersonal Violence, 8,* 155-168.

Deblinger, E., & Heflin, A. H. (1996). *Treating sexually abused children and their nonoffending parents: A cognitive behavioral approach.* Thousand Oaks, CA: Sage.

Dell, P., & Eisenhower, J. W. (1990). Adolescent multiple personality disorder: A preliminary study of eleven cases. *Journal of the American Academy of Child and Adolescent Psychiatry, 29,* 359-366.

Dimock, P. (1988). Adult males sexually abused as children: Characteristics and implications for treatment. *Journal of Interpersonal Violence, 3,* 203-221.

Dixon, J. C. (1963). Depersonalization phenomena in a sample population of college students. *British Journal of Psychiatry, 109,* 371-375.

Dolan, Y. (1991). *Resolving sexual abuse: Solution-focused therapy and Ericksonian hypnosis for adult survivors.* New York: W. W. Norton.

Eibender, A. J., & Friedrich, W. N. (1989). Psychological functioning and behavior of sexually abused girls. *Journal of Consulting and Clinical Psychology, 57,* 155-157.

Ekstein, R. (1966). *Children of time and space, of action and impulse.* New York: Appleton-Century-Crofts.

Elkind, D. (1967). Egocentrism in adolescence. *Child Development, 38,* 1025-1034.

Everly, G. (1989). *A clinical guide to the treatment of the human stress response.* New York: Plenum.

Everly, G. (1993). Neurophysiological considerations in the treatment of posttraumatic stress disorder: A neurocognitive perspective. In J. P. Wilson & B. Raphael (Eds.), *International handbook of traumatic stress syndromes.* New York: Plenum.

Evers-Szostak, M., & Sanders, S. (1992). The Children's Perceptual Alteration Scale (CPAS): A measure of children's dissociation. *Dissociation, 5,* 91-95.

Fagan, J., & McMahon, P. P. (1984). Incipient multiple personality in children: Four cases. *Journal of Nervous and Mental Disease, 172,* 26-36.

Femina, D. D., Yeager, C. A., & Lewis, D. O. (1990). Child abuse: Adolescent records vs. adult recall. *Child Abuse & Neglect, 14,* 227-231.

Ferreira, A. (1963). Family myth and homeostasis. *Archives of General Psychiatry, 9,* 457-463.

Finkelhor, D. (1979). *Sexually victimized children.* New York: Free Press.

Finkelhor, D., & Browne, A. (1985). The traumatic impact of child sexual abuse: A conceptualization. *American Journal of Orthopsychiatry, 55,* 530-541.

Fivush, R. (1993). Developmental perspectives on autobiographical recall. In G. S. Goodman & B. L. Bottoms (Eds.), *Child victims, child witnesses: Understanding and improving testimony* (pp. 1-24). New York: Guilford.

Fossum, M., & Mason, M. (1986). *Facing shame: Families in recovery.* New York: W. W. Norton.

Fraser, G. A. (1991). The dissociative table technique: A strategy for working with ego states in dissociative disorders and ego-state therapy. *Dissociation, 4,* 205-212.

Friedman, H., Krakauer, S., & Rohrbaugh, M. (1989). Time-line vs. standard genograms: An experimental comparison [Summary]. *Proceedings and Abstracts of the Annual Meeting of the Eastern Psychological Association, 60,* 13.

Friedman, H., Rohrbaugh, M., & Krakauer, S. (1988). The time-line genogram: Highlighting temporal aspects of family relationships. *Family Process, 27,* 293-303.

Friedrich, W. N. (1988). Behavior problems in sexually abused children: An adaptive perspective. In G. E. Wyatt & G. P. Powell (Eds.), *Lasting effects of child sexual abuse.* Beverly Hills, CA: Sage.

Friedrich, W. N. (1990). *Psychotherapy of sexually abused children and their families.* New York: W. W. Norton.

Friedrich, W. N. (1993). Sexual victimization and sexual behavior in children: A review of recent literature. *Child Abuse & Neglect, 17,* 59-66.

Friedrich, W. N. (1995). *Psychotherapy with sexually abused boys: An integrated approach.* Thousand Oaks, CA: Sage.

Friedrich, W. N., Grambsch, P., Broughton, D., Kuipers, J., & Beilke, R. L. (1991). Normative sexual behavior in children. *Pediatrics, 88,* 456-464.

Friedrich, W. N., Grambsch, P., Damon, L., Koverola, C., Wolfe, V., Hewitt, S., Lang, R., & Broughton, D. (1992). Child sexual behavior inventory: Normative and clinical comparisons. *Psychological Assessment, 4,* 303-311.

Friedrich, W. N., Urquiza, A. J., & Beilke, R. L. (1986). Behavior problems in sexually abused young children. *Journal of Pediatric Psychology, 11,* 47-57.

Gardner, G., & Olness, K. (1981). *Hypnosis and hypnotherapy with children.* New York: Grune & Stratton.

Gelinas, D. J. (1983). The persisting negative effects of incest. *Psychiatry, 46,* 312-332.

Gil, E. (1991). *The healing power of play: Working with abused children.* New York: Guilford.

Gil, E. (1996). *Treating abused adolescents.* New York: Guilford.

Gil, E., & Johnson, T. C. (1993). *Sexualized children: Assessment and treatment of sexualized children and children who molest.* Rockville, MD: Launch.

Goldston, D., Turnquist, D., & Knutson, J. (1989). Presenting problems of sexually abused girls receiving psychiatric services. *Journal of Abnormal Psychology, 98,* 314-317.

Gomez-Schwartz, B., Horowitz, J. M., & Cardarelli, A. P. (1990). *Child sexual abuse: The initial effects.* Newbury Park, CA: Sage.

Goodwin, J., Cheeves, K., & Connell, V. (1989). In J. Goodwin (Ed.), *Sexual abuse: Incest victims and their families* (2nd ed.). Chicago: Year Book Medical Publishers.

Gordon, B., Schroeder, C., & Abrams, J. M. (1990a). Age and social-class differences in children's knowledge of sexuality. *Journal of Clinical Child Psychology, 19,* 33-43.

Gordon, B., Schroeder, C., & Abrams, J. M. (1990b). Children's knowledge of sexuality: A comparison of sexually abused and nonabused children. *American Journal of Orthopsychiatry, 60,* 250-257.

Gould, C. (1993). Presentation in A. L. McCulley (Producer/Director), *Dissociation in children* [Videotape]. Nevada City, CA: Cavalcade Productions.

Gould, C., & Graham-Costain, V. (1994). Play therapy with ritually abused children. *Treating Abuse Today, 4,* 4-10, 14-19.

Graham-Costain, V. (1993). Presentation in A. L. McCulley (Producer/Director), *Dissociation in children* [Videotape]. Nevada City, CA: Cavalcade Productions.

Green, R. (1994). Atypical psychosexual development. In M. Rutter, E. Taylor, & L. Hersov (Eds.), *Child and adolescent psychiatry: Modern approaches.* Oxford: Blackwell Scientific.

Groth, A. N. (1979). Sexual trauma in the life histories of rapists and child molesters. *Victimology, 4,* 10-16.

Grove, D., & Panzer, B. I. (1991). *Resolving traumatic memories: Metaphors and symbols in psychotherapy.* New York: Irvington.

Harter, S. (1983). Developmental perspectives on the self-system. In E. M. Hetherington (Ed.), *Handbook of child psychology: Socialization, personality, and social development* (4th ed.). New York: John Wiley.

Hartman, C. R., & Burgess, A. W. (1988). Information processing of trauma: Case application of a model. *Journal of Interpersonal Violence, 3,* 443-457.

Hartman, C. R., & Burgess, A. W. (1993). Information processing of trauma. *Child Abuse & Neglect, 17,* 47-58.

Herman, J. L. (1992). *Trauma and recovery: The aftermath of violence—from domestic abuse to political terror.* New York: Basic Books.

Herman, J. L., & Schatzow, E. (1987). Recovery and verification of memories of childhood sexual trauma. *Psychoanalytic Psychology, 4,* 1-14.

Hindman, J. (1989). *Just before the dawn.* Ontario, OR: AlesAndria Associates.

Hoffman, L. (1981). *Foundation of family therapy: A conceptual framework for systems change.* New York: Basic Books.

Hooper, C. (1992). *Mothers surviving child sexual abuse.* London: Tavistock/Routledge.

Hornstein, N. L. (1991, October). *The treatment of MPD in children and adolescents.* Paper presented at Treatment of Dissociation and Multiple Personality Disorders Conference, Baltimore.

Hornstein, N. L. (1996). Complexities of psychiatric differential diagnosis in children with dissociative symptoms and disorders. In J. L. Silberg (Ed.), *The dissociative child: Diagnosis, treatment, and management.* Lutherville, MD: Sidran.

Hornstein, N. L., & Putnam, F. W. (1992). Clinical phenomenology of child and adolescent dissociative disorders. *Journal of the American Academy of Child and Adolescent Psychiatry, 31,* 1077-1085.

Hornstein, N. L., & Silberg, J. (1995). *Diagnostic and therapeutic issues in childhood dissociative disorders.* Paper presented at the 12th Annual Meeting of the International Society for the Study of Dissociation, Orlando, FL.

Hornstein, N. L., & Tyson, S. (1991). Inpatient treatment of children with multiple personality/dissociative disorders and their families. *Psychiatric Clinics of North America, 14,* 631-648.

Hyde, N. D. (1990). Voices from the silence: Use of imagery with incest survivors. In T. A. Laidlaw & C. Marmo (Eds.), *Healing voices: Feminist approaches to therapy with women* (pp. 163-193). San Francisco: Jossey-Bass.

International Society for the Study of Dissociation, Standards of Practice Committee. (1994). *ISSD guidelines for treating dissociative identity disorder (multiple personality disorder) in adults.* Skokie, IL: Author.

Irwin, H. J. (1996). Traumatic childhood events, perceived availability of emotional support, and the development of dissociative tendencies. *Child Abuse & Neglect, 20,* 701-707.

James, B. (1989). *Treating traumatized children: New insights and creative interventions.* Lexington, MA: Lexington.

James, B. (1990). Practice: The dissociatively disordered child. *Advisor, 3,* 8-10.

Johnson, R., & Shrier, D. (1987). Past sexual victimization by females of male patients in an adolescent medicine clinic population. *American Journal of Psychiatry, 144,* 650-652.

Johnson, T. C. (1993). Preliminary findings. In E. Gil & T. C. Johnson, *Sexualized children: Assessment and treatment of sexualized children and children who molest.* Rockville, MD: Launch.

Karen, R. (1994). *Becoming attached: Unfolding the mystery of the infant-mother bond and its impact on later life.* New York: Warner.

Karp, C. L., & Butler, T. L. (1996). *Treatment strategies for abused children: From victim to survivor.* Thousand Oaks, CA: Sage.

Kaufman, J., & Zigler, E. (1987). Do abused children become abusive parents? *American Journal of Orthopsychiatry, 57,* 186-192.

Kendall-Tackett, K. A., Williams, L. M., & Finkelhor, D. (1993). Impact of sexual abuse on children: A review and synthesis of recent empirical studies. *Psychological Bulletin, 113,* 164-180.

Klein, R. (1989). Countertransference with the borderline patient. In J. Masterson & R. Klein (Eds.), *Psychotherapy of the disorders of the self: The Masterson approach.* New York: Brunner/Mazel.

Kluft, R. P. (1984). Multiple personality in childhood. *Psychiatric Clinics of North America, 7,* 121-134.

Kluft, R. P. (1985). Childhood multiple personality disorder: Predictors, clinical findings, and treatment results. In R. P. Kluft (Ed.), *Childhood antecedents of multiple personality.* Washington, DC: American Psychiatric Press.

Kluft, R. P. (1996). Outpatient treatment of dissociative identity disorder and allied forms of dissociative disorder not otherwise specified in children and adolescents. *Child and Adolescent Psychiatric Clinics of North America, 5,* 471-494.

Kluft, R. P., & Fine, C. G. (Eds.). (1993). *Clinical perspectives on multiple personality disorder.* Washington, DC: American Psychiatric Press.

LaPorta, L. D. (1992). Childhood trauma and the multiple personality disorder: The case of a 9-year-old girl. *Child Abuse & Neglect, 16,* 615-620.

LeDoux, J. (1994). Emotion, memory and the brain. *Scientific American, 270,* 50-57.

Levine, E. S. (1980). Indirect suggestions through personalized fairy tales for treatment of childhood insomnia. *American Journal of Clinical Hypnosis, 23,* 57-63.

Littner, N. (1960). The child's need to repeat his past: Some implications for placement. *Social Service Review, 34,* 128-148.

Main, M., & Solomon, J. (1990). Procedures for identifying infants as disorganized/disoriented during the Ainsworth strange situation. In M. Greenberg, D. Cicchetti, & M. Cummings (Eds.), *Attachment in the preschool years.* Chicago: University of Chicago Press.

Malenbaum, R., & Russell, A. T. (1987). Multiple personality disorder in an eleven-year-old boy and his mother. *Journal of the American Academy of Child and Adolescent Psychiatry, 26,* 436-439.

Malinosky-Rummell, R. R., & Hoier, T. S. (1992). Validating measures of dissociation in sexually abused and nonabused children. *Behavioral Assessment, 13,* 341-357.

Maltz, W. (1991). *The sexual healing journey: A guide for survivors of sexual abuse.* New York: HarperCollins.

Manion, I. G., McIntyre, J., Firestone, P., Ligezinska, M., Ensom, R., & Wells, G. (1996). Secondary traumatization in parents following the disclosure of extrafamilial child sexual abuse: Initial effects. *Child Abuse & Neglect, 20,* 1095-1110.

Mann, B. J., & Sanders, S. (1994). Child dissociation and the family context. *Journal of Abnormal Child Psychology, 22,* 373-388.

McCann, I. L., & Pearlman, L. A. (1990). *Psychological trauma and the adult survivor: Theory, therapy, and transformation.* New York: Brunner/Mazel.

McElroy, L. P. (1992). Early indicators of pathological dissociation in sexually abused children. *Child Abuse & Neglect, 16,* 833-846.

McGoldrick, M., & Gerson, R. (1985). *Genograms in family assessment.* New York: W. W. Norton.

McMahon, C. E., & Sheikh, A. A. (1986). Imagination in disease and healing processes: A historical perspective. In A. A. Sheikh (Ed.), *Anthology of imagery techniques.* Milwaukee, WI: American Imagery Institute.

Meiselman, K. C. (1978). *Incest: A psychological study of causes and effects with treatment recommendations.* San Francisco: Jossey-Bass.

Mendel, M. P. (1995). *The male survivor: The impact of sexual abuse.* Thousand Oaks, CA: Sage.

Mennen, F. E., & Meadow, D. (1995). The relationship of abuse characteristics to symptoms in sexually abused girls. *Journal of Interpersonal Violence, 10,* 259-274.

Mian, M., Marton, P., & LeBaron, D. (1996). The effects of sexual abuse on 3- to 5-year-old girls. *Child Abuse & Neglect, 20,* 731-746.

Minuchin, S., & Fishman, H. C. (1981). *Family therapy techniques.* Cambridge, MA: Harvard University Press.

Morrow, K. B., & Sorell, G. T. (1989). Factors affecting self-esteem, depression, and negative behaviors in sexually abused female adolescents. *Journal of Marriage and the Family, 51,* 677-686.

Myers, J. E. B. (1992). *Legal issues in child abuse and neglect.* Newbury Park, CA: Sage.

Nemzer, E. (1996). Psychopharmacological interventions for children and adolescents with dissociative disorders. In J. L. Silberg (Ed.), *The dissociative child: Diagnosis, treatment, and management.* Lutherville, MD: Sidran.

Nilsson, L., & Archer, T. (1992). Biological aspects of memory and emotion: Affect and cognition. In S.-A. Christianson (Ed.), *The handbook of emotion and memory: Research and theory.* Hillsdale, NJ: Lawrence Erlbaum.

Ornitz, E. M., & Pynoos, R. S. (1989). Startle modulation in children with post-traumatic stress disorder. *American Journal of Psychiatry, 147,* 866-870.

Ornstein, P. (1995). Children's long-term retention of salient personal experience. *Journal of Traumatic Stress, 8,* 581-605.

Pearce, J. W., & Pezzot-Pearce, T. D. (1997). *Psychotherapy of abused and neglected children.* Guilford: New York.

Pearlman, L. A. (1997). *Constructivist approach to trauma treatment.* Workshop sponsored by the Centre for Treatment of Sexual Abuse and Childhood Trauma, Ottawa.

Pearson, G. (Ed.). (1968). *A handbook of child psychoanalysis.* New York: Basic Books.

Perry, B. (1996). Incubated in terror: Neurodevelopmental factors in the "cycle of violence." In J. D. Osofsky (Ed.), *Children, youth and violence: Searching for solutions.* New York: Guilford.

Peterson, G. (1991). Children coping with trauma: Diagnosis of "dissociation identity disorder." *Dissociation, 4,* 152-164.

Peterson, G. (1993). Presentation in A. L. McCulley (Producer/Director), *Dissociation in children* [Videotape]. Nevada City, CA: Cavalcade Productions.

Peterson, G. (1996). Treatment of early onset. In J. L. Spira (Ed.), *Treating dissociative identity disorder.* San Francisco: Jossey-Bass.

Peterson, G., & Putnam, F. W. (1994). Preliminary results of the field trial proposed criteria for dissociative disorder of childhood. *Dissociation, 7,* 212-219.

Piaget, J., & Inhelder, B. (1969). *The psychology of the child.* New York: Basic Books.

Prior, S. (1996). *Object relations in severe trauma: Psychotherapy of the sexually abused child.* Northvale, NJ: Jason Aronson.

Putnam, F. W. (1989). *Diagnosis and treatment of multiple personality disorder.* New York: Guilford.

Putnam, F. W. (1991). Dissociative disorders in children and adolescents: Developmental perspective. *Psychiatric Clinics of North America, 14,* 519-532.

Putnam, F. W. (1993). Dissociative disorders in children: Behavioral profiles and problems. *Child Abuse & Neglect, 17,* 39-46.

Putnam, F. W. (1994). Dissociative disorders in children and adolescents. In S. J. Lynn & J. W. Rhue (Eds.), *Dissociation: Clinical and theoretical perspectives.* New York: Guilford.

Putnam, F. W. (1996). Child development and dissociation. *Child and Adolescent Psychiatric Clinics of North America, 5,* 285-301.

Putnam, F. W. (1997). *Dissociation in children and adolescents: A developmental perspective.* New York: Guilford.

Putnam, F. W., Helmers, K., Horowitz, L. A., & Trickett, P. K. (1995). Hypnotizability and dissociativity in sexually abused girls. *Child Abuse & Neglect, 19,* 645-657.

Putnam, F. W., Helmers, K., & Trickett, P. K. (1993). Development, reliability, and validity of a child dissociation scale. *Child Abuse & Neglect, 17,* 731-741.

Putnam, F. W., & Peterson, G. (1994). Further validation of the Child Dissociative Checklist. *Dissociation, 7,* 204-209.

Pynoos, R. S., & Nader, K. (1993). Issues in the treatment of posttraumatic stress in children and adolescents. In J. P. Wilson & B. Raphael (Eds.), *International handbook of traumatic stress syndromes.* New York: Plenum.

Pynoos, R. S., Steinberg, A. M., & Goenjian, A. K. (1996). Traumatic stress in childhood and adolescence: Recent developments and current controversies. In B. A. van der Kolk, A. C. McFarlane, & L. Weisaeth (Eds.), *Traumatic stress: The effects of overwhelming experience on mind, body, and society.* New York: Guilford.

Reagor, P. A., Kasten, J. D., & Morelli, N. (1992). A checklist for screening dissociative disorders in children and adolescents. *Dissociation, 5,* 4-19.

Rhue, J. W., & Lynn, S. J. (1991a). Storytelling, hypnosis and the treatment of sexually abused children. *International Journal of Clinical and Experimental Hypnosis, 31,* 198-214.

Rhue, J. W., & Lynn, S. J. (1991b). The use of hypnotic techniques with sexually abused children. In W. C. Webster & D. J. O'Grady (Eds.), *Clinical hypnosis with children.* New York: Brunner/Mazel.

Riley, R., & Mead, J. (1988). The development of symptoms of multiple personality disorder in a child of three. *Dissociation, 1,* 41-46.

Rosenberg, E. (1995). *Growing up feeling good.* New York: Puffin.

Rosenfeld, S. (1981). Some comments on clinical casework. In D. Daws & M. Boston (Eds.), *The child psychotherapist and problems of young people.* London: Wildwood House.

Russell, D. E. H. (1986). *The secret trauma: Incest in the lives of girls and women.* New York: Basic Books.

Rutter, M. (1971). Normal psychosexual development. *Journal of Child Psychology and Psychiatry, 11,* 259-283.

Sanders, B., & Giolas, M. H. (1991). Dissociation and childhood trauma in psychologically disturbed adolescents. *American Journal of Psychiatry, 148,* 50-54.

Santostefano, S., & Calicchia, J. (1992). Body image, relational psychoanalysis, and the construction of meaning: Implications for treating aggressive children. *Development and Psychopathology, 4,* 655-678.

Seligman, M. E. P. (1975). *Helplessness: On depression, development, and death.* San Francisco: W. H. Freeman.

Shalev, A. Y. (1996). Stress versus traumatic stress: From acute homeostatic reactions to chronic psychopathology. In B. A. van der Kolk, A. C. McFarlane, & L. Weisaeth (Eds.), *Traumatic stress: The effects of overwhelming experience on mind, body, and society* (pp. 77-101). New York: Guilford.

Sheikh, A. A., & Panagiotou, N. C. (1975). Use of mental imagery in psychotherapy: A critical review. *Perceptual and Motor Skills, 41,* 555-585.

Shirar, L. (1996). *Dissociative children: Bridging the inner and outer worlds.* New York: W. W. Norton.

Silberg, J. L. (Ed.). (1996a). *The dissociative child: Diagnosis, treatment, and management.* Lutherville, MD: Sidran.

Silberg, J. L. (1996b). Interviewing strategies for assessing dissociative disorders in children and adolescents. In J. L. Silberg (Ed.), *The dissociative child: Diagnosis, treatment, and management.* Lutherville, MD: Sidran.

Silberg, J. L. (1996c). Psychological testing with dissociative children and adolescents. In J. L. Silberg (Ed.), *The dissociative child: Diagnosis, treatment, and management.* Lutherville, MD: Sidran.

Silberg, J. L. (1997). *Guidelines for treatment of dissociation in children.* Proposal prepared for the International Society for the Study of Dissociation, Skokie, IL.

Silberg, J. L., & Waters, F. (1996). Factors associated with positive therapeutic outcome. In J. L. Silberg (Ed.), *The dissociative child: Diagnosis, treatment, and management.* Lutherville, MD: Sidran.

Sirles, E. A., Smith, J. A., & Kusama, H. (1989). Psychiatric status of intrafamilial child sexual abuse victims. *Journal of the American Academy of Child and Adolescent Psychiatry, 28,* 225-229.

Spiegel, D. (1984). Multiple personality as a post-traumatic stress disorder. *Psychiatric Clinics of North America, 7,* 101-110.

Stanton, M. D. (1992). The time line and the "why now?" question: A technique and rationale for therapy, training, organizational consultation and research. *Journal of Marital and Family Therapy, 18,* 331-343.

Terr, L. C. (1988). What happens to early memories of trauma? A study of twenty children under age five at the time of documented traumatic events. *Journal of the American Academy of Child and Adolescent Psychiatry, 27,* 96-104.

Terr, L. C. (1990). *Too scared to cry: Psychic trauma in childhood.* New York: Harper & Row.

Terr, L. C. (1991). Childhood traumas: An outline and overview. *American Journal of Psychiatry, 148,* 10-20.

Tobias, B., Kihlstrom, J. F., & Schacter, D. L. (1992). Emotion and implicit memory. In S. A. Christianson (Ed.), *The handbook of emotion and memory: Research and theory.* Hillsdale, NJ: Lawrence Erlbaum.

Trepper, T. S., & Barrett, M. J. (1989). *Systemic treatment of incest: A therapeutic handbook.* New York: Brunner/Mazel.

Trujillo, K., Lewis, B. O., Yeager, C. A., & Gidlow, B. (1996). Imaginary companions of school boys and boys with dissociative identity disorder/multiple personality disorder: A normal to pathologic continuum. *Child and Adolescent Psychiatric Clinics of North America, 5,* 375-391.

van der Kolk, B. A. (1994). The body keeps the score: Memory and the evolving psychobiology of posttraumatic stress. *Harvard Review of Psychiatry, 1,* 253-265.

van der Kolk, B. A. (1996a). The body keeps the score: Approaches to the psychobiology of posttraumatic stress disorder. In B. A. van der Kolk, A. C. McFarlane, & L. Weisaeth (Eds.), *Traumatic stress: The effects of overwhelming experience on mind, body, and society.* New York: Guilford.

van der Kolk, B. A. (1996b). Trauma and memory. In B. A. van der Kolk, A. C. McFarlane, & L. Weisaeth (Eds.), *Traumatic stress: The effects of overwhelming experience on mind, body, and society* (pp. 279-302). New York: Guilford.

Van Gijseghem, H., & Gauthier, M. (1994). Links between sexual abuse in childhood and behavioural disorders on adolescent girls: A multivariate approach. *Canadian Journal of Behavioural Science, 26,* 339-352.

Vincent, M., & Pickering, M. R. (1988). Multiple personality disorder in childhood. *Canadian Journal of Psychiatry, 33,* 524-529.

Waldschmidt, C., Graham-Costain, V., & Gould, C. (1991, November). *Memory association in play therapy with children with multiple personality disorder.* Paper presented at the Eighth International Conference on Multiple Personality/Dissociative States.

Waters, F. S. (1989). Non-hypnotic therapeutic techniques for multiple personality in children [Summary]. In B. G. Braun (Ed.), *Proceedings of the Sixth International Conference on Multiple Personality/Dissociative States.* Chicago: Rush.

Waters, F. S. (1996). Parents as partners in the treatment of dissociative children. In J. L. Silberg (Ed.), *The dissociative child: Diagnosis, treatment, and management.* Lutherville, MD: Sidran.

Waters, F. S., & Silberg, J. L. (1996a). Promoting integration in dissociative children. In J. L. Silberg (Ed.), *The dissociative child: Diagnosis, treatment, and management.* Lutherville, MD: Sidran.

Waters, F. S., & Silberg, J. L. (1996b). Therapeutic phases in the treatment of dissociative children. In J. L. Silberg (Ed.), *The dissociative child: Diagnosis, treatment, and management.* Lutherville, MD: Sidran.

Watkins, J. G., & Watkins, H. H. (1992). *Hypnosis and ego-state therapy.* Paper presented at the International Conference on the Study of Multiple Personality and Dissociation, Chicago.

Weiss, M., Sutton, P., & Utrecht, A. J. (1985). Multiple personality in a ten-year-old girl. *Journal of the American Academy of Child and Adolescent Psychiatry, 24,* 495-501.

Wherry, J. N., Jolly, J. B., Feldman, J., Adam, B., & Manjanatha, S. (1994). The Child Dissociative Checklist: Preliminary findings of a screening instrument. *Child Sexual Abuse, 3,* 51-66.

White, M., & Epston, D. (1990). *Narrative means to therapeutic ends.* New York: W. W. Norton.

Wieland, S. (1997). *Hearing the internal trauma: Working with children and adolescents who have been sexually abused.* Thousand Oaks, CA: Sage.

Williams, L. M. (1994). Recall of childhood trauma: A prospective study of women's memories of child sexual abuse. *Journal of Consulting and Clinical Psychology, 62,* 1167-1176.

Williams, M. B. (1991). Clinical work with families of MPD patients: Assessment and issues for practice. *Dissociation, 4,* 92-98.

Williamson, J., Borduin, C., & Howe, B. (1991). The ecology of adolescent maltreatment: A multilevel examination of adolescent physical abuse, sexual abuse, and neglect. *Journal of Consulting and Clinical Psychology, 59,* 449-457.

Yates, A. (1991). Childhood sexuality. In M. Lewis (Ed.), *Child and adolescent psychiatry: A comprehensive textbook.* Baltimore: Williams & Wilkins.

# Index

Abuse-focused model, 21-22, 41-42
Abuser, placing the abuse with the, 80, 100-101
Adolescents:
    age-appropriate behaviors, 164-165
    control over situations, trying to gain, 27-28
    dissociation, 115-116, 120-124, 127-129
    guilty, I am (internationalization), 27
    infatuation with and older person, 27
    intrusive thoughts, 30
    issues relevant to, addressing, 132
    memories of abuse/lack of protection, 31-32
    metacognitive processes, lack of, 146-148
    negative experience, therapy as a, 206-208
    positive experience, therapy as a, 208-214
    self-blame, 11
    self-definition, 8-9
Adoption, 83-84, 139

Advice, 207
Age-appropriate behaviors, 162-165
Ages, Sandy, xiv
Aggressive behavior, 9-10, 26, 137
Alcohol, 82
Alliances/abuses/losses/shifts, identifying family, 88-89
Ambivalent feelings, 13-14, 33
Angry alters of adults with dissociative identities, 137
Animals, children taking on behaviors of, 144
Anxiety:
    decreasing, structural guidelines for, 26
    grounding techniques, 31, 49
    imaging not to be used for high, 48
    normal response, 25
Arousal system, 10, 26
Atmosphere in the therapy room, 208-214
Attachment experiences, positive/negative, 3, 5, 40
Attention seeking as normal, 27

Attention to the child, sexual abuse pro-
    viding, 15-16
Avoiding old events and feelings, 187,
    191-194
    *See also* Resistance, child's


Behaviors, imaging and learning new, 63-
    68
Betrayal and closeness, juxtaposition of,
    14, 33-34
Beyond the abuse, existence, 97
Biological tendency and dissociation, 118
Blank slate, therapy with a, 206-207
Body as an important and healthy part
    of self, 159-162
Body feeling, cutting off, 16
    *See also* Dissociation
Boundaries, sexual abuse as disrespect-
    ful of, 15, 34-36
Bowen, Murray, 80


Chaotic, I feel (internationalization), 13-
    14, 32-33
Child Behavior Checklist, 123
Child Dissociative Checklist (CDC), 122
Children:
    animals, children taking on behav-
        iors of, 144
    children who molest children, 153-154
    control of the conversation, estab-
        lishing the child as in, 176-178
    diagnosing dissociation in, 120-124
    dissociation and clinical observations
        with school-age, 125-127
    dissociation and clinical observations
        with the young child, 124-125
    educating the family/child about dis-
        sociation, 139-143
    fragmented self and dissociation, 116
    self-regulate, ability to, 8
    therapy, child-focused, 39-41
    voices, intrusive, 144-145
    *See also* Resistance, child's
Children's Perceptual Alteration Scale, 122
Cimermanis, Bev, xiv
Closeness and betrayal, juxtaposition of,
    14, 33-34

Cognitive therapy, 134
Comfort objects, 31
Compulsive behaviors, 167-170
Confrontation, direct, 207
Consistency and safety in therapeutic
    setting and therapist's reactions, 132
Conte, Jon, xiv
Control, my sexuality means no (inter-
    nationalization), 16, 37
Control of the conversation, establishing
    the child as in, 27-28, 176-178
Coping strategies, 18, 22, 40, 138
    *See also* Dissociation
Corticosteroids, 12
Countertransference, 40
Court cases and imaging, 44, 48-49
Cross-sectional views of relationships
    within a family. *See* Genograms
Curiosity, sexual, 28


Damaged, I am (internationalization), 9,
    23-25
Dearning, Penny, xiv
Decision making, fear of, 12
Defenses, sensitivity to a child's, 49-50
Demeanor, therapist, 209
Denial, 17, 18, 48
Depersonalization, 116
Depression, 3, 82
Developmental stages/tasks, 40, 88
Dichotomous responses, 154
Discrete behavioral states model, 120
Dissatisfaction, sexual, 172
Dissociation:
    acceptance by the therapist of child's
        inner experiences, 131
    adolescents, clinical observations
        with, 127-129
    communication between parts, en-
        couraging, 62-63
    defining, 17-18
    diagnosing, 120-124
    dissociative disorder of childhood
        (DDoC), 117
    dissociative identities, 117, 137
    educating the family/child, 130, 131,
        139-143

environment, working with the, 134-139

examples of, 114

feeling states, increasing the awareness within a child of, 130

hypnosis, 131

integration of all the parts, 131-133

internal dynamics of, exploring the, 25, 143-148

International Society for the Study of Dissociation, 134

Kluft's four-factor theory, 118-119, 129-131

McElroy's model, 119

normal to dysfunctional, 115-116

play therapy, 132-133

psychopharmacological interventions for, 133-134

Putnam's model, 120

resistance, 181, 183-184

school-age child, clinical observations with the, 125-127

summary, 148-149

therapy room, within the, 38-39

triggers that activate, 131

Watkins and Watkin's model, 119-120

young child, clinical observations with the, 124-125

Dissociative Experience Scale, 115, 123

Dissociative Features Profile (DEP), 123

Distorted messages and distortion of reality, 17-18

Distress, identifying points of, 58-60

Distrust of people and of the future, 3-4, 34

Documentation and imaging, 50

Drugs, 82

Dynamic interactive process, therapy as a, xiv

Dysregulation, 10, 26


Educating the family/child about dissociation, 130, 131, 139-143

Ego states, 119-120

Egocentric thinking, 10

Emotional distress, 82

Emotions, I have no (internationalization), 17-18, 38

Emotions, imaging and exploring, 60-62, 68

Entrances and exits of important people and timelines, 95

Environment influencing coping mechanisms, 22

Escape mechanisms, 17-18
  See also Dissociation

Exhibitionism, 152

Exits and entrances of important people and timelines, 95

Experiences and messages, recognizing/understanding early, 98-100

Extreme sexual abuse, 15, 114, 118

Eye contact, therapist's making, 209


Families:
  dissociation and therapists working with, 134-139

  educating the family/child about dissociation, 130, 131, 139-143

  resistance, 197-200

  separate place from the child where parents talk, 130

  special status in, sexual abuse providing, 15-16

  See also Genograms; Timelines

Fantasy and reality, differentiating, 48, 115

Feeling states, increasing the awareness within a child of, 130

Feelings, my sexuality means no (internationalization), 16, 37

Flashbacks, 137, 212
  anxiety, relieving, 49

  frightening, 75

  grounding techniques, 31

  physical sensation memories, 24

  traumatic imaging, 43

  working with, imaging and, 54-56

Flexibility in the therapist's approach, 210

Forced or pushed into therapy, 206

Foster home placement, 84, 139

Frayne, Jill, xiv

Frightening feelings/scenes from imaging, 75-76


Gender issues and sexual abuse, 153, 154-155

Genograms:
   alliances/abuses/losses/shifts, identifying family, 88-89
   confusing to read, 81
   context for viewing both abuse and family response, 80
   creating, 82-87
   markings used, 81-82
   messages and myths passed down within a family, 103-111
   patterns in the family, identifying, 89-90
   relationships and experiences set down in concrete form, 81
   role of sexual abuse in the family, 90-92
   structure to the child's story, providing, 92-94
   summary, 112
Good things happen when I'm sexual (internationalization), 15-16, 36-37, 40
Grounding techniques, 31, 49
Group home placement, 84
Guided imagery, 46
Guilty, I am (internationalization), 10-11, 26-29, 100

Hate, 33
Healing experiences and dissociation, 119
Hearing the Internal Trauma: Working With Children and Adolescents Who Have Been Sexually Abused (Wieland), xi, 4
Helplessness, learned, 9-10
Hippocampus, 12
Homosexuality, 170-171
Hyperresponsivity of the biological systems caused by abuse, 9-10, 24-25, 133-134
Hypnosis, 46, 47-48, 131

Imaginary playmates, 115
Imaging:
   abuse-related internalization of self, working through the, 57-58
   connecting with the part that was abused, 51-53
   defining, 45-46

developing the image, 72-76
dissociation, 62-63
distress, identifying points of, 58-60
emotions, exploring, 60-62
flashbacks, 54-56
hypnosis, 47-48
initiating the, 68-72
not be used, when imaging should, 48-50
"now self" to help the "younger self," using the, 53-54
positive therapy experience, 211
pseudomemories, 46-47
skills, learning new, 63-68
summary, 77
terminating the imaging, 76-77
therapeutic, 43-44
traumatic, 43, 44
Immature impulsive responding, 18
Infants. See Children
Infatuation with an older person, 27
Information processing model, 5
Integrated contextual model, 5
Internal dynamics of dissociation, exploring the, 143-148
Internalization model, xii
   ambivalent feelings, 13-14
   boundaries, sexual abuse as disrespectful of, 15
   closeness and betrayal, juxtaposition of, 14
   common characteristics of sexual abuse experiences, 6, 7
   context within which the event(s) occurred, 4
   distorted messages and distortion of reality, 17-18
   egocentric thinking, 10
   good things happen when I'm sexual (internationalization), 36-37
   helplessness, learned, 9-10
   intrusion, 8-9
   memories of abuse/lack of protection, 13
   perceptions of and reactions to new experiences, 3-4
   physiological reactivity, 9-10
   psychodynamic trauma-focused therapy, xii

self-blame, 11
sensorimotor/emotional modalities, 12-13
sexualized behaviors, 15-17
simplification, 6, 8
summary, 19
threats, 11-12
working models, 2
See also Therapy
International Society for the Study of Dissociation, 134
Interventions, therapist's, 188-190, 195-196, 209-211
Intrusion, 8-9, 25, 30

Kanigsberg, Ellie, xiv
Kluft's four-factor theory, 118-119, 129-131

Labels, use of diagnostic, 25, 207
Laberge, Thérse, xiv
Lees, Ann, xiv
Literature/studies on trauma/child development and sexual abuse, 117-120, 214
Longitudinal views of relationships within a family. See Timelines

Mamon, Maggie, xiv
Masculinity, society's concept of, 154
Masturbation, 152
McElroy's model, 119
Medications and dissociation, 133-134
Melodic tones and imaging, 71
Memories of abuse/lack of protection:
dissociation, 128
false, 46-47
intrusive/suppressed/repressed, 13, 17, 30-32
negative therapy experiences, 207
physical sensation memories, 24
timelines, 96-97
Messages and myths passed down within a family:
identifying, 103-108
new messages, creating, 110-111
questioning, 107, 108-110

Metacognitive processes, lack of, 146-148
Metaphor of play, 191
Models for understanding the dynamics and effects of sexual abuse:
information processing model, 5
integrated contextual model, 5
traumagenic factor model, 4-5
See also Internalization model
Multigenerational diagrams. See Genograms
Multiple personalities, 117
"Multiple Personality in Childhood" (Kluft), 129
Mylination of the hippocampus, 12
Myths. See Messages and myths passed down within a family

Negative feelings, my sexuality means (internationalization), 16, 37
Negative space and imaging, 73
Neurobiological effects, 26
New positive messages, identifying and practicing, 110-111
New situations, fear of, 12
Nurturing and dissociation, 119

Observing behaviors and diagnosing dissociation, 121, 124-129
Oke, Susan, xiv
Orientation, sexual, 170-171

Panic attacks, 212
Parents. See Families
Peer sex play, 152
Perceptions and reactions to new experiences, 2-4
Physical sensation memories, 24
Physiological reactivity, 9-10, 24-25, 133
Pigeon, Helen, xiv
Play therapy, 48, 132-133, 191
Pleasurable sensations for the child, sexual abuse providing, 15-16
Positive attachment experiences, 3, 40
Positive messages, identifying and practicing new, 110-111
Posttraumatic stress (PTSD), 24

Powerlessness, sense of, 9, 25-26
Preschool child. *See* Children
Pseudomemories, 46-47
Psychic reasoning, 48
Psychodynamic trauma-focused therapy, xii, 22
Psychopharmacological interventions for dissociation, 133-134
Psychophysiological mechanisms by which dissociation may occur, 119-120
Psychosexual development, normal, 25, 28, 151-153
Psychotherapy, psychodynamically aware, 134
Puberty, 152, 159
Putnam's model, 120

Questioning messages and myths, 107, 108-110

Regression, 181, 184-185
Relationship-focused therapy, 40
Relationships, dysfunctional, 171-172
Repetition of words and imaging, 71
Replay of abuse, 172-174
Repression, 18
Resistance, child's:
    discomfort with feelings, 188, 193-194
    dissociation, 183-184
    forget or put experience behind, wanting to, 187, 191-193
    healthy aspect of, 180, 190, 196-197
    helping children through the resistance, 190-197
    patterns of, 186
    recognizing resistance, 181-186
    regression, 184-185
    secondary gain, 190, 196
    summary, 202-203
    therapist interventions, inappropriate, 188-190, 195-196
    time-out, 185-186
    transference, 182-183
    understanding, 186-190
Resistance, the parent's, 197-200
Resistance, the therapist's, 200-202

Responsibilities on the child, avoiding putting inappropriate, 29-30
Responsible for, I am (internationalization), 11-12, 29-30
Revictimization, 3
Ritual abuse, 48
Role of sexual abuse in the family, 90-92
Role-play, 66-68

Safety, disruption in sense of personal/world, 14
Safety and consistency in therapeutic setting and therapist's reactions, 74-75, 132
Salins, Lalita, xiv
Schizophrenia, 48
School-age child, clinical observations with the, 125-127
    *See also* Children
Secondary gain, 190, 196
Self:
    before the abuse/during the abuse/and now, 101-103
    body as an important and healthy part of, 159-162
    fragmented, repeated dissociation and the, 116
    in relation to others, awareness of, 40
    sexuality as a positive aspect of, 165-167
Self-abuse, 9
Self-blame, 11, 79
Self-caring, 30
Self-comforting, 30
Self-definition, 8-9
Self-evaluation, 106
Self-rating/reporting scales, 120, 122
Self-regulate, ability to, 8
Self-system, dissociative experience linked to a part of the, 118-119, 130
Self-theory, 5
Sensation, sexuality becomes linked to a lack of, 16-17
Sensorimotor/emotional modalities, 12-13
Seppanan, Linda, xiv
Setting of the therapy room, 208-209
*Sexual Healing Journey* (Maltz), 166

Sexuality:
  as a positive aspect of self, 165-167
  age-appropriate behaviors, 162-165
  body as an important/healthy part
    of the self, 159-162
  compulsive behaviors, 167-170
  developmental level beyond that of
    the child, sexual activity at a, 150
  dissatisfaction, sexual, 172
  effects of abuse on sexual develop-
    ment, 153-155
  normal sexual development, 25, 28,
    151-153, 155-159
  orientation, sexual, 170-171
  relationships, dysfunctional, 171-172
  replay of abuse, 172-174
  summary, 178-179
  therapeutic process, 174-178
Sexualized behaviors, 3
  children who molest other children,
    153-154
  good things happen when I'm sexual
    (internationalization), 15-17, 36-37,
    40
  reinforcing, 15-16, 36-37, 151
  therapy sessions, 35, 163-164, 175-176
Simplification and sexual abuse models,
  6, 8
Skills, imaging and learning new, 63-68
Societal myths connected with childhood sexual abuse, 105
Soothing tones and imaging, 71
Special status in the family, sexual abuse
  providing, 15-16
Structure to the child's story, genograms
  providing, 92-94
Suicidal ideation, 3, 82, 212

Temperament, 22
Terminology avoided, xiv
Therapy:
  abuse-focused model, 21-22
  acceptance by the therapist of child's
    inner experiences, 131
  betrayal and closeness, juxtaposition
    of, 33-34
  boundaries, 34-36
  chaotic, I feel (internationalization),
    32-33

child-focused therapy, 39-41
cognitive, 134
damaged, I am (internationalization),
  23-25
dissociation, 38-39
as a dynamic interactive process, xiv
guilty, I am (internationalization), 26-
  29
hearing something different than
  what therapist says, 37-38
inappropriate interventions, 188-190,
  195-196
memories of abuse/lack of protection, 30-32
as a negative experience, 206-208
perpetrator, happening of abuse
  placed with the, 80
play, 132-133
as a positive experience, 208-214
powerless, I am (inter-
  nationalization), 25-26
psychodynamic abuse-focused approach, 22
reconnecting to the process of normal
  sexual development. See Sexuality
resistance, therapist's, 200-202
responsible for, I am (internationalization), 29-30
safety and consistency in therapeutic
  setting and therapist's reactions,
  132
setting of the therapy room, 208-214
sexuality, discussions of, 37, 174-178
summary, 41-42, 214-216
time, problem of limited, 212
See also Genograms; Resistance listings; Timelines
Thinking, therapist explaining the development of, 27
Threats from sexual abuse, 11-12
Time in therapy experience, problem of
  limited, 212
Timelines:
  creating, 95-98
  difficult to construct, 95
  entrances and exits of important peo-
    ple, 95
  experiences and messages, recognizing/
    understanding early, 98-100

memories of abuse/lack of protec-
    tion, 96-97
messages and myths passed down
    within a family, 103-111
placing the abuse with the abuser/
    environment, 100-101
self before the abuse/during the abuse/
    and now, identifying the, 101-103
summary, 112
vertical axis for important dates, 94
Time-out, 181, 185-186
Toddlers. *See* Children
Transference, 181, 182-183
Trauma Symptom Checklist for Children,
    122

Traumagenic factor model, 4-5
Traumatic imaging, 43, 44, 76
Tree diagram, family. *See* Genograms
Trigger responses, 31, 66, 131, 146

Voices, intrusive, 144-145

Watkins and Watkin's model, 119-120
Whelan, Chris, xiv

Year by year, working through timelines,
    97

# About the Author

**Sandra Wieland,** Ph.D., is Assistant Clinical Professor at the University of Ottawa and has a private practice in Victoria, British Columbia, Canada. Formerly, she was Director of the Centre for Treatment of Sexual Abuse and Childhood Trauma in Ottawa. Prior to that, she was associated with the Children's Department at the Royal Ottawa Psychiatric Hospital and developed the hospital's program for children who had been sexually abused and their families. She has been active in increasing awareness across Canada of the need for specialized therapy for children who have been abused. For this work, she received Ottawa's Woman of Distinction Award in Health, Science, and Technology. She has presented workshops and training courses across Canada and the United States on topics related to sexual abuse and, in particular, working with children and adolescents who have been sexually abused. She is the author of *Hearing the Internal Trauma: Working With Children and Adolescents Who Have Been Sexually Abused* (Sage, 1997). Her present research and writing are focused on the role of parents with children who have been abused, and she is currently working on a book for these parents.